Respectable Radical

Radical Men, Movements and Ideas

GENERAL EDITOR: A. F. THOMPSON,
WADHAM COLLEGE, OXFORD

Forthcoming titles in the series:

Keir Hardie
K. C. MORGAN

Arthur Henderson
R. I. MCKIBBIN

The General Strike
G. A. PHILLIPS

Dictatorship or Partnership:
*A History of the Trade Unions and the Labour Party
in Great Britain*
R. SHACKLETON

The Left-Wing Intelligentsia in the 1930s
STUART SAMUELS

Labour or Tory?
The Working-Class Movement on Merseyside
P. J. WALLER

Respectable Radical

George Howell and Victorian Working Class Politics

F. M. LEVENTHAL
Boston University

Weidenfeld and Nicolson
5 Winsley Street London W1

SBN 297 00224 4

Printed in Great Britain by Cox & Wyman Ltd,
London, Fakenham and Reading

In Memory of David Edward Owen

Contents

Editor's Introduction

The aim of this series is to bring together a variety of studies by historians and others of the development of the Left in recent times. Its eventual purpose is to provide a general survey of the impact of radical men, movements, and ideas on both sides of the Atlantic. The first volumes, however, are concerned with the Left in Britain, and in particular with the evolution of the Labour Movement, whose chequered history throws so much light on problems which face the would-be reformer in any advanced society.

The main objective of the Left is always 'a radical reform' of the existing order in the interests of 'the people'; but the meaning of the term 'radical' varies with time, place, and circumstance. The history of the British Labour Movement illustrates this fluctuating relationship between constant and variable, ends and means. If it is to be understood, the Movement has to be set against the background of nineteenth-century Radicalism from which it emerged, and its activities in the twentieth century must be related to the changing conditions which have modified its beliefs and governed its destinies.

The immediate need is for scholarly but readable studies of those aspects and phases of the Movement which are of increasing interest both to students and to the general reader. In part, this means filling the more important gaps in our existing knowledge; but it also means adding new dimensions to what is familiar and opening up new perspectives in the light of changes in the historian's methods and the range of research in allied disciplines upon which he can now draw.

The reader must also be offered a choice of approach. The projected studies will therefore consist of four main types: the biographical, covering intellectuals as well as men of action; the structural, analysing the organization of the Movement and setting its activities in their economic and social context; the ideological, exploring the role of ideas and their promoters in these activities; and the episodic, dealing with the interaction of men, movements, and ideas in moments of crisis or in areas of crucial importance for the Left.

A. F. Thompson

Acknowledgements

This book grew out of a dissertation submitted in 1967 for the doctorate in history at Harvard University. Although the basic conception of the work is much the same as in its original version, it has been completely rewritten and considerably shortened. The dissertation, entitled 'George Howell, 1833–1910: A Career in Radical Politics', was awarded the De Lancey K. Jay Prize by Harvard University in 1968.

In the course of my research on the nineteenth-century labour movement I have been fortunate in receiving the advice and encouragement of many historians in both England and the United States, among them the late Professor Reginald Bassett, Dr Stephen Coltham, Professor R. W. Greaves, Dr Royden Harrison, and Mr Raymond Postgate. Mr Chimen Abramsky kindly gave me access to his microfilms of the minutes of the London Trades Council, and Professor Herman Ausubel and Professor Michael Wolff furnished me with material I could not otherwise obtain. Mr William Abrahams, Professor H. J. Hanham, Professor Standish Meacham, and Mr A. F. Thompson have all read the manuscript at various stages and improved it by their suggestions. My wife Jean grappled with my prose, proof-read successive drafts, and eased the burdens of composition by her patience and confidence. I am particularly grateful to my friend Professor Peter Stansky for his invaluable criticism. My greatest debt is to the late Professor David Owen, with whom I began the study of Victorian history more than a decade ago and who guided my research and my career with the wisdom and unfailing kindness that only his students can fully appreciate. Whatever virtues this book has owe more than I can say to his ideas, and its dedication to his memory is an inadequate expression of my gratitude. Neither he nor any of those acknowledged above is responsible for its deficiencies.

I am obliged to the staffs of numerous libraries: those of Harvard University, the British Museum, the Newspaper Library at

Colindale, University College (London, Imperial College, Cambridge University, the British Library of Political and Economic Science, the Goldsmiths' Library, the Bodleian Library, the Bethnal Green Library, as well as those of the House of Commons, the Trades Union Congress, the London County Record Office, the National Liberal Club, and, most of all, the Bishopsgate Institute.

I should also like to acknowledge the generosity of Harvard University in awarding me a Frank Knox Memorial Fellowship and a Jens Aubrey Westengard Scholarship which made my research in England possible.

F.M.L.

Kirkland House
Cambridge, Massachusetts
May, 1969

Introduction

Despite its relevance to an understanding of social history, the biography of ordinary men, to borrow Sir Lewis Namier's phrase, has traditionally been neglected because of the scarcity of documentary evidence. Historians of working-class life have generally approached their subject in terms of the collective experiences of identifiable groups. Illuminating as such studies have often been, they reinforce the bias of anonymity, the tendency to regard working men primarily as part of the 'mob' or the 'people', rather than as actual historical characters. Furthermore, they fail to provide the analysis in depth of psychological motivation and social aspirations that an individual case study can offer. Although one must be wary of generalizing about working-class life from the experiences of particular labour leaders, these prominent figures are often the only ones about whom much is known. Unfortunately, the biographical literature on British working-class leaders of the last century is of little value to the student of labour history. With the exception of a few classic works, like the autobiographies of Samuel Bamford and William Lovett, most surviving biographies and memoirs have either been exercises in hagiography by devoted disciples or exemplary success stories of the 'workbench to Treasury bench' type.

This book attempts to study a chapter of English labour history – chiefly the third quarter of the nineteenth century – through the career of George Howell, a working-class politician and trade unionist. Howell was neither more representative nor more significant than many of his contemporaries. He did, however, bequeath to posterity an enormous quantity of personal and public papers which are the principal source for this biography. While the lives of other labour leaders, like Robert Applegarth and W. Randal Cremer, for whom no comparable documentary material survives, have been recorded in commemorative works, almost nothing except a brief note in the *Dictionary of National Biography* has been published about Howell. The survival of his manuscript collection would itself justify the study which follows, but its underlying objective is to assess the social and political attitudes of a characteristic mid-Victorian artisan, whose ideas exemplify the prevailing Liberalism of the politically-conscious labour aristocracy of his generation. To a great extent the nature of this material has determined the character of a Howell biography: the focus must of necessity be on his career in the labour movement, a career made possible and given scope by the growth of popular institutions, such as trade unions and voluntary organizations for agitation, in the middle years of the nineteenth century.

Although it would be unreasonable to claim that Howell exerted an appreciable influence in Victorian politics, he was a notable participant in almost every phase of the political activity of working men from the decline of Chartism to the rise of the Labour Party. Until recently, these years have been regarded as a barren period in the history of the British labour movement. The multiplicity of Howell's activities furnishes evidence for a reassessment of this transitional era, those years in which most articulate working-class leaders looked to the patronage of their social betters for the solution to their problems. Howell was firmly committed to the removal of the disabilities which impeded labour's social and political advancement, but his perspectives were shaped by the dominant cultural values of his day. The ideal of self-help, instilled alike by the forces of Benthamite Radicalism and religious dissent, vitiated the class consciousness of mid-Victorian artisans, fostering accommodations within the existing order rather than rebellion against it. Born in the troubled years of the reform agitation, the New Poor Law, and militant Chartism, Howell's generation of labour leaders reached maturity in the atmosphere of lessened tension generated by mid-Victorian prosperity. Impervious to the profound sense of alienation among the victims of the Industrial Revolution, these representatives of the artisan *élite* aspired to become proper Victorians, and some of them ended their lives as moderately eminent ones.

Howell's career illustrates the way in which the development of working-class institutions furnished professional opportunities for their most capable and ambitious members. From the moment he abandoned bricklaying in the mid-1860s, he managed, often somewhat precariously, to support himself by holding official positions within the labour movement. After a period as Secretary of the

Reform League, the first organization effectively to mobilize the working classes on behalf of franchise extension, he helped to establish the Trades Union Congress, serving as the first Secretary of its Parliamentary Committee. Admittedly, in the larger political context, he was little more than a petty functionary, but his years of service brought him some prominence and a means of subsistence, enabling him ultimately to realize his greatest ambition: to become one of the first working men to secure election to Parliament.

In a vital sense, however, Howell was justified in regarding himself a failure. In spite of the recognition accorded him by his associates and his middle-class benefactors, the security and affluence he so desperately craved eluded him throughout his life. Although he attained 'respectability', he was never able to climb into the bourgeoisie, to achieve that status compounded of material comfort and self-confidence to which he aspired. Only in his last years did he come to realize that even in a society as socially mobile as Victorian England, the route to fame and fortune, except for the unusually talented, was effectively circumscribed by the circumstances of one's origins. Howell lacked both the opportunity and the capacity to transcend his relatively humble background, and whatever success he did achieve was strictly within the context of working-class politics. The precepts that dominated his life were, in fact, chimerical: self-improvement and industry did not always bring commensurate rewards. Perhaps the ultimate irony of Howell's career was that his inflexibly Gladstonian Liberalism and his opposition to socialist welfare measures, so characteristic of his own generation, alienated him from the progressive elements in the labour movement by the end of the century, making him almost an anachronism in his own lifetime.

Abbreviations

BM   British Museum
HC   Howell Collection, Bishopsgate Institute, London
LCRO London County Record Office
LS   Liberation Society
LSE   British Library of Political and Economic Science,
        London School of Economics
LTC   London Trades Council
LTRA Land Tenure Reform Association
OBS   Operative Bricklayers' Society

B

I

The Making of an Artisan

George Howell was born on 5 October 1833, in Wrington, Somerset, a quiet village remembered chiefly as the birthplace of John Locke.[1] Situated in a valley between Broadwell Down and the Mendip Hills, Wrington's most notable feature was its fifteenth-century church, whose towers are considered among the finest in Somerset. Little is known of Howell's ancestry, but the family's origins seem to have been in Wales, perhaps descending from Howells of Carnarvon. A dominant figure in his early years was his grandmother Charity Welsh, a Wrington woman, whose daughter Mary married Edwin John Howell at the St James Parish Church in Bristol on 4 November 1832. Edwin Howell, who was born in 1809, was, like his father before him, a mason by trade, although after his marriage he struck out on his own and became a general builder, sub-contracting projects in the vicinity of Wrington. Three years his senior, Mary Howell bore him eight children: George, the eldest, was followed by four more sons and three daughters during the next nineteen years. Despite his strenuous occupation Edwin Howell was not a robust man. Consumptive as a child, he was afflicted with recurrent illness – as George was to be as well – and he died at the age of fifty-nine.

During the first decade of his life George Howell's family moved frequently as his father changed from one construction job to another. His earliest childhood memory appears to have been the summer of 1836 and the departure of a group of Wrington villagers for the West Indies, where the liberation of the slaves had created a demand for free white labour. The depression of the 1830s created widespread unemployment even in largely non-industrial Somerset, and although the mastery of a trade ensured a relatively advantageous position for Edwin Howell, he often had difficulty in finding jobs. A devoted husband and father, he was perpetually bothered by economic anxiety, never certain from one month to the next that he would be able to support his family. His son's subsequent concern with bettering his own material condition reflected the constant insecurity which threatened domestic happiness during childhood. Before the Howells moved from Wrington to neighbouring Banwell in the early part of 1838, George entered the village school, where the rudiments of reading were taught by a local schoolmistress, the primer being the New Testament.

The Howell and Welsh men were almost all employed in the building trade, and it is probable that George's parents met through this occupational connection. In 1838, shortly after moving to Banwell, Edwin Howell's father, two of his brothers, and two of his brothers-in-law found work in Monmouthshire. With the prospect of better opportunities, Edwin Howell transported his family from Banwell to Pontypool in the autumn of that year. He joined his relatives working on the construction of the Newport waterworks. While the coal mines and canal barges meant new excitement to George, accustomed to the rustic Somerset landscape, he was not yet old enough to comprehend the economic distress and unrest which plagued South Wales in these years. Yet not even a young child can fail to be stirred by a parade, and on 3 November 1839 he was treated to an historic one. A large group of Pontypool ironworkers and colliers marched through the town on their way to the abortive Newport 'rising' of 4 November, the 'nearest thing to an armed revolt that Chartism produced'.[2] As radicals and free traders, Edwin Howell and his brothers were sympathetic to Chartism, but they were not politically active. Economic and religious distinctions separated them further from the rebellious Chartist labourers of the region.

If the impact of the depression in Monmouthshire was severe before the Newport incident, it worsened in the period which followed. In 1840 economic crisis forced Edwin Howell to move his family yet again in search of employment, this time to Bristol. For the next three years he worked as a sub-contractor for bridges on the Bristol and Exeter railway. The family lived relatively prosperously in the Bedminster section of Bristol, where George attended a Church of England boys' school and the local Anglican Sunday School. Working-class prosperity was, however, invariably precarious, and in 1843 a lawsuit destroyed the brief interlude of security. As a sub-contractor, Edwin Howell was obliged to obtain the money to pay for his materials and labourers from the chief contractor. In this kind of relationship a hierarchy of financial responsibilities operated; if any component member defaulted, the entire structure collapsed. During the railway boom of the 1840s risky speculations frequently ended in just such disasters for those involved. When his chief contractor defaulted over several thousand pounds owed to Howell, the latter took legal action. Ignorant of the intricacies of litigation, Howell failed to file certain essential documents, negligence which rendered him liable to prosecution for contempt of court. On top of this, the solicitor who was handling his case vanished in the middle of the proceedings. Despite the apparent validity of Howell's claim, the court decided against him. Legal costs were applied for, security was demanded, and in its absence a writ was issued for his arrest. The expenses of the case had exhausted the family's resources, and they found themselves suddenly reduced to penury. To avoid the local bailiff and constable, Howell fled to Taunton, where one of his brothers was engaged in business.

In Taunton the ruined man became seriously ill, and for several weeks his life appeared to be in danger. Mary Howell hastened to her husband's side, leaving her four children in the charge of a distant relative, who mistreated them in their mother's absence. Ten-year-old George was removed from school and sent into the streets to pick up lumps of coal that dropped from passing carts bound for the city. He entered a squalid world of vagrant children and paupers; for George the nightmare was a brief one, for others it was an all-too-familiar pattern in the Hungry Forties. Howell recalled in later years, 'I seemed to have grown into manhood all at once, for care and suffering developed a self-reliance which was abnormal in one so young. I had a brother to care for, and that burthen caused me to forget any privation or troubles of my own.'[3] The commitment to the ethic of self-help was implanted at an early age; practical necessity anticipated the lessons of Smilesian truths that his later reading would impress upon him.

When Edwin Howell recovered from his illness, Mary returned to collect her temporarily abandoned children. The family once again settled in Wrington, almost six years after their initial, hopeful departure. Howell's father was often away in the years that followed, desperately trying to recoup his fortune. The recurrent absence of his father and the identification of this absence with economic necessity permeated Howell's thinking in these years of development. Imbued at an early age with a consciousness of the hazards of working-class life, he came to regard *petit bourgeois* respectability as a bulwark against the hardship he had known in his youth. His ambivalence towards his own background derived in part from his identification of emotional satisfaction with financial security. The unity of the family seemed to be contingent on material fortune, rather than ensuring protection against economic uncertainty.

There were by this time five Howell children, and it was incumbent upon the eldest to begin working, for the family needed the small contribution he might make. Full-time schooling now became impossible, although Howell was able to continue his education sporadically at night or when there was no work to be found.[4] For several months he held a succession of farm jobs, protecting harvested wheat from scavenging birds and driving a plough – the ordinary unskilled agricultural jobs that working-class children took on in rural districts. During one of his father's longer stays in Wrington, Howell was able to return to day school for more rudimentary arithmetic and geography. Day school had to be abandoned once again before he turned twelve, although in the autumn and winter of 1845 he did attend evening classes. For all practical purposes Howell's formal education was finished, and the eagerness with which he later sought to instruct himself was commensurate with the deficiencies in his schooling. Howell did continue to attend Sunday School, but although some reading was taught, the early nineteenth-century Sunday School was more concerned with social correction than with intellectual cultivation, instilling in the children of the labouring classes the solid, and seemingly appropriate, virtues of discipline, industry, and piety.[5]

At the age of twelve George – like earlier generations of Howells and Welshes – embarked on a career in the building trade. For the next two years he worked as his father's assistant. Long stints on construction sites were interspersed with occasional intervals at school, an irregular schedule which reinforced Howell's insecurity. His initial duties were those of a mortar boy, mixing the mortar and carrying it – on his head – to the building site. The work was arduous, and the hours ordinarily from 6 a.m. to 6 p.m. Father and son had to walk the five miles from their home to Nailsea, where they worked on a mineshaft. Edwin Howell's next job was the excavation of trenches, tunnelling, and masonry for an aqueduct to supply Bristol with water. This vast project was built in sections by groups of masons and labourers, each under the supervision of a sub-contractor. George now graduated from mortar boy to time-keeper, responsible for the hours and pay of those employed by his father. Hired by the day, the workers on these jobs received their wages fortnightly. They were paid in truck rather than cash, a custom which enabled many sub-contractors – not evidently including Howell – to obtain a commission from the stores which the men frequented. (The practice of truck payment was one against which George Howell agitated in his later trade union efforts.) Before the completion of the first part of his project, Edwin Howell contracted for both the excavation and masonry of an additional segment. Here George worked alongside the navvy foreman, gaining experience in making fuses, in drilling, and taking his turn at the wheelbarrow.

Howell's autobiographical reflections never waver from their tone of filial piety, and it is difficult to determine the character of parental influence. As the eldest son, George seems to have been subjected to warnings about the necessity of perseverance and steady application. His father demanded relentless obedience and industry, and his severity commanded more respect than affection. For several years George saw little of him, and this lack of paternal attention may have been a factor in his over-solicitous regard for his own son during his brief life. The relations of father and son suffered a greater strain when George started working for his father. Concerned with upright behaviour in the home, Edwin Howell was even more rigorous in his demands as an employer. The dual role meant that George had to strive through physical labour for fatherly approval. The elder Howell was no more indulgent to his son, despite his immaturity, than to other workers, and George constantly struggled to prove his merit. This need to assert his worth and the dread of inadequacy constantly figured in his adult life, a recurrent source of anxiety in his relations with others.

The solemnity of his home and community instilled a moral fastidiousness in Howell, a quality alarming in one so young – though perhaps the greatest part of it was a product of later developments. A true Victorian sense of propriety, a tendency towards priggish self-righteousness manifested itself at an early age. Religious teaching sanctioned the repression of joyful impulses, but, in any case, playfulness was a luxury in which Howell could rarely afford to indulge. Unflagging industry, the price exacted by economic circumstances, had to be transmuted into a moral virtue, and the capacity for humour suffered in the process. In the years ahead his earnestness was enhanced by the striving for respectability. The social ideals of the era reinforced childhood constraints. At the end of the century Howell noted with self-congratulatory zeal:

With all my experience during these years, I was spared that villainous knowledge which depraves. Scenes of revelry and riot, of debauchery and vice, filthy language, ribaldry, and coarse oaths I seldom heard, and then only with disgust – as foreign to my nature and to my bringing up. All this I owe to my home influence and perhaps to my own innate nature.[6]

Howell's self-portrait obscures the natural liveliness of adolescence, but he does recall occasional opportunites for swimming and tree-climbing, for poaching and hikes to Wells and Glastonbury. The most festive local event was the annual Club Feast, held on the first Wednesday after Whitsun. The members of the 'Sick Club' (an embryonic friendly society) went in procession to the church accompanied by banners and a band. The religious service was followed by a fair and refreshments at the houses of local gentry. Leisure hours were, however, infrequent, and Howell ordinarily devoted them to reading works like Foxe's *Book of Martyrs, Pilgrim's Progress, Robinson Crusoe, Gulliver's Travels,* and Hannah More's *Bible Rhymes.*[7]

By the time Howell was fourteen, he was eager to escape the strenuous outdoor life, which had not only taken its toll in his father's health, but was causing his own to suffer. Wrington, which had no industry at all before the 1840s, offered few prospects. Most of the villagers were either employed in agriculture or local trade. When rudimentary industrialization began, it did so in the traditional pattern of cottage production. Messrs Durham, a Bristol boot and shoe manufacturer, put out some of its work to a Wrington craftsman, who established a shop in the rear of his house and took in village boys as apprentices. Towards the end of 1847, after a brief and unhappy period working for a glazier, Howell bound himself as an apprentice to the shoemaker, appropriately named Crispin. The three-year agreement stipulated that he was to receive one shilling per week as pocket money after the first six months and a regular weekly wage after the first year. The hours arranged were even longer than those prevalent in the building trade: from 6 a.m. to 8 p.m., although when there was an unusual quantity of work they might begin an hour earlier or end several hours later. Still, the work was indoors and far less taxing than what Howell had been accustomed to. The workshop was a comfortable, well-ventilated room, and Crispin encouraged conversation among his workers, often leading them himself in hymn singing during the long days.

Among English trades the shoemakers had a reputation for Radicalism and included many Chartists and freethinkers in their number. The traditional artisan trades had been the source of political ideas and leadership for working-class culture, and the close-knit workshop environment of the shoemakers was especially suited to the awakening of political consciousness.[8] The free-ranging discussions during work exposed Howell to new ideas, and they formed the substance of secondary education for the curious young mind. Fortunately the vigorous conversation did not offend his moral sensibility: 'the workshop was pretty free from swearing and lewd talk, as neither the Wesleyan [Crispin] nor the Mormon [one of the journeymen] favoured it'.[9] Politics and religion were heatedly debated, the former with Radical unanimity, the latter with sectarian diversity. The revolutions of 1848 evoked an enthusiastic response, the liberal movements in France, Poland, and Italy attracting new partisans in the distant Somerset village. Domestic political events did not pass unnoticed: Howell and his companions applauded the pathetic revival of Chartist protest at Kennington Common and lamented its rapid demise.

Howell's shop mentor, Sam Cross – a journeyman shoemaker, Deist, and Chartist – inducted his young follower into a local Chartist group.[10] Despite a membership card – for which he paid a shilling – Howell's Chartism was no more than an adolescent fancy – intense and thoroughly naïve. None the less, the principles which Cross inculcated set the framework within which the political ideas of the later reformer developed. For future working-class leaders like Howell, Chartism, however feeble by this time, offered the rudiments of political experience and ideological guidelines which would bear fruit in the franchise agitation of the 1860s. In a very real sense Howell's generation were the political heirs of the Chartist leaders and, in the case of Howell himself, of William Lovett. The younger leaders inherited not only a commitment to parliamentary reform and a democratic suffrage, but also a belief in the instrumentality of agitation and the practicability of institutional change. Like Lovett, Howell was concerned not merely with the vote, but with the spiritual and intellectual improvement of his class through education and propaganda. Both men shared a moderate, reformist outlook and accepted the social tenets of their age; modification within the existing framework of society, not a revolutionary transformation of it, would suffice for working-class advancement.

Contemporary Radical and working-class newspapers furnished the text for the workbench discussions. Circulation figures of such periodicals are deceptive: in the shop, as in the public house, a single copy satisfied the needs of many workers who were either illiterate or too poor to purchase their own. Howell's own experience underlines the importance of these journals in shaping working-class culture. For those who had left school and for whom books were difficult to obtain, newspapers represented the main source of information about the outside world. Not only were the political tempests of the 1840s fully reported, but political attitudes were subtly moulded. Extensive coverage of liberal movements abroad helped to safeguard the British labour movement from undue xenophobia. From the French Revolution to the advent of the First International, the Radical Press attempted to arouse the sympathies of English workers for revolutionary movements on the Continent. In Howell's workshop several newspapers were taken regularly, to be read aloud by one of the better readers. The Chartist *Northern Star* and the *Working Man's Friend,* a serious penny journal published by John Cassell, were especially well-received, and through them Howell learned of the exploits of men like Kossuth, Mazzini, and Garibaldi.[11] Often the men exchanged these newspapers for others with workers in neighbouring shops.

In the latter part of 1848 the Wesleyan Methodists held a series of revival meetings in the Wrington chapel. At the suggestion of his Methodist employer Howell attended and was promptly converted. His family was nominally Anglican, and Howell had been baptized and reared in the established church. Although attracted to the Wesleyans by the emotional appeal of revivalism, his conversion does not appear to have stemmed from a deep spiritual crisis. It was neither despair nor an overwhelming sense of sin, but rather the uncertainties of premature adulthood which motivated him. No longer subject to his father's direction, Howell was experimenting with new attachments, new guidelines for conduct. Although by no means frivolous, his conversion to Wesleyanism was, in some sense, a spiritual counterpart of his Chartist involvement. It was a normal phenomenon of adolescence, a reflection of the transition from the limited horizon of juvenile preoccupations to the more complex intellectual and spiritual life of the adult.

Until his conversion religion had played only a peripheral part in Howell's life; henceforth it became the main focus of his energy, as his increasing religious activity demonstrates. The young Wesleyan became a confirmed and proselytizing teetotaller and took part in a temperance demonstration in Cheddar in 1850. He was recruited as a Sunday School teacher, although his advanced educational ideas – the suggestion, for example, that writing as well as reading be taught – found little favour with his superiors, who regarded writing as too secular a pursuit for the Sabbath. In addition to his weekly classroom duties, Howell occasionally delivered sermons in outlying villages.

The workshop and the chapel combined to stimulate an insatiable appetite for knowledge, although his efforts were directed more towards acquiring encyclopedic information than to satisfying intellectual curiosity. This pattern of compulsive, unsystematic reading was common among self-instructed artisans, true of Bamford and Lovett as well as of Howell. These avid students had little practical guidance in the world of books, little sense of what was valuable for or appropriate to untutored minds.[12] The motivation for such striving was not wholly intellectual. Samuel Smiles and other publicists convinced Victorian artisans that books were the avenue to success. Reading thus served a utilitarian function, for only through books could the artisan acquire the accomplishments essential for social advancement.

In 1850 a Wesleyan preacher friend introduced him to the *British Controversialist*, a new magazine aimed at members of mutual improvement societies, which often carried suggestions of worthwhile books.

At first [he wrote the Editor some years later] I found your pages were altogether unsuitable to my condition. . . . After reading several of the articles over and over again and purchasing some of the books mentioned in the courses of reading in the first volume I began to see the light and to like the *Controversialist* for its own sake.

Early in 1852 he wrote to Samuel Neil, the Editor, requesting information on books which dealt with the British Constitution. A reply arrived with the next issue. Howell readily acknowledged his debt to 'the training I have given myself through the *Controversialist*' and the books suggested to him by Neil for turning him into a 'politician'.[13] Howell was similarly to assist the next generation of working men with bibliographical hints in the columns of the *Bee-Hive* in 1874. A *Controversialist* series on 'The Art of Reasoning' prompted him to borrow Locke's *Essay on Human Understanding* from the village rector, John Vane, who tried at the same time and without success to persuade him to return to the Church of England.

Much of his reading in these years followed typical working-class patterns. His Wesleyan class leader – a self-taught local miller – lent him *Paradise Lost* and G. H. Watts's *On the Improvement of the Mind*, as well as various religious periodicals. His enthusiasm for Milton, whom he cherished as 'my teacher', was a characteristic response, shared by Bamford and Mark Rutherford's Zachariah Coleman.[14] The combination of Puritanism and liberal political attitudes commended itself especially to young evangelical minds, flirting for the first time with Radicalism.[15] The Miltonic influence inspired him to attempt the composition of religious verse, which the *Working Man's Friend*, to whom he sent a sample in 1850, did not deem worthy of publication. Howell also read George Crabbe, whose depiction of rural life he could appreciate, and two working-class poets, Robert Bloomfield and the Northamptonshire peasant, John Clare. An introduction to Plutarch opened up historical literature for him, and an exposure to the French and English revolutions convinced him of the heroic quality of Oliver Cromwell. Religious tracts, as one might expect, comprised the largest portion of his reading; a dutifully-saved five shillings enabled him to buy John Gregory Pike's *Persuasives to Early Piety*, John Wesley's *On Christian Perfection,* and Richard Baxter's *A Call to the Unconverted*. In 1851 Howell helped his Wesleyan employer and the local vicar to establish a free reading room in Wrington. For the first time he began to read *The Times,* and he now had access to philosophical works formerly inaccessible.

Shortly before his eighteenth birthday Howell made his first trip to London, indeed his initial journey away from the Somerset-Monmouthshire area. Naturally he attended several Evangelical lectures in Exeter Hall, but for once religion took second place to secular attractions. Like countless other tourists in London in 1851, he spent most of his time at the Crystal Palace exhibition. As he recollected nearly half a century later,

I cannot express my feelings as I entered that vast palace of iron and as I glanced around the multifarious and magnificent collection of the products of the world there represented. All dreams of fairy land were eclipsed in a moment. I wandered over its vast space and its numerous galleries, noting here and there the wondrous things collected together, from the huge pyramid of coal, to the almost deafening hum of machinery, from the splendid collection of works of art to the fabrics of all countries. I listened to the strains of music and I watched the vast multitudes as they wandered about the transepts and other parts of the building.[16]

Wrington must have seemed unbearably humdrum in contrast when Howell returned after his brief trip. His term of apprenticeship ended in 1851, and although he remained for a few months as an 'improver' under Sam Cross, he was eager to escape the confines of the obscure village. 'I was ambitious', he wrote, 'to fly alone. I wanted a wider field. Wrington was too small a place for me to continue to live in.'[17] Early the next year he and two friends set out for Weston-super-Mare, where shoemaking work was promised. He joined the local Athenaeum and participated in discussions there. Livelier than Wrington, Weston still did not satisfy his restlessness, and within weeks of his arrival Howell removed himself to Bristol, his home from 1840 to 1843. Here he was to remain for nearly three years, until the attraction of London became irresistible.

In the nine years since his departure from Bristol as a boy of ten, Howell's life had been guided by the two principal events of his youth: the acquisition of a trade and his conversion to Wesleyanism. Both the essential gravity of his character and the requisite devotion to toil found their justification in his new faith. The puritanical streak in Methodism – and in the artisan ethic as well – suited Howell's fastidious and upright character. Through dedication to work – an economic necessity in any case – he would find favour in God's eyes, to be revealed in worldly success. Whatever reassurance religion offered of ultimate salvation, it was the hope of reward in this life which made the rigours of working-class life tolerable for him. The pleasures and temptations against which Methodist teaching counselled were ones he had willingly denied himself. While reinforcing his sense of duty, it did not instil any inclination towards submissiveness; indeed the prescription of obedience and industry concealed an underlying ambiguity. Without denying that moral indiscipline could lead to social rebelliousness, it was equally clear that moral rectitude encouraged self-reliance. The logical outcome of education and perseverance was ambition for self-betterment, not a humble acceptance of inferior status. For Howell, as for many others, the injunction to moral self-improvement had a material corollary. Wesleyanism offered an answer to the doubts and dilemmas of the young man, troubled by his own youthful energy: it seemed to give his career purpose, to allay his insecurity, and to justify his restless ambition.

Bristol promised new channels for Howell's religious enthusiasm. Instead of the sparsity of Wrington activities, he now found a range of organizations competing for his attention. Upon his arrival he joined a Reformed Methodist chapel in St Thomas' Street, immediately volunteering as a Sunday School teacher. The Young Men's Improvement Society, affiliated with the chapel, occupied his leisure hours. Here Howell and other young artisans read high-minded essays and debated public questions, hoping to raise the level of knowledge of all through intellectual interchange.[18] Equipped with arguments from the *British Controversialist*, Howell became a leader in the group, obtaining valuable experience in public speaking, which he put to good use at temperance meetings. On Sundays he inveighed against the evils of liquor in the Bristol slums and began to speak on labour questions. His first such speech was on the Master and Servant Act, delivered at a Bristol club house in 1852.[19]

To supplement these activities Howell organized an informal study group, but the self-imposed regimen proved too strenuous for the less dedicated participants. Howell was forced to admit that the endurance required ensured a greater number of victims than survivors:

So intent were a few of us upon rigorous self-improvement that we determined to meet all through the spring and summer months at 4 o'clock in the morning to read and discuss some chosen authors, for a full hour and a half, before we set off for work, as each of us began at 6 a.m. The books first chosen were: Coleridge on 'Method', Archbishop Whateley's 'Logic' and his 'Rhetoric'. Sunday mornings we were to meet at 6 a.m. and continue until 8. The books for Sundays were Paley's

Natural Theology and his evidences of Christianity, and Bishop Butler's *Analogy*. Two of the five soon fell away, then a third; two only were left. We continued steadfastly at our self-imposed task, until after some months my only companion failed me, and I was left alone.[20]

Since he shunned more convivial gatherings in public houses, Howell's recreation consisted chiefly of lectures and sermons. At the meetings he attended at the Broadmeat Rooms, Henry Vincent, the celebrated Chartist orator, and itinerant Wesleyan preachers spoke. A widening range of contacts brought somewhat greater catholicity of interest, permitting even occasional attendance at Secularist and Unitarian meetings. A founder of the Young Men's Christian Association in St James's Square, Howell once read a paper on Byron, hardly the most likely subject for one of such puritanical disposition, at a meeting there. The opening of the YMCA meant the availability of a reading room with a large selection of reviews, newspapers, and journals. Tea meetings at the chapel – the refreshments consisting of tea and 'British temperance wine' – and group singing in private homes enlivened an otherwise sober existence.

Above all, his religious preoccupation spurred Howell on to yet more intensive reading. With characteristic self-satisfaction he later recorded,

Let those educated at Rugby or Eton, preliminary to Oxford or Cambridge, sneer. They are put through courses of study early; I had to begin where they left off. I had to feel my way, in spare hours, with sparse means, and no real guide to help me or point the way. Books, only books were my masters, teachers, counsellors and friends at that early date.[21]

Although familiar with Wordsworth and Byron by this time, Howell continued to avoid Shakespeare until he had obtained the reluctant approval of his Methodist class leader, whose suspicion of imaginative literature reflected conventional Evangelical attitudes.[22] Emerson's *Representative Men* proved inspirational, but a more memorable literary discovery was Harriet Beecher Stowe's *Uncle Tom's Cabin*, which appeared in England in 1852. Despite his bias against fiction, Howell was captivated by the sentimental abolitionist tract. Shortly thereafter he attended his first stage performance – a dramatization of the novel – and was as deeply moved as he had been reading it. 'Of all in that theatre', he recalled, 'perhaps no one, not even a school girl or a seamstress, felt so absorbed, or gave vent to feelings of emotion as I did.'[23]

Upon his arrival in Bristol Howell had obtained work with the Durham shoe firm, but transferred to another shop after a short while. There he continued his craft until his parents moved to Bristol in 1853, at which time Howell returned to their home as a boarder. Having taken some building land on which he was putting up houses, Edwin Howell prevailed upon his son to return to the family trade. The masons' union, however, prohibited more than one son – in this case George's younger brother Charles – from pursuing his father's craft, except after serving a full apprenticeship. Howell could not face another apprenticeship, especially in a trade in which he had past experience. At the age of twenty, then, Howell became a bricklayer rather than a mason and, consequently, was excluded from stonecutting or carving. This reversion to his father's employ did not at first arouse misgivings, despite a sixty-hour week of arduous labour. The work was familiar, consisting of mixing mortar and cement, fixing roofs, and constructing drains. During evenings or in poor weather he could still devote himself to his books and to the chapel.

After a year of working under his father the yearning for new adventures, and especially for the splendours of London, revived. Ever since his first visit Howell dreamed of returning. The limitless horizons of the capital seemed to guarantee opportunities for betterment which did not exist in the setting he knew. Now that he had rejoined the large family – there were now seven other children – independence was even more appealing. Life in Bristol had its rewards, with its busy religious activities and the companionship of like-minded young men, but its more pedestrian virtues paled beside the ostentatious qualities of London. By 1854 his plans became unalterable and preparations for the change began:

I went [to London] to take part, if fortune favoured me at all, in the stirring events of the time, political, intellectual, religious, industrial, and social. To do this I must succeed in my handicraft; upon this too I had made up my mind. In the winter of 1854–5 I saved all I could; I read industriously with more method and to some purpose.[24]

In addition – although this was perhaps a reflection of hindsight – he had already begun to formulate three distinct goals, which were unlikely to be attained were he to remain buried in Somerset. With confidence in the potential of self-help, the Bristol bricklayer aimed to write a book, to speak in Exeter Hall, and to enter Parliament. That such fantasies could in fact be realized is, at least in part, a vindication of the Smiles philosophy; that such aspirations existed suggests the extent to which the ideals of a bourgeois society infected young Victorian artisans. These three ambitions represented not merely the culmination of his intellectual, religious, and political endeavours; it also implied a sense of commitment to the existing community, unqualified by feelings of alienation or exclusion. Howell's identification with the interests of his fellow workers did not preclude the desire to rise above these circumstances. Indeed from this period – if not earlier – one can discern in Howell what Royden Harrison has defined as the ambivalent attitude of the mid-Victorian working man: 'Liberalism at the front of the mind, and old working-class sentiments and traditions at the back of it.'[25] Working-class life and culture had formed his youth, liberal values defined his later years. Inevitably a tension – even a conflict – was to persist between the two elements, since they produced contradictory reactions to the economic system. On the one hand, Howell desired its transformation by, and for the benefit of, the labouring classes, but at the same time he yearned for success within, and according to the standards of, the system. Hence the combination of identifying with the working class while struggling for bourgeois acceptance, of the sense of superiority to his peers and the self-effacement in the company of his social and intellectual betters. This uncertainty of status enhanced his insecurity: the higher he tried to climb, the more unsteady the rungs of the ladder became.

By the age of twenty-one the main lines of Howell's character were already apparent. Wesleyanism and the artisan ethic had infused him with a determination to improve his situation. His experiences, especially in Crispin's workshop, had aroused a Radical political sensibility, which he, like other labour leaders throughout the century, had no difficulty in reconciling with his Methodist piety. Wesley's exhortation to submission seemed to be belied by practice in the Methodist chapel itself, where all classes might attain a moral equality that might have a political equivalence. In fact the reformed Methodist chapels, in which working men acquired skills as organizers and public speakers, prepared them for the duties of democratic citizenship. A shifting of attention from individual – and chiefly spiritual – preoccupations to public life did not imply an abandonment of Methodist ideals; it did, however, determine the perspective from which Methodist politicians viewed public affairs.

In his earnest dedication, in his concern for organizational details Howell showed clearly the Methodist stamp. The attitudes and diligence which he had brought to religious pursuits were transferred to political and industrial questions in the late 1850s and 1860s. In a practical sense as well, the religious activities in Bristol had trained him for unknown fields of action. The chapel, the temperance groups, and the YMCA provided experience in public speaking and in organizational problems.

Yet, despite the certainty of purpose which religion generated, it could not entirely overcome anxieties. Piety protected the fallible creature from moral backsliding, but in the reorienting of energies towards the affairs of men, there was no comparable defence against failure. Self-righteousness was less effective in human relations than in one's relations with God; personal ambition in worldly matters was harder to satisfy than spiritual longings. Howell's lingering fears of inadequacy were reflected in a tendency towards defensiveness in his dealings with others that would aggravate political conflicts.

In the summer of 1855, as Howell contemplated his departure from Bristol, he could not foresee the new opportunities London would bring. Within a decade he was to abandon the trade he had come to pursue and to discover in working-class politics a new career, though one with little occupational security. His youthful ambitions were to be fulfilled, but not without hardship and disillusionment. Most significantly, London would introduce him to other young men from the provinces, and with them he was to shape the course of the labour movement in the next generation.

A Political Apprenticeship in London

George Howell arrived in London in July 1855 with neither friends nor the prospect of a job, carrying a letter of introduction from the Bristol YMCA to the Aldersgate Street branch as his passport to fortune. Not yet twenty-two, he was equipped for the new world he was about to discover with little more than youthful exuberance and ambition. Although he possessed a craft, his opportunity to practise it would depend less on his own industriousness than on prevailing trade conditions. Years later, with the perspicacity of hindsight, he could appreciate the overconfidence with which he confronted the London scene:

My ideals were scarcely those of the class of workmen with whom I was to come into contact. The book world was my ideal, but I had no fitting preliminary training for the use of my pen as a mode of even assisting me to get a crust. In character I was almost puritanical, a total abstainer, which in itself was scarcely a recommendation in the building trades at that date. I was strongly imbued with religious convictions, which I can only describe as puritanical protestantism. I was modest, even to shyness, and yet there was a firm self-reliance, natural to my character. I do not think that the idea of not succeeding ever entered into my head.[1]

After spending his first night at a temperance hotel near Paddington Station, Howell presented himself at the Aldersgate YMCA. Members of the staff informed him that they could help him in securing a position as a clerk or shop assistant, but not as a 'mechanic'. In his Bristol experience craftsmen and clerks mingled socially, forming the core of the improvement societies, but Howell soon discovered that class distinctions were sharper in London, and that respectable institutions were less accessible to working men than they had been in Bristol. He was, moreover, stunned by the social exclusiveness which prompted their rejection of his membership application:

I was clean and decent, having a black frock coat and vest, but also had corduroy trousers. This settled the business for I was looked at first by one, then by another, and at last I was told by the officer in attendance that I could not come dressed like that. My face burned with indignation and shame, that the Young Men's Christian Association closed its doors against the colours and material of a workman's trousers.[2]

To have his hard-earned respectability questioned was an affront not easily borne; he had not diligently sought to improve himself in order to endure such humiliating encounters.

Even before the general recession of 1857, the building trades were hurt by the high interest rates prevailing during the previous three years, which restricted new construction. By the winter of 1856–7 some 25,000 building trades workers in London were unemployed – approximately a quarter of the labour supply.[3] In such depressed conditions jobs were difficult to find and more difficult to retain. Men were hired by the week but could be dismissed by the day, and they had no security against the displeasure of their employers. Possessing neither personal contacts nor union affiliation, Howell had the added disadvantage of youth. However, after a week of fruitless searching, he accepted a job as an 'improver', a position inferior to that of a journeyman bricklayer, at wages of a guinea for the standard $58\frac{1}{2}$-hour week. His pay was lower than average for an artisan in the London building trades – ordinarily 32s – but the scarcity of work left him little choice and was, in any case, higher pay than an unskilled labourer received.[4] His foreman gave him the opportunity to earn extra money repairing stoves and boilers, the additional work raising his earnings to something approximating the average artisan wage.

The project, on which Howell was to work for a year, was the construction of a crescent of houses in the Caledonian Road, in the vicinity of the cattle market, a region then still largely undeveloped. He found lodgings with the masons' foreman and, once settled, immediately sent to Bristol for his treasured books. For Howell, as for many mid-Victorian working men, housing presented a serious problem in view of the lack of cheap and abundant public transport.

Frequently beginning work at 6 a.m., he found the trains, which did not operate until later in the morning, useless. The relatively high price of tickets would in any case have precluded their regular use. A worker might be obliged to walk many miles every day or to shift his lodgings frequently as he moved from job site to job site. This nomadic aspect of working-class life was an important factor in labour opposition to extended residential qualifications in franchise reform bills.

It is impossible to reconstruct Howell's movements at all times in the period from 1856 to 1862. A list of his jobs would in itself be a partial history of the architectural development of mid-Victorian London. In the late 1850s he worked on the City Road section of the main drainage scheme, sponsored by the new Metropolitan Board of Works. Several years later he was employed in the construction of Scott's new Foreign Office building. There were additional jobs in Islington, Greenwich, Camberwell, Chelsea, and in the large slum areas north and west of the City. Some of these projects reflect the expansion of London building in areas which were still virtually rural; others provide evidence of the renovation in this period of the dilapidated residue of an earlier era of expansion.

Hiring methods in the building trades in the late 1850s increased the uncertainty of employment. Although Howell began to receive first-class bricklayer's wages immediately after his period as an 'improver' and by 1859 was working as a deputy foreman, there were many days when work was unavailable or when weather conditions made it unfeasible. A bricklayer might travel to his job site by 6 a.m. only to find that his employer had no use for his services on that day. Since hiring was usually done only at that time of the morning, it would be at once too late to secure employment in some other location. Hence a day's labour – and wages – might be lost. Once Howell became a foreman, his situation was more secure, but there were still idle days, which were not – as in the case of some of his acquaintances – to be squandered in drink. Instead he used such occasions for tours of the British Museum and the National Gallery. His antiquarian interests drew him to the archaeological and the natural history exhibits, but in these infrequent visits nothing excited him more than the reading room, and he longed for a permit which would allow him to enter this sanctuary of men of learning. When he received his ticket in 1859, he regarded it as a privilege whose spirit was not to be violated by reading 'any work of fiction or general literature'.[5]

The long hours of physical labour ordinarily left little time for devotional and intellectual pursuits. At first Howell used his Sundays to sample London's religious offerings. Despite his professed Methodism, he enjoyed an eclectic mixture of Nonconformist, Anglican, and Secularist services, although he attended the heterodox South Place Chapel with some regularity. Increasingly Sundays were given over to lectures at the Hall of Science and even more to Chartist meetings, which continued even after the movement itself had effectively expired. Throughout the decade between Howell's arrival and the formation of the Reform League, older Chartists, like Benjamin Lucraft, Robert Hartwell, and John Bedford Leno, mingled with young Radicals at numerous debating halls and public houses in London, reinforcing with personal ties the ideological bond between Chartism and later reform movements. There were other new political contacts in the 1850s which helped to mould Howell's developing political consciousness: the prominent Secularists, George Jacob Holyoake and Charles Bradlaugh, the foreign exiles, Giuseppe Mazzini and Louis Kossuth, and the socialist pioneer, Robert Owen, then in his ultimate spiritualist phase. In the early 1860s Howell came to know Karl Marx, John Malcolm Ludlow, the Christian Socialist, and several of the English Positivists, most notably Professor Edward Spencer Beesly and Frederic Harrison.[6]

The extent of the influence of foreign exiles on men like Howell is difficult to assess. Continental revolutionaries radiated a romantic aura which working-class leaders found intoxicating. The nationalist struggle for freedom evoked a warm response among Englishmen seeking to win greater political and industrial rights for themselves. The very exoticism of men like Garibaldi and Kossuth appealed to working men accustomed to the domestic species of artisan and middle-class reformer. If Kossuth and Mazzini were uprooted failures, they appeared to Howell as crusaders for nationalist and liberal ideals which he shared. But if he derived a vicarious pleasure from the exploits of foreign revolutionaries, he showed a marked reluctance to adapt their techniques to domestic problems.

The example of Marx – with whom Howell became acquainted through the formation of the First International – indicates that personal contact and admiration implied little comprehension of theory. In a characteristically exaggerated journalistic reminiscence, Howell recalled,

There is perhaps but one man living who knew more of Marx in those years than I did – that man is Mr. W. R. Cremer. Many of those who shout his name never held converse with him, never even saw him. I speak not of his writings – they mostly came later – I speak of the man as I knew him – simple, confiding, yearning for the redemption of humanity.[7]

He was certainly unfamiliar with Marx's early theoretical and polemical writings, and their personal relations – highly embellished in his depiction – did not stimulate closer investigation of Marxian doctrine. Howell, like many of his working-class associates, exhibited a kind of benighted blindness about Marx's prescriptions for capitalism. They never realized that he did not share their convictions about the practicability of reforming society but looked to its reconstruction. Howell would have repudiated the notion of implacable class antagonism, which stood as an affront to his faith in the efficacy of self-help and middle-class benevolence. With Marx, as with Mazzini, men like Howell assimilated only those ideological precepts – the importance of working-class organization, international proletarian solidarity – which were palatable, disregarding others which offended the tenets of their Radical Liberalism.

Given its identification with such disparate figures as Mazzini, Marx, Ernest Jones, and John Bright, it is hardly surprising that mid-Victorian working-class Radicalism lacked a consistent theoretical framework. Many of the intellectual godparents of the labour movement did have certain general characteristics in common: Jones, Beesly, Marx, and Bright, for example, were all middle class in origin. All were sympathetic to working-class aspirations and criticized the existing order for its injustice to the working man, and it mattered little that their diagnoses were poles apart. What was most significant about these friends of the people was that they appeared to be on the right side, in opposition to the conservative élite which kept England divided into two nations. Middle-class patronage was cherished partly because of the prevailing deference of working men and partly because it seemed to provide a respectable veneer for popular protest. If the patrons were themselves mutually antagonistic, it was possible to select from them only those doctrines which could be harmonized with the political and social ethos of the artisan.

Until 1858 or 1859 Howell's involvement in political affairs was largely passive – an inquisitive acolyte, eager to absorb the political wisdom of the Radical prophets, whether they were Chartists or foreign propagandists. More important for his development in these years were the numerous informal groups in which he took part – improvement societies, debating clubs, and temperance organizations – more cosmopolitan versions of associations he had known in Bristol. Through such groups Howell met other aspiring working-class politicians and began to establish a network of connections within which he was to construct a career. The movement in the building trades was to give this element cohesion and to serve as the catalyst in the development of working-class Radicalism in the 1860s.

Many of these informal and ephemeral groups met in public houses, and Howell – drinking lemonade or ginger beer – found that his sobriety gave him an advantage in public speaking over somewhat incapacitated associates. The poet and printer J. B. Leno was the guiding spirit of an informal group of young workers who met regularly in the Windsor Castle pub in Holborn, and Howell occasionally took part.[8] He attended meetings of a Chartist group (probably the North London Political Union) in Islington, led by Benjamin Lucraft, and of a 'foreign affairs committee', which, like those founded by David Urquhart at the time of the Crimean War, sought to stimulate popular discussion of diplomacy. As a member of the Wheatsheaf Yard temperance society, Howell organized lectures which he and other members delivered all over London. The circuit was devised on the Wesleyan model, with Howell, Lucraft, and Charles Bartlett, a plasterer and lifelong friend, offering their services, and the societies addressed paying the speaker's expenses in return. The inspirational lecture series continued for two years but was abandoned once local societies lost interest and refused to reimburse the speakers. For a time Howell took part in another young men's improvement society in Camberwell, and in 1857 he established the Milton Club at a coffee house near Islington Green for the purpose of studying Milton's political writings. 'All of this kind of work,' Howell noted, 'gave me experience and confidence on the platform, so that I was not unprepared for that wider sphere which opened up to me in the industrial movement of 1859 and the movements which grew out of it.'⁹

His compulsive self-improvement, which the Aldersgate YMCA had failed to appreciate in 1855, persisted all through the early London years. Soon after Howell's arrival, he enrolled in a series of classes on penmanship, commercial arithmetic, and book-keeping – prerequisites for a clerical career, but not for that of a brick-layer. He subsequently attended geometry and architectural drawing classes at the Charterhouse School of Art, established by the Reverend William Rogers, a pioneer in working-men's educa-tion in the City.¹⁰ Since linguistic facility was one sign of culture, Howell was determined to remedy the deficiencies of his educa-tion in this field. He attended classes in Latin and Greek, taught by an old Chartist named Clarke, and later others in French. In addition, he made half-hearted attempts to learn Italian and Spanish on his own. It seems likely that Howell's increasingly fre-quent encounters with Continental Radicals stimulated him to learn foreign languages, but as with so many of his other intellectual experiments, there was more pretension than system in his effort.

The core of Howell's intellectual medicine was a massive dose of classic English prose – Bacon, Milton, Hume, Gibbon, Burke, Macaulay, and Carlyle. He had by this time overcome some of his earlier puritanical misgivings about fiction, regarding it as a suffici-ently respectable form of literature to warrant his reading Scott, Bulwer Lytton, Dickens, and Thackeray, although not within the confines of the British Museum Reading Room. In general, his choice of reading followed the suggestions of the *British Controver-sialist* or accepted canons of merit. Books were regarded essentially as tools of self-improvement, rather than a source of pleasure, and the appeal of a book was proportionate to its accepted significance. But at least the areas of Howell's exploration became somewhat less parochial than in earlier years: theology gave way to politics and economics in reading, just as it had done in his public activities. James Mill and David Ricardo superseded Richard Baxter and John Wesley as favoured authors. For relaxation Howell and his friend Bartlett read and discussed works on geology and astronomy. Among the books chosen for recreational reading were Thomas Dick's *Celestial Scenery* and *Siderial Heavens*, the phrenologist George Combe's *Constitution of Man Considered in Relation to External Objects,* and G. H. Lewes' *The Physiology of Common Life.*

In this dogged pursuit of education no intellectual exercise seemed too taxing, no book too ponderous, despite the physical strain of bricklaying. The quest for encyclopedic knowledge overcame fatigue and discouragement, justifying the effort to assimilate whole areas of impractical information.

The rich cultural resources of London and the occasional glimpses of notable men of letters enhanced Howell's fascination with the world of scholars and gentlemen. His later connection with John Stuart Mill and with the Positivists seemed to demonstrate that intellectual barriers could be surmounted with less difficulty than social ones. With the knowledge that books afforded, Howell felt he could communicate with Thomas Hughes or Goldwin Smith on an intellectual plane in spite of his social inferiority, but he never quite appreciated the distinction between wisdom and information, between the intellectual and the man who had simply read many books. His obsequious efforts to ingratiate himself with the celebrities he did come to know were matched by a pathetic sense of awe towards the ones he merely viewed from afar.

Appropriately enough, it was *On Heroes, Hero-Worship, and the Heroic in History* which aroused Howell's admiration for Carlyle, whom he occasionally saw wandering alone at night along Cheyne Walk, when he was living in Chelsea in 1861. He found this physical closeness exhilarating and even had 'the temerity literally to walk in [Carlyle's] footsteps, but always at a respectful distance behind him'.[11] Such diffidence was less apparent in his limited contact with T. H. Huxley. 'Of all the men whom I have known', he wrote, 'there was no one to whom I was attracted so much as towards Professor Huxley.'[12] Howell attended his lectures to working-class audiences in 1860 'On the Relations of Man to the Lower Animals' and a further series in 1863 on 'Our Knowledge of the Causes of the Phenomena of Organic Nature'. These talks at the Museum of Practical Geology in Jermyn Street sharpened Howell's interest in science and converted him to the theory of evolution. In 1866 or 1867 he persuaded Auberon Herbert to introduce him to Huxley at a breakfast meeting, and once Howell forgot his initial timidity, they conversed happily about economics and labour problems.[13] The two met occasionally in later years at meetings on technical education, an interest they shared. In the 1870s Howell encouraged his son to attend Huxley's lectures and conceived the notion of placing the boy under his tutelage. Whether such a proposal, reflecting Howell's high, and probably misguided, aspirations for his son, would have earned Huxley's blessing is impossible to determine, since the boy's illness and premature death precluded its realization.[14]

Through public and intellectual activities Howell's early preoccupation with religion was tempered in the years of adjustment to London. The character of political and social life in the capital exerted a humanizing influence. Formerly sheltered among the self-righteous young Wesleyans of Bristol, Howell now had to cope with the more worldly society of working-class Radicals. If the economic environment was more abrasive, so too was the social *milieu*. Howell reconciled himself to the rowdier tone of London politics, developing even a mild tolerance for alcohol, although he never overcame the abhorrence for drunkenness which resolute abstinence had instilled in him. Family life also made him rely less on religion for emotional solace. On Christmas Day, 1856, he married his landlady's sister, Dorcas Taviner, the youngest daughter of George Taviner, a Wiltshire farmer. Dorcas shared few of her husband's political interests, but she provided a home and companionship during the rare intervals when Howell was not involved in organizational work. The marriage was a moderately happy one – at least until the death of their only child, George Washington Taviner Howell, in 1880. It was only after Howell's own retirement and his wife's death in 1897 that the company of women became an important source of pleasure for him. For most of his active life he was preoccupied with affairs of politics and labour, not with those of the heart.

The Dispute in the Building Trades

The builders' struggle, which began in 1858, was a watershed in the history of the British labour movement in the nineteenth century. Following a period of working-class quiescence, the conflict stimulated new political and industrial activity, generating a moderately coherent strike organization and leaving in its wake the component elements of working-class politics in the next two decades. The immediate consequences of the dispute were the foundation of the London Trades Council in 1860, the establishment of that exemplary 'new model' union, the Amalgamated Society of Carpenters and Joiners, the reorganization of the Bricklayers on similar principles, and the setting-up of the *Bee-Hive*, the most influential labour newspaper of its time. In addition, as its most recent chroniclers have reiterated, the strike and lockout among the London builders made the First International possible.[15] These developments coincided with a renewal of the Chartist belief that political rights were an essential preliminary to social and economic reform. This revival, coupled with the sprouting of new institutional forms for labour agitation, explains the belated conversion of British trade unions to political action.

Perhaps the most significant achievement of the builders' struggle, in view of such wide ramifications, was 'the bringing together of men who for years, rightly or wrongly, were regarded as the leaders of the Labour movement. They became also practically leaders in all subsequent political movements for at least a quarter of a century.'[16] These men included George Odger, W. Randal Cremer, Edwin Coulson, George Potter, William Allan, Robert Applegarth, and George Howell. In their trade union history Sidney and Beatrice Webb identified an inner core of leaders whom they labelled the 'Junta'. Consisting of Applegarth, Odger, Coulson of the Bricklayers, Allan of the Amalgamated Society of Engineers, and Daniel Guile of the Ironfounders, the Junta, according to the Webbs, became in the early 1860s 'a cabinet of the Trade Union Movement'.[17] For the first time 'the leaders of working-class politics stood together in a compact group, united by close personal friendship'.[18] Later labour historians have disputed the Webbs' account, stressing not only their exaggeration of institutional novelty, but their tendency to anticipate the formation of the Junta and to overestimate its inner coherence.[19]

The chronology and personal ties were, in fact, far more subtle than the Webbs seemed to realize. The split between Potter and the Junta faction, which they rightly stress, only began to develop in 1861 and, reaching a climax in 1865, it diminished in the last years of the decade. Daniel Guile, initially a supporter of Potter, did not join the others until 1867 and was not a major figure in the movements of the early 1860s. It was really only in 1867, with the establishment of the Conference of Amalgamated Trades, that a pattern of collective action became recognizable. Even more significant was the preoccupation with politics of Odger and Applegarth – and Howell – which Allan and Coulson did not share. It was political, rather than industrial, agitation which was of primary importance in the years between the collapse of the builders' strike and the passage of the Second Reform Bill. Although Applegarth, who had become Secretary of the ASCJ in 1862, was at the centre of the political movements, the other dominant figures tended to be men who operated largely outside the trade union context. It was not the union leaders, but aspiring politicians, like Howell, Odger, and Cremer, who organized the political agitation, ultimately joining forces with middle-class Radicals.

The 'close personal friendship' to which the Webbs refer was at best intermittent and was always vitiated by practical considerations. Although they could act effectively on industrial matters, Coulson and Allan were reluctant to take up the reform question before 1866 and remained aloof from political activity. Compared to Odger or Potter, Coulson was an obscure figure, whose influence John Malcolm Ludlow – who came to know most of these men in the course of the builders' struggle – denied.[20] If the Junta and their associates exhibited remarkable harmony in their war against Potter, it was an alliance based on expediency. Howell and Coulson despised each other, an antipathy stemming from rivalry within the Operative Bricklayers. Applegarth and Cremer shared a similar enmity. Howell quarrelled at some time with everyone but Applegarth, and the ill-tempered, abusive Cremer antagonized most of his colleagues until he left them to devote his energies to international conciliation, for which he was knighted and awarded a Nobel Peace Prize.

The movement for a nine-hour day in the building trades originated with the London stonemasons in 1853, but little progress was made until other trades took up the struggle five years later. In January 1858 George Potter, then Chairman of the small Progressive Society of Carpenters and Joiners, convened a meeting to reopen the hours question. Representatives of fourteen London carpenters' societies agreed to join in a nine-hour campaign, and their delegates met throughout the spring of 1858. When the master builders denied a plea by the carpenters for a Saturday half-holiday, the masons lent their support and were followed shortly thereafter by the bricklayers, the plasterers, and the painters. In September Potter organized a Building Trades Conference of delegates from each of the five trades which sought to mobilize labour to agitate for the nine-hour day.

The master builders repeatedly refused either to reconsider the demand for a shorter day or to receive a deputation. After months of futile approaches the Conference finally selected five London firms at which workers would attempt to deliver a nine-hour petition. Three of these firms simply rejected the petition, but at Trollope and Sons in Pimlico a mason was discharged for daring to present one. On 21 July 1859 the masons on the Trollope project in Knightsbridge decided to strike in defence of the victimized mason. The other participating trades proved their loyalty by joining the masons in the subsequent walk-out, demanding the nine-hour day as well as the reinstatement of the dismissed mason as the conditions of their return. The master builders countered with a general lockout, and within ten days 24,000 workers were unemployed.[21]

In September the master builders offered to reopen their doors to those workmen who would subscribe to what came to be called the Odious Document, which made the renunciation of trade union affiliation a condition of employment. The Conference remained defiant, and only a few workmen accepted the employers' terms. This challenge to trade union survival aroused the anger of uninvolved unions, who now began to offer financial assistance to the beleaguered London trades, obliged to support their own men as well as the unaffiliated majority of the strikers. The Amalgamated Society of Engineers, the prototype of the new-style union, contributed nearly £3,500.[22]

Only the stonemasons, among the trades represented by the Conference, broke away from Potter's alliance and began to negotiate independently. At this sign of disunity the Conference decided in November to end the strike against Trollope's and defer their demand for the shorter day, thus concentrating their protest against the weakest aspect of the enemy policy – the Odious Document. Several firms withdrew it in the following months, and in February 1860 the Central Association of Master Builders abandoned it unconditionally. By the end of the month the strike was over. It was a pyrrhic victory for the workers: they had managed to survive the employers' challenge to the right of association and had demonstrated their financial staying power. None the less, the struggle had proved expensive: the Conference had distributed nearly £23,000 in lockout pay.[23] The funds of the unions were depleted and their structural viability tested almost to the breaking point.

In March the Bricklayers withdrew from the Conference, in which only the carpenters, the plasterers, and the painters now remained. The Bricklayers insisted that their resignation implied no disillusionment with the Conference, but simply a recognition of the need for financial rehabilitation.[24] Potter, who had earned considerable notoriety by his conduct of the strike, was unwilling to permit the movement to disintegrate. Despite the misgivings of affiliated unions, he used the executive council of the Conference to summon representatives from all parts of the country to a meeting in Derby in January 1861. Its purpose was to extend the scope of the existing organization and to re-kindle the agitation for shorter hours. Representing the 2,400 members of the Operative Bricklayers' Society, Howell was one of five London delegates at the gathering.[25]

Although he had long been sympathetic to trade unionism, Howell had not joined the Bricklayers until the strike showed him that there was 'some real work to be done'.[26] By now a deputy foreman, he decided in August 1859 to identify himself with the cause of reform by becoming a member. As he later stated in his testimony to the 1867 Royal Commission on Trade Unions, 'I had no objection to the society at any time, but that which induced me to join was that a practical question was coming on upon the reduction of the hours of labour in which question I felt a great interest, and I decided to cast in my lot with the society at once.'[27] As a newcomer to the Operative Bricklayers, Howell played an exceedingly minor role in the 1859–60 strike and lockout, although his intelligence soon won recognition in his appointment to the committee revising union rules. By autumn of 1859 he was serving as a union delegate at the weekly building trades meetings in Shaftesbury Hall.[28] Throughout this period he was generally without work and obliged to rely on Conference strike pay, which fluctuated between 2s and 6s per week,[29] in addition to a small subsidy paid by his own union. By the end of 1860 Howell's effectiveness as a debater and his organizational skill won him new prominence within the Bricklayers, as his selection as representative to the Derby Conference indicates.

The meeting at Derby established a United Kingdom Association for Shortening the Hours of Labour in the Building Trades, with Potter as its Secretary. Although Howell was active in formulating the objectives of the new group, he had been denied the authority to commit the OBS to any course of action and returned to London to find his union unwilling to identify itself with Potter's proposals. Most of the building trades unions now preferred to act independently, thus preventing Potter from continuing to manage the agitation. The Bricklayers, with some reluctance, did agree to collaborate with other societies in sending nine-hour petitions to employers. This new provocation led the master builders to retaliate by introducing payment by the hour – generally 7d – rather than by the day. Not only did this permit dismissal at an hour's notice, but the marginal wage increase over the old rate of 32s per week concealed the fact that payment by the hour made a nine-hour day almost unenforceable. By shifting their ground from hours to wages, the employers undercut the operatives' effort to limit the length of the work day. Moreover, additional payment for overtime was to be eliminated.

Resistance was now carried on principally by the bricklayers and stonemasons, who struck against the innovating employers. While the association of master builders urged general approval for the new procedure, many of the smaller firms accepted the demand of the masons and bricklayers for a 55½-hour week at the old rate of pay – in other words, the ten-hour day with a Saturday half-holiday. The bricklayers continued to strike until October 1861, and the stonemasons held out until the middle of the next year. This struggle – far more sporadic and disorganized than the battle against the notorious Document – proved largely abortive: in the end it secured the concession of the short Saturday, with a readjustment of wages to the old rate, but the hour system became the conventional pattern of employment.

As a result of his new prominence within the Operative Bricklayers, Howell came to play a much more active role in this dispute than he had in the earlier strike. When a builder named Kelk announced in March 1861 that he would impose the hour system, the OBS summoned a meeting of his employees at which Howell, as union spokesman, urged resistance to payment by the hour. Deputations were appointed to the innovating firms, and on 21 March Howell was elected as a member of the newly formed Bricklayers' strike committee.[30] This mark of recognition of the ambitious young bricklayer was gratifying not merely in bringing him his first position of responsibility, but also for its material rewards: during the seven months that the strike committee functioned

Howell and his associates were paid at the standard wage rate of
33s per week.[31] The appointment ensured Howell's election to the
executive of the new London Trades Council two months later.

The efforts of the workers' deputations met with mixed success.
The few employers who withdrew the hour system were troubled
no further. The bricklayers' strike continued against those employers – like Kelk – who defied the union's appeal and was soon joined
by the masons and plasterers. To publicize their campaign the
OBS held a mass meeting in St James's Hall on 25 March, at which
Howell justified the renewed strike action to the assembled workers.
Several of the affected employers sent an agent to the provinces to
obtain replacements for the London operatives, and the union dispatched Howell as its representative to counteract the blandishments of the builders' recruiter. Visiting Manchester, Liverpool,
Plymouth, and other towns in the South and West, Howell
effectively impeded the enlistment of blackleg labourers.

In early April a master builder named Jackson questioned
Howell about the possibility of a settlement on any terms other
than the nine-hour demand. Jackson informed him that many of
the builders were not averse to the Saturday half-holiday and hoped
for a compromise on that basis. Howell reported his discussion to
a union meeting on the 10th, and the Society accepted Jackson's
terms, with the stipulation that wages be raised per ten-hour day in
order to maintain the weekly rate of 33s. Some of the employers
settled on these conditions, although they shortened the half-
holiday by eliminating the dinner hour. This concession attracted
provincial workers seeking the now-more-favourable London
opportunities. The bricklayers soon found that new demands were
being made on their virtually depleted funds at the same time that
their unity was being increasingly eroded. At a meeting on the 25th
the desperate Society resolved to continue the fight, but they were
now forced to impose 1s per week levy on members for the duration
of the struggle against the recalcitrant firms.

When the Brighton builders decided to emulate the London
employers by instituting the hour system, Howell was dispatched
to Sussex to warn the bricklayers there to secure at least the London compromise. On 29 May Howell was re-elected to the strike
committee, and for the next five months he and his two colleagues
continued visiting picketing workers, negotiating with employers,
composing letters to provincial societies and to newspapers, and

attending nightly strike meetings in various parts of London. By mid-October the bricklayers decided to abandon their resistance. The compromise terms had been accepted by many, though not all, of the employers, but the union found itself financially incapable of continuing the strike. Their expenditure for the period had exceeded £1,850, and it had been necessary to resort to levies and loans from sympathetic societies, as well as private subscriptions, in order to meet expenses.[32]

The strike had been a failure in general terms, but for Howell it proved to be an unanticipated opportunity to begin a career in public life. Although unemployed for most of the period from 1859 to 1861, for seven months Howell had earned good wages for doing the kind of work that prepared him for the organizational duties that comprised much of his activity in the years to come. He continued to work as an artisan for nearly four more years, but he was no longer the obscure artisan who had hesitated to join a trade union. There had in fact been 'some real work to be done', not merely in the interest of labour conditions, but in the interest of his own career.

The London Bricklayers

The London Order of the Operative Bricklayers demonstrated its resiliency by overhauling its organization and embarking on an aggressive programme of expansion. If effective agitation was to be waged against the employers, it was essential for the union to possess funds sufficient to sustain its members during periods of unemployment. Militancy without solvency was futile, since the union could ensure solidarity only if it compensated men adequately for loss of work. Once a union's funds were exhausted, the employers invariably regained the upper hand and settled disputes on their own terms.

While the fight against the hour system was still raging in 1861, the London Order's constitutional revisions committee proposed a reorganization on the lines of the new-model craft unions, of which the Amalgamated Society of Engineers served as prototype. What appealed to the Bricklayers were the carefully devised financial and administrative arrangements that enabled these unions to attain unprecedented stability. By shifting their emphasis to friendly benefits and the protection of craft interests, such unions lost their revolutionary character and universal appeal. Increasingly they preferred conciliation to the sort of confrontation which might threaten their financial resources, but this cautious outlook strengthened trade unionism during a period in which its right to survive was repeatedly questioned.

A London Order circular of the early 1860s spelled out the redefinition of the union's functions:

The Society shall be established for the purpose of supporting its members when out of employment, travelling relief, and for the burial of deceased members and their wives; and also to secure to its members all the rights, rules, customs and privileges of the trade; to regulate the price and lessen the hours of labour, and generally to ameliorate the condition and advance the general interest of the trade.[33]

Howell's preamble to the revised 1867 edition of the Society's rules mentioned 'sickness, accident, and superannuation' among the new benefits.[34] Although the reconstructed union abandoned its concern with apprenticeship regulation – an obsession of the old-fashioned societies – it did stipulate a minimum of three years of bricklaying as a condition of membership. Moreover, potential members had to be under forty-five years of age, a restriction that stemmed from the new emphasis on benefits. Inevitably the insurance aspect of unionist activity demanded regular increases in contributions by members. Between 1861 and 1868 the entrance fee was raised from 7s 6d to 10s per member, and the weekly subscription rose from 3d to 10½d. The affiliated metropolitan 'lodges' elected a seven man executive council for staggered six-month terms, with all members eligible for re-election. One feature of Coulson's policy of sponsoring affiliated lodges outside London was the association of eight provincial representatives with the executive. The new professionalism of the amalgamated union is evident in the recasting of the job of General Secretary. Elected annually by a democratic vote of the entire membership, he was provided with an office and initially a weekly salary of two pounds.[35] Responsible to the executive council, he had the duty of keeping the accounts, but wide discretionary powers inevitably devolved upon the only full-time paid official. Despite the centralization implicit in the authority of the Secretary and the council, the Operative Bricklayers, like the Engineers, was run on a federal basis, with the local branches retaining their own funds and ultimate elective power. While the office of Secretary acquired remarkable security

of tenure – Coulson held the post until 1891 – both he and Applegarth of the ASCJ faced frequent attacks from dissident members,
who used local branches as a base for subversion.

The Bricklayers mingled a preoccupation with conciliation and
benefits with a sense of class-consciousness, directing their enmity
towards the capitalist rather than towards capitalism. In a series of
articles aimed at attracting new members, Howell, enlisted as chief
propagandist, argued that operatives could only make their influence felt through a union with large membership and tight organization. 'By constantly associating together, feelings of friendship and
unanimity will be the result. We shall get to understand that the
interest of one is the interest of all.'[36] However, the power which
worker-solidarity generated should not be dissipated in violence; it
must be cautiously exerted to 'protect the weak against the strong
and realize the greatest good for the greatest number'. Trade union
strength must not be used aggressively, but rather to provide the
worker with 'protection to enable him to resist the attempted in-
fringement of his rights and privileges'.[37] In industrial activity – as
later in politics – the working-class inclination was almost invariably
towards amelioration rather than revolution. Howell praised the
agitation for shorter hours, but he also shared his associates' reluctance to resort to militant tactics: 'Why cannot both parties meet
and settle the question without strikes? Whoever refuses, whether
man or employers, are justly to blame for the results. If the demands be unjust or ill-timed, all the more necessary is it that it
should be discussed with calmness and settled without strife.'[38]
Despite this retreat from violence, Howell's propaganda disclosed
an unabating hostility towards 'the avariciousness and injustice of
the employing class'.[39] Persistent union effort – as in the disputes of
1859–61 – was needed in order to resist the 'aggressions of unprin-
cipled capitalists',[40] whose chief goal seemed to be the oppression of
defenceless workers.

In September 1861 Howell started the *Operative Bricklayers'
Society Trade Circular and General Reporter*, with the assistance of
his strike committee associates, Charles Shearman and Henry
Noble. During the four months of his editorship, the paper reflected Howell's interest in the education and moral improvement of
his fellow workers. His introductory editorial cautioned that 'unity
without knowledge is most likely to prove abortive. It is not numbers alone which we require – we need intelligence also.' He

expressed the hope that the monthly journal would become 'the channel for the communication of thought between man and man, and will enable us to discuss topics of general interest to the whole trade'.[41] In addition to reports on branch and executive meetings and information on trade conditions around the country, Howell sought to provide columns for correspondence, for articles on the workman's library, and for discussion of public affairs. While the journal was under Howell's control, unions were advised to abandon their hostility to political involvement on the grounds that they had a duty to 'watch over the welfare of their members politically as well as socially'.[42] After the publication of the fourth issue in December, illness forced Howell to resign the editorship, but worsening relations with the General Secretary may have hastened his retirement.

While the two men differed little on basic trade union policy, Howell joined in the complaints against Coulson's reckless sponsorship of branches affiliated with the London Order in areas traditionally within the Manchester orbit.[43] Howell's concern with politics also clashed with Coulson's indifference to these matters, although, under Applegarth's influence, the Secretary was won over to his rival's viewpoint. If Howell's challenge to his leadership increased the friction, a strong personal antipathy lay at the root of the conflict. A competent, even dynamic leader, Coulson was a coarse, obstinate man, lacking the social graces which Howell admired. Single-minded in his attention to trade questions, he found Howell's versatility suspect, symptomatic of a shifty unsteadiness. In addition, Coulson distrusted his younger rival's cleverness. Within scarcely two years of his entry into the Society, Howell had piloted through a constitutional reconstruction (which ironically strengthened Coulson's position), managed the strike committee, and established the *Trade Circular*. His self-seeking tactics and undeniable competence posed a threat to Coulson's domination of the union. With his friend Shearman and the former Secretary, Henry Turff, he began a systematic campaign to undermine Coulson's authority, widening a breach which ultimately led Howell to resign from the London Order in 1871 and to join the Sheffield Lodge of the Manchester Unity the next year.

Howell always polled well in the executive council elections, occasionally, as in 1862, 1864, and 1865, receiving more votes than any other candidate. On the other hand, he consistently failed in his efforts to displace Coulson as General Secretary. The votes seemed to disappear. Thus while Howell received 626 votes in the council election in December 1862, he could muster only 138 votes to Coulson's decisive poll of 726 in the contest for the Secretaryship.[44] After an open quarrel with Coulson over his representation of the Society at the Birmingham Trades Union Congress and over the Markley affair in 1869,[45] Howell decided to contest the leadership for the third and final time, but in the July 1870 election he finished a poor second with 147 votes to Coulson's 500.[46] Despite this rivalry, Coulson found it difficult to avoid utilizing Howell's talents. He served as the Bricklayers' delegate to the London Trades Council until replaced by Coulson himself in September 1862. In 1863 he was once again called upon to make peace with the injured Manchester Unity of Bricklayers.

Coulson's expansionist policy repeatedly jeopardized relations with London's northern counterpart, which saw its influence dwindling in the face of encroachments by London Order branches. In 1861 Howell had secured an arrangement between London and Manchester, whereby they agreed to collaborate in tramp relief and expressed mutual intentions to seek greater unity in trade policy. The northern society, a larger, but less enterprising union, stipulated that the London Order refrain from opening affiliated lodges where Manchester Unity branches already existed. Howell accepted these terms in September 1861, only to find the agreement violated the following March, when a group of Wolverhampton bricklayers, who had seceded from the Manchester Unity, received permission from the London officials to open as an affiliated branch. Terrified lest Coulson's more aggressive union supplant them entirely, Manchester revoked the 1861 accord in retaliation.

In September 1863 Howell secured another settlement with Manchester, but his report to the OBS warned that

tampering further with their lodges will only widen the breach between the two bodies and produce ill-feeling where harmony should prevail. We broke the engagements; therefore we should conciliate, and we believe it our duty to remove the cause of complaints. . . . Let them work, and wish them God speed, but don't throw obstacles in their way, and depend upon it, they will be only too glad to see us prosper if we work honestly and in good faith.[47]

This advice was disregarded, and the truce proved to be only a temporary one: the conflict was to be rekindled six years later. In 1865 Howell's services were again enlisted, this time as delegate to the new International Working Men's Association, with which the OBS became the first union to affiliate, thanks in large measure to Howell's manœuvring.[48]

It is clear that Howell and Coulson were able to forget their mutual antipathy when required in order to further policies they both favoured. In the International, in the 1865 London Trades Council struggle against George Potter, and later in the work of the Conference of Amalgamated Trades, vital working-class interests pushed personal grievances into the background. None the less, Coulson emerged indisputably as the victor in the contest within the Operative Bricklayers' Society. Howell's attempt to wrest the leadership was repeatedly foiled, and his failure reinforced his inclinations towards political, rather than industrial, activity.

The London Trades Council

The London Trades Council developed from the delegate meetings held during the winter of 1859–60 to co-ordinate support for the striking building workers. Once the conflict over the Document had been resolved, the working-class organizers felt that it would be valuable to establish a permanent 'trade committee so as to be able, on emergency, to call the trades together with dispatch, for the purpose of rendering each other advice or assistance'.[49] With Thomas Jones of the Tinplate Workers' Society as the first Secretary, the Council was launched in July 1860. Howell appears to have helped devise the original proposals, but he did not join the Council until May 1861, when he was elected to the fifteen-member executive.[50] Along with Odger and Cremer, he was instrumental in promoting a rule unlikely to arouse enthusiasm among many of the trade unionists: 'That the duties of the Council shall be to watch over the general interest of labour, political and social, both in and out of Parliament; to use their influence in supporting any measure likely to benefit Trades' Unions; also to publish (if necessary) an Annual Trades' Union Directory.'[51] During the next five years, chiefly through the medium of the London Trades Council, Howell and Odger, with the support of Applegarth and Cremer, struggled to convert the trade unions to a belief in the efficacy of political action. Although individual members participated readily in Radical movements of the early 1860s, it was not until the end of 1866 that the politically timid unions agreed to add their voices to the reform agitation.

Within three weeks of his arrival on the executive, Howell replaced the provisional appointee, Thomas Jones, as Secretary, a position he combined at first with service on the Bricklayers' strike committee.[52] The earliest formulation of the rules had not foreseen a salaried officer, but the need for some remuneration soon became apparent. Although Howell never received a regular stipend, the Council decided that the Secretary should – at least in theory – be paid £6 per year.[53] For nearly a year he received no compensation at all, but between May and September he was granted £6 in several instalments.[54] When Odger became Secretary, his wages were paid only slightly less irregularly. The rules stipulated that the Secretary's function was to keep the minutes and accounts, but, in practice, he managed the finances and general affairs of the body. In the London Trades Council, as in most working-class societies at the time, the single official found himself responsible for all matters of business and policy, subject only to the intermittent check by the membership. Howell found that the large initial expenditure on a trade union directory, the first of its kind in England, meant that he had

to start [his] secretarial duties with a debt, and very soon the enthusiasm of the trades had mostly evaporated. I practically had to wait upon the various Societies for a small grant towards the cost of the Council, for printing and postage – for that comprised the whole of our expenditure – and towards the debt. We had nothing to pay for a meeting room, inasmuch as the Bell Inn, Old Bailey, was always open to us. . . .[55]

All the trades represented on the Council were obliged to contribute to its maintenance, but at first only at the rate of 2s per 100 members every year. The principal sources of income were the three large societies which came increasingly to dominate the Council, especially once their secretaries joined the executive – the Bricklayers, the Engineers, and the Carpenters.

Despite its lack of funds, the London Trades Council struggled to win recognition and to establish itself as an effective spokesman of labour interests. Although the rules prohibited action unless in response to an appeal, the Council assumed the responsibility for investigating trade distress and recommending to affiliated bodies support for worthy strikers. It had no authority to impose levies on

these societies, but it could grant credentials to those seeking assistance and enjoin its affiliates to provide aid. Moreover, it increasingly arrogated to itself the power to summon delegate meetings
not only over trade questions, but over public issues of general
interest to the working class as well.

Before the end of 1861 the Council became embroiled in the
question of participation in political affairs. Howell consulted
Professor Beesly and James Stansfeld, the Radical Member of
Parliament, on possible political action, and Odger encouraged
societies to take up the question of political reform, arguing that
trade unions were the only organizations which could deal with the
subject effectively. The repercussions were inauspicious: the Engineers, the strongest and wealthiest of the Council's component
elements, disapproved.[56] The political faction, led by Howell and
Odger, resigned itself to a policy of non-intervention in politics for
the time being. In his annual report Howell noted the defeat of
Odger's initiative:

The Council . . . resolved not to take up political questions as a Council; but as most of the members of the Council are in favour of reform,
they determined to co-operate with other bodies, not as a Council, but
as individuals. . . . They will strictly adhere to their functions of watching over the interests of Trade Unions and confine themselves to such
measures as affect us as workmen.[57]

Politics were, however, more difficult to ignore than some of the
unions imagined. In December 1861 the General Neapolitan
Society of Working Men appealed to the Council for help in promoting Italian unity and for advice on the organization of labour.[58]
Replying on behalf of the Council, Howell welcomed the fraternal
greetings of the Italian workmen and affirmed the Council's sympathy for the cause of Italian freedom. Despite the warm tone of
the address, he explained in no uncertain terms that the fusion of
political and social goals, characteristic of the Mazzinian working-
class societies of Italy, evoked little enthusiasm in England. 'Our
trade societies are not constituted on a political basis,' he informed
them, '[but] are more of a social character, their objects being to
promote the well-being of their members in all matters appertain-
ing to their daily toil.' Justifying the moderation of his countrymen,
Howell continued, 'We bend our energies to the development of
our social interests, and earnestly strive to better our condition as

workmen; for we feel that this will ultimately lead to political power.'[59]

The address, one of several which Howell wrote, illustrated the ambivalence of English artisans towards Radicalism at home and abroad, most striking in their participation in the International Working Men's Association. Dedicated to international working-class solidarity, they applauded enterprises abroad on behalf of greater liberty regardless of the means employed to secure this end. If they were willing to condone foreign revolutions, politically-conscious artisans disavowed similar tactics at home. Since they already possessed a large degree of civil and religious liberty, they felt that the common goals of all workers had been at least partially attained in England. Given such distinctions it was only appropriate that the character of domestic agitation should be more conciliatory, conducted through the agency of trade societies seeking modest objectives. Not only were these organizations the principal channels for working-class reform agitation, but they also assured that it would be parochial and limited in outlook. Just as the new model respectability curbed militancy in industrial affairs, so too it guaranteed that working-class Radicalism would reject violence.

Most of Howell's tasks during his tenure as Secretary of the London Trades Council were less dramatic than communications with foreign agitators. Letters to newspapers defended London trade societies against allegations of complicity in the Sheffield outrages, in which violence had been employed against non-unionists. Meetings were arranged to mobilize support for the bricklayers and the masons. The Council investigated appeals from other unions and granted credentials to the weavers, coopers, and shoemakers, as well as the building workers. In addition, Howell corresponded frequently with societies in Glasgow, Liverpool, Manchester, and Bristol, seeking assistance or offering counsel.[60]

Recurrent illness, which forced Howell to relinquish the editor-ship of the Bricklayers' *Trade Circular,* made it difficult for him to perform his secretarial duties. On several occasions he expressed his intention to resign, but in April 1862 he was re-elected to the Council and continued in office.[61] Poor health was not the only deterrent to the discharge of his functions; the conflict within the OBS threatened to undermine his position completely. In view of their enmity, it is not surprising that Coulson schemed to remove Howell from the Council as the Bricklayers' representative. In May

1862 Howell threatened resignation, claiming that his position would be untenable were he to cease representing his union. His friends rallied to his defence, protesting that 'in consequence of the liability of a delegate to be removed at the caprice of a few in his own trade, it was . . . advisable that the Secretary should not depend upon such a slender thread'. A resolution was passed declaring that the Secretary would not be obliged to represent a particular union, but that 'he should be a good society man and be answerable to the Council only for his conduct'.[62] His tactics having failed, Coulson sought to appease the ill-feeling which the incident had provoked in a letter expressing regret at 'the misunderstanding between the Secretary of the Council and his own trade'.[63] The damage was irreparable, however, and in July Howell submitted his resignation. In August Odger replaced him as Secretary, and a month later Coulson took his place as the Bricklayers' delegate.

His health and the conflict with Coulson were only partly responsible for Howell's retirement. Since the end of the hours dispute Howell and his colleagues on the strike committee had been denied work by vindictive London builders for their part in the struggle. Shearman and Noble left London, but Howell was reluctant to give up his Council position. He hoped the boycott would prove temporary, but foremen were afraid to hire him unless he changed his name. At last he was obliged to look for work outside London, where his identity carried no stigma. In the summer of 1862 Howell found work in Kingston-on-Thames and moved his family there, only to find himself unemployed when jobs became scarce in the winter. During the next year and a half he moved several times in search of work, to Surbiton, Long Ditton, and elsewhere in Surrey. He did not return to London until June 1864, when a former employer, Henry Dove, an Islington church builder, offered him a job as a foreman, a position he was to retain until he was appointed Secretary of the Reform League in April 1865.

Howell reappeared on the London Trades Council as a 'special delegate' in March 1865 and was re-elected to membership in August. By this time he had become Reform League Secretary and was again serving on the Bricklayers' executive, as well as on the General Council of the International. The LTC provided a useful base of operation from which to co-ordinate relations between the League and the trade societies. His role as 'special delegate' in March and April served a different purpose: the antagonism between the Junta and Potter reached a climax when the London Trades Council passed a vote of censure on Potter at a special delegate meeting in March 1865. The details of the battle have been fully described elsewhere;[64] what is significant here is that Howell was from the outset identified as an anti-Potter partisan. The Council, in fact, recalled Howell to reinforce the Junta faction in the contest. At a delegate meeting on 29 March he indicted Potter for convening meetings in support of the North Staffordshire puddlers' strike without consulting the LTC. Howell had attended one of these unauthorized meetings two weeks earlier, at which Potter's supporters had voted down his critical resolution insisting that 'the proper body to take up this question is the Trades Council'.[65] When the Council gathered for its annual conference on 28 August he led the attack on Potter's irresponsible meetings, castigating him for having 'thrown the apple of discord in amongst them'. Potter, he claimed, 'aimed at the annihilation of the Council by repudiating and denouncing its authority'.[66]

Howell remained on the Council until 1867, when its activities were, for all practical purposes, subsumed in the Conference of Amalgamated Trades. For the services he performed during his years of participation, he reaped substantial benefits. Although outdistanced by Coulson within his own union, he had found a new stage on which to promote his career. His stint as Secretary provided valuable organizational experience, and in the following years he was able to ally himself more closely with the Junta, thus laying the foundation for his accession to the Secretaryship of the Reform League.

3
The Revival of Reform Agitation

In March 1861 Richard Cobden, disheartened by the political inertia which seemed to sustain Palmerstonian rule, remarked to his friend William Hargreaves,

> I wonder the working people are so quiet under the taunts and insults offered them. Have they no Spartacus among them to lead a revolt of the slave class against their political tormentors? I suppose it is the reaction from the follies of Chartism which keeps the present generation so quiet. However, it is certain that so long as five millions of men are silent under their disability, it is quite impossible for a few middle class members of Parliament to give them liberty.[1]

The Roman parallel was an inappropriate one, rarely echoed in the pronouncements of working-class leaders of the day, except, perhaps, in the somewhat patronizing references to the plight of foreign labourers. In his address to the Neapolitan Society of Working Men a year later Howell stressed the contrast between the relative freedom prevalent at home and the survival of tyranny abroad. English workers, he observed, 'had thrown off the shackles of despotism'.[2] If the image of slavery was inapplicable, Cobden's assessment of the political temper was more perceptive. In the late 1850s and into the 1860s political timidity, heightened by the failure of Chartism and the spread of economic benefits, dampened the impulse towards militant reform agitation.

Cobden was right to stress 'the reaction from the follies of Chartism', but he failed to perceive the tenacity of democratic aspirations even in a tranquil period. The workers concentrated on obtaining their share in the new free trade prosperity and on strengthening their trade unions, but they never abandoned their earlier goal of full political rights. Whatever the weaknesses of Chartism as a popular movement, it had bequeathed to the next generation a political ideology around which agitation could be renewed in more auspicious times. The reform movement of 1865–7 developed from the workers' conviction that they had a moral right to come 'within the pale of the Constitution', not from a sense of grievance, as Cobden intimated, against a condition of political subjection. As with so many other labour demands in this period, agitation for the suffrage reflected a desire to participate in the existing system, not, as was true of the more intransigent Chartists, to transform it.

Chartism had provided a political creed for its heirs, but it had also demonstrated how not to organize a national movement. The radical character of the Charter would alone have spelled disaster, but the cogency of its programme had been diluted by Feargus O'Connor's agrarianism and Bronterre O'Brien's anti-capitalist call for public ownership and land nationalization. In the absence of effective central direction, rival leaders, each with his own followers and programme, contended for domination of the amorphous movement. Chartism fell victim more to the factionalism which plagued its history than to official hostility. In the quixotic O'Connor the movement discovered its own Spartacus, but if his demagoguery inspired one generation of working men, it warned the next against similar tactics. The Reform League never produced an O'Connor; its ultimate domination by men like Howell marked a victory for the policy earlier identified with William Lovett. While the Reform League derived its ideology from Chartism, its structure imitated that of the Anti-Corn Law League. With a concise, cautious platform and centralized authority, the Reform League would never match the heroic posture of Chartism, but at the same time it would manage to avoid most of the pitfalls which its predecessor encountered at every turn.

It was certainly true, as Cobden warned, that so long as the working classes refrained from political organization, the ameliorative efforts of bourgeois reformers were futile. John Bright had been preaching the merits of a wider franchise to redress the balance against the power of the landed interest since his arrival at Westminster in 1846, and his return to Parliament as a member for Birmingham after his 1857 defeat foreshadowed a renewed effort to promote suffrage reform. While he did not share the reservations of most politicians about the dangers of a more democratic franchise, not even the Rochdale Radical endorsed an indiscriminate extension of the vote. Despite Bright's growing enthusiasm for popular participation as a counterweight to aristocratic privilege, the workers were slow to accept his leadership. His hostility to trade unionism and factory legislation, his coolness to the question of Polish freedom, and, most of all, his opposition to full manhood suffrage retarded an effective alliance until 1866. The bonds were undoubtedly strengthened during the campaign in support of the Union during the American Civil War, when Frederic Harrison, a proponent of the alliance between Bright and the workers, was able to report that 'the leading Radicals among the London working men are ready to adopt [Bright and Cobden's] lead in a way they never were before'.[3] This was somewhat exaggerated: even such a manifestation of common sympathy could not compensate – at least initially – for Bright's repudiation of the full democratic programme.

In fact, the working classes were neither as quiet as Cobden implied, nor as dependent on the leadership of men like Bright as they imagined. If the immediate post-Chartist years proved singularly unfruitful in successful agitation, the breakdown of national solidarity after the Crimean War and the economic decline of 1857–8 did reawaken latent social tensions. The nine-hour movement among artisans, especially in the building trades, provided a fillip to their class-consciousness. Chartist activity, which had never completely disappeared, actually revived in a spate of suffrage organizations in London, Newcastle, Manchester, Rochdale, and York.[4] While it is apparent that Radical and working-class political activity overlapped rather than merged in a cohesive movement, this very fragmentation guaranteed a wide appeal, both elements attracting separate groups of adherents. What was significant about the reform movement on the eve of the 1860s was the revival of simultaneous agitation – despite a variation in goals – within different classes. If the middle-class Radicals sought a more restricted reform than the artisans did, both groups were now – as in the 1830s – moving in the same direction. The distinction lay in the extent of desired changes, not in the notion of change itself, and both groups could sanction at least tenuous collaboration. Between 1859 and 1865 a unified reform movement did not take shape, but rather successive waves of political agitation provoked by disparate and often unforeseen events. If many of these incidents were foreign and of no obvious relevance to English workers, the politically-conscious artisans themselves, influenced by sympathetic Radical politicians and intellectuals, chose to link the democratic cause abroad with the reform question at home. Thus the spontaneous indignation aroused by the failure of liberalism in Europe stirred the self-awareness of the English workers, reinforcing their traditional demand for greater political power.

Several months after Howell and George Odger failed to convert the London Trades Council to the idea of political involvement, they decided to promote a reform society for trade unionists outside the Council. After a preliminary meeting in October 1862 the Trades Unionists' Manhood Suffrage and Vote by Ballot Association was launched with Thomas Grant Facey, a printer, as Secretary *pro tem.* and Odger as Chairman. Odger's appointment, together with the presence of Howell, Applegarth, and Cremer on the executive, linked the new body to the London Trades Council, whose political counterpart it hoped to become. As in the case of the Reform League, which the organization prefigured, individual and society membership was encouraged. Individual members, who paid an initial fee of one penny, were invited to form branches, and trade societies could constitute themselves as branches as well. Both were to send representatives to a central council which would direct agitation in the form of meetings, petitions, addresses, and deputations to the House of Commons. The basis of the campaign was a professed belief in 'the natural and God-given rights of every man to equal political rights'.[5] Despite an enthusiastic endorsement by the *Bee-Hive* the Association aroused scant interest among the London trades, and, after several introductory meetings, it subsided into inactivity until May 1864. Its revival at that time coincided with the establishment of the Universal League to secure many of the same objectives. Presumably the working-class leaders had not yet settled on an effective structure for the reform movement and were still casting about for alternatives. The resurrection of the trade unionist organization did, however, emphasize their leaders' belief that agitation should be waged within the existing trade-union framework. At a 26 May meeting the executive council appointed deputations to visit societies and seek their participation in a manhood suffrage conference, originally scheduled for July.[6] This conference, held in fact on 13 September, once again urged an active movement among the trades for franchise extension.[7] Howell addressed an anniversary dinner of the South Kensington brick-layers' lodge on the need to abandon anti-political parochialism and to work for reform through the Manhood Suffrage Association.[8] Several further meetings were held, but by the spring of 1865 the Association had been absorbed into the Reform League.

If the working men were reluctant to respond to the reformers' appeal, their interest was more readily engaged by events abroad, most notably the American Civil War. While their initial reaction was uncertain and, at times, ambivalent, it is clear that by the end of 1862, and especially after the Emancipation Proclamation, the masses rallied to the Northern side. From the outset they had abhorred slavery, the horrors of which had been luridly portrayed in the immensely popular *Uncle Tom's Cabin*, but the sense of identification with the democratic cause grew into a self-sacrificing devotion to Lincoln and the future of the Union. 'For years,' Howell wrote, 'one test of a man's Liberalism was – What was he on the American question?'[9] His own attitude had at first been equivo-cal. In the Bricklayers' *Trade Circular* he declared that in America 'man is pitted against his brother, without any great principle being involved, except, indeed, that of self-government by the Southern-ers'. But he went on to note that 'the Southerners are only fighting for greater despotic power in relation to slavery'.[10] The first con-cern of English working men was the organization of relief for the Lancashire cotton workers, whose livelihood had been ruined by the Northern blockade of Southern ports. In October 1862, three months after his resignation as Secretary, Howell urged the London Trades Council to take action on behalf of the cotton workers, and a month later this advice was heeded by a London Working Men's Central Committee to collect money from trade societies for Lanca-shire relief.[11]

London trade unionists convened a public rally on 26 March 1863, to express working-class sympathy with the American struggle and with Negro emancipation. Arranged by Professor E. S. Beesly, this gathering in St James's Hall marked the culmination of efforts to unite Bright's crusade with the enthusiasm of the working classes. Although the guests included Goldwin Smith, John Stuart Mill, James Stansfeld, Henry Fawcett, and Frederic Harrison – not to mention Karl Marx and Henry Adams among the audience – the occasion took on an avowedly working-class aspect. Except for Beesly and Bright, all the speakers were London trade unionists.[12]

Moving the first resolution of the evening, Howell deprecated the slave-owners' attempt to destroy the Union and criticized those public men in England who favoured the Confederacy. In an attempt to justify the earlier equivocation of many working men, he admitted that it was unusual for trade unionists to denounce a revolution. Had it arisen as a result of tyranny and oppression, he suggested, they would have felt obliged to sympathize with its objectives, since it was their duty to fight in defence of liberty and progress. There was, in fact, not a single principle for which the South struggled that would warrant the approval of 'lovers of freedom'. Howell summoned his fellow workers 'to raise their voice loud and strong against the attempt which was being made to establish an independent kingdom, having for its chief cornerstone slavery'.[13]

Although working men participated in pro-Union meetings throughout the year, the St James's Hall rally was an important milestone. Not only did it furnish testimony to the democratic sympathies of the workers: it markedly advanced the coalescence of Bright and his supporters with the politically-conscious artisans. As Howell later reminded him, 'Your presence with us on the American question in St James's Hall gave a great impetus to the political tendencies of the unions, and aided us greatly in our endeavour to bring them into the political arena.'[14]

Other foreign events had a similar catalytic effect on political agitation, furthering collaboration among the classes for common ends. In the autumn of 1862, for example, a Working Men's Garibaldian Fund Committee held a series of Hyde Park meetings to express their solidarity with the Italian patriot. When a proposed visit by their hero was announced, the preliminary committee was absorbed by another, led by Robert Hartwell, the ex-Chartist and future editor of the Bee-Hive, to plan a public demonstration to greet him. At the same time a middle-class City of London Demonstration Committee was formed. Plans ceased upon the postponement of Garibaldi's visit, to be revived in March 1864 in preparation for his April arrival in London. The two groups collaborated in arranging the ceremony of welcome at Nine Elms Station. On 11 April several hundred representatives of the two committees and a number of MPs assembled at the train station, and a procession of many thousands of artisans escorted Garibaldi on his triumphal journey to Stafford House, the London residence of the Duke of Sutherland.

The subsequent announcement of Garibaldi's premature departure, ostensibly for health reasons, aroused suspicions of political
intrigue that no official assurances could allay. Stansfeld and other
prominent Radicals believed that the General had made up his own
mind to cancel an intended provincial tour. Perhaps he had become disillusioned with admiring English hosts, prepared to
applaud his exploits, but unwilling to offer practical assistance. The
real cause of the change in plans was not, in any case, as significant
as the impression created among the incipient reform groups, for
whom the incident served as yet another spur to political action.
On 23 April a Working Men's Shakespeare Tercentenary Committee turned a Primrose Hill commemorative celebration into a
protest meeting against Garibaldi's alleged expulsion. After the
gathering, which had been addressed by Beesly, Harrison, William
Shaen, and Edmond Beales, was dispersed by the police, some
sixty of their number reconvened at the Adelaide Arms, near Chalk
Farm. Resolutions were passed against the 'forcible suppression' of
the demonstration, and a deputation was appointed to present their
complaints to the Home Secretary. Howell, a member of both the
Garibaldi and Shakespeare committees, proposed a national political organization to widen the scope of their agitation, a suggestion
which was to bear fruit in the formation of the Reform League
within the next year.[15] The Garibaldi committee continued to meet
during the next few months to solicit contributions and discuss the
right of public meeting, but by the summer the new Universal
League took over the organization of such activities.

During the course of the Garibaldi agitation Radicals and working-
class leaders – although in this case excluding Bright and his
followers – joined forces also on behalf of Polish independence.
Sympathy for the Polish struggle for freedom dated back to the
1830 uprising and had been kept alive by Polish exiles in London
and English Radicals, whose Russophobia led them to champion
any apparent victims of Czarist tyranny. In response to the 1863
revolt the London Trades Council sponsored a mass meeting on
28 April. Attended by the usual amalgam of Radicals, Positivists,
and trade union leaders, the meeting resulted in a resolution calling
upon the government to declare itself in favour of Polish independence.[16] Several meetings later the collection of working men and
middle-class Radicals established the National League for Polish
Independence, with the London barrister Edmond Beales as

President and the Marquis Townshend – or Lord Raynham as he then was – as Treasurer. While its objective was to muster 'moral and pecuniary aid' for the Polish cause, the League refused to disavow war if that were the only way to prevent Poland's absorption by Russia.[17]

The Garibaldi and Polish movements converged to achieve a more inclusive blending of middle-class Radicals and trade unionists than the domestic reform effort had been able to achieve alone. The different spheres of activity tended to overlap, bringing one group into contact with another. Beales and Howell, as well as Beesly, Applegarth, and Coulson, joined the second phase of Garibaldi agitation after taking part in the Polish campaign. Conversely, Potter, Cremer, Samuel Morley and the Leicester MP, Peter A. Taylor, came to the Polish agitation from the 1862 Garibaldi committees. The interpenetration of these movements fostered a political alliance that straddled class lines. Association with politically-involved trade unionists convinced middle-class Radicals, whose contact with them had previously been limited, that 'men who can take so genuine an interest in the destinies of foreign nations are fit henceforth to share in ruling their own'.[18]

Amid these waves of activity the Marquis Townshend, one of the few aristocrats who genuinely supported the reform movement, invited a group of Radicals and trade union representatives to the unveiling of his plans for a Universal League for the Material Elevation of the Industrious Classes on 14 December 1863. Its objects were more comprehensive than any previous body, aiming at the social, economic, and political advancement of working men. In addition to the reduction in the hours of labour, the League proposed to promote franchise extension, the international fraternity of workers, and wider recreational and educational opportunities. J. B. Leno was named Chairman and Garibaldi Honorary President, the latter a precedent that the Reform League was to follow. The vice-presidents included Beales, J. A. Nicholay, and Captain E. Dresser Rogers, all of whom were to become Reform League officials. Townshend, the Treasurer and principal financial supporter, obtained rooms for the Universal League at 18 Greek Street. The office provided a welcome alternative to the back room of public houses as a meeting-place for politically active trade unionists, as well as a home for the International Working Men's Association launched some months later.[19] Howell was a latecomer to its councils, but by June 1864, after his return to London, he became an active member.

In May the Universal League sponsored meetings to consider the right of public assembly and the amendment of the Master and Servant Act, but once Gladstone announced his conversion to parliamentary reform the organization shifted its emphasis to the suffrage question. Howell took part in a 17 May meeting which, while applauding Gladstone's declaration, insisted that 'manhood suffrage was the only basis on which any effective agitation could be sustained'.[20] A Universal League Reform Committee, which Beales felt would strengthen Gladstone's hand, was formed, and on 20 June the League officially committed itself to the principle of manhood suffrage.[21] Beales presided over a large public meeting at the Freemasons' Tavern two days later at which Howell moved the main resolution stating 'that the time has arrived when the unenfranchised masses of the people of this country should be admitted to a share in the right of election of members to the House of Commons by that right being extended to all resident and registered male persons of sound mind and unconvicted of crime'. Howell added that democracy did not mean the predominance of one class over another, but rather 'the just equality of all before the law'. The delegates present proposed to establish a special committee to raise money, convene meetings, and set up district branches in order to implement their political programme.[22]

Townshend objected to this concentration on the franchise question, regarding the proliferation of reform committees as a means of removing the League from his control. His response was to 'amalgamate' the earlier Reform Committee with the League, in other words, to stifle it before it could effectively take off on its own.[23] Although the League lingered on for another year, it was evident by the first annual meeting of 27 July that its achievements had not matched its expectations. The report to the membership might boast that the organization had 'inaugurated the new franchise movement',[24] but Townshend resisted this exclusively political orientation and, in doing so, prevented his creation from maintaining the leadership of the new reform drive. This antipolitical reaction, unleashed by the League's founder, was a factor in the revival of the Trades Unionists' Manhood Suffrage Association in 1864. Moreover, the Universal League did continue to furnish premises throughout the autumn and winter of 1864–5 at which plans for a Reform League could be hatched, despite the hesitations of Townshend and the suspicions of Potter's *Bee-Hive* clique.

One additional source of reform energies was the International Working Men's Association, as much a product of Continental Radical currents as of traditionally English ones. In early September 1864 a committee drawn from Universal League members planned a public meeting to welcome a deputation of Paris workers who were planning to reply in person to a fraternal message sent by George Odger.[25] At this inaugural meeting of the First International, held on 28 September in St Martin's Hall, the chairman, Professor Beesly, traced its derivation to the attendance of French workers at the Polish demonstration in July 1863. Replying to Odger's plea for a 'fraternity of peoples', Victor LeLubez, a French *emigré* and prominent member of the General Council in its early years, proposed the formation of a central committee in London representing working men from all the affiliated countries. The delegates, including workers from Germany, Italy, and Poland, not to mention France and England, approved the French suggestions as the basis of the new association and elected a provisional council of thirty-three delegates to implement them.[26] Howell, who described the gathering as 'most enthusiastic', was appointed to the predominantly English body.[27]

At the first meeting of the Council on 5 October Odger was elected Chairman and Cremer General Secretary.[28] Characteristically vague in their expectations for the new body, the English delegates were unable to agree on a programme. George Wheeler and J. B. Leno even suggested merging it with the Universal League, in whose Greek Street offices the Council met until the beginning of 1866, but this suggestion was promptly scotched.[29] It was at this point that Karl Marx, who had played no role in organizing the St Martin's Hall meeting, intervened decisively. With the encouragement of the Council leaders, he prepared the deliberately unprovocative Inaugural Address and Provisional Rules, thus providing ideological guidelines for the amorphous body. These rules adopted virtually unaltered from Marx's draft, characterized the function of the association as furnishing 'a central medium of communication and co-operation between Working Men's Societies existing in different countries and aiming at the same end, viz., the protection, advancement, and complete emancipation of the working classes'.[30]

While working-class leaders like Howell identified their own struggles with those of embryonic European – and American – democracy, the principal motive for their support of the International was to safeguard their trade union interests. They believed that it would increase international solidarity and perhaps prevent the importation of strike-breaking European labourers.[31] The new association represented the culmination of successive attempts, dating back to the 1790s, to foster systematic communication between British and Continental workers. But if their foreign counterparts entertained notions of proletarian uprisings and the overthrow of capitalism, the English trade unionists were by no means infected with similar expectations, regarding the International not as the engine of world revolution, but rather as one of several instruments for the promotion of social and political reform. More receptive to the sentimental and ambiguous doctrines of Mazzini than to Marx's 'scientific socialism', the English members found in the International – at least at its inception – a tolerance for ideological opacity which allowed them to mingle bourgeois liberal and Marxist doctrines, with little sense of their fundamental incompatibility.

In describing the programme of the International Howell later remarked that 'a Gladstone or a Bright could have accepted [it] with a good conscience'.[32] This assessment assumed with some justification that his English colleagues shared his objectives for the International, goals which would indeed have given little offence to radically-inclined Liberals. The subsequent renunciation of these moderate principles he blamed on the importation of 'wild, abstract continental theories', the 'ravings' of middle-class intellectuals who diluted the proletarian composition of the International and were responsible for the ultimate dissension and decay.[33] In fact, the 'pernicious' foreign influences brought the International to life and nurtured it on an avowedly socialist programme, even though most of the English workers seemed to remain oblivious to the permeation by more extreme ideological currents. It was Marx's intellectual ascendancy which raised the association to international notoriety, although by 1867 – and the passage of the Reform Act – it began to stagnate in England, and within a few years was to crumble under the assault of Bakunin and the anarcho-syndicalists.

With the promulgation of the basic charter of the First International Marx acquired a pre-eminence within the General Council never effectively challenged in England. The influence of Odger and Cremer rapidly declined, their places taken by reliable agents of Marx, like George Eccarius, a German tailor. At no point did Howell figure prominently in the affairs of the organization. Although he was named to the General Council every year until 1869, he was rarely in evidence after the summer of 1866.[34] Most active during the first year, he was appointed to the key standing committee in November 1864 and was re-elected the following September. In November he was also named as a deputy to visit trade societies in order to solicit potential members.[35] His prize was the Operative Bricklayers, whose affiliation he secured in February 1865, the first trade union to join the International. Having served as intermediary, Howell was nominated as the Bricklayers' representative on the General Council.[36]

Marx was later to claim that Howell's withdrawal from the International was the result of disappointed ambition. Howell had 'canvassed keenly the "proud position" of editor [of the *Commonwealth*]. Having failed in his "ambitious" attempt [in February 1866] he waxed sulky, his zeal grew less and less, and soon after he was no more heard of.'[37] It is evident that the split over the *Commonwealth* – not so much in February as during the summer – exacerbated tensions within the General Council. Its minutes in July testify to disputes between Howell and Cremer over the newspaper, with Howell complaining that certain of Cremer's remarks 'reflected on him'.[38] No details of the argument survive, but Howell's known sensitivity to criticism, his undeniable ambition, and the growing coolness between the General Council and the Reform League contributed to his disenchantment with the International. Despite his nominal ties with the General Council until 1869, he began to find himself ideologically out of step, opposing, for example, its endorsement of land nationalization and of Fenian terrorism. Most of all, however, it was the pressing demands of his Reform League work which forced Howell to curtail his participation in other groups. During its first years he found it useful to retain membership in associated working-class bodies. Hence he remained active in the London Trades Council, the Operative Bricklayers, and the International. Within them he served his political apprenticeship, acquiring the essential bureaucratic skills and personal contacts for his later work. Those organizations which prepared the way for the Reform League also prepared the way for Howell's career in Radical politics.

Howell's proposal for a national franchise movement in April 1864, although enthusiastically received, was not rapidly implemented. The efforts of the Trade Unionists' Manhood Suffrage Association and the Universal League to initiate a popular campaign through the existing organizational framework continued for almost another year. The new International diverted London labour leaders from their overriding concern with franchise reform and, to some extent, delayed an effective alliance with bourgeois reformers by stirring up latent proletarian militancy. In the face of middle-class resistance to manhood suffrage and trade union indifference, the impetus for a major undertaking was dissipated in fruitless meetings and ineffectual organizations. It was not until the beginning of 1865 that the diverse currents could be blended into a single movement.

At the end of January Randal Cremer announced at a meeting of the General Council of the International that efforts were being made to organize a manhood suffrage meeting.[39] Cremer was apparently referring to the work of Mason Jones, a well-known Irish Radical orator and journalist, who approached Edmond Beales at this time about the possibility of promoting franchise agitation in London. Beales warned Jones that the working men would respond to nothing less than a programme of manhood suffrage and the ballot. Unaware of the feuds in which he was currently embroiled, they sought out George Potter, suggesting that he summon the London reform and trade union groups to a mass meeting. Potter, who appreciated all too well the bickering and rivalries which split these groups, was sceptical about the feasibility of bringing them together. Jones assured him that if the workers were prepared to take up the question in earnest, a number of influential men, including several MPs, would lend personal and financial support. While arrangements were made for a meeting at St Martin's Hall, Mason Jones sought the co-operation of the veteran Chartist, Ernest Jones, who offered his assistance on the condition that the new movement pledge itself to full manhood suffrage and not yield to the watered-down schemes of the 'Manchester tricksters' in the National Reform Union.[40]

Attended by a large and representative body of working-class reformers, the St Martin's Hall meeting on 23 February inaugurated the Reform League to obtain registered and residential manhood suffrage and the ballot. With Mason Jones and Beales as intermediaries, a committee was appointed to negotiate with middle-class Radicals and to invite their collaboration. Robert Hartwell, who presided over the St Martin's Hall gathering, was named Provisional Secretary. On 11 March the committee met with John Bright, Charles Elt, Acton Smee Ayrton, Peter A. Taylor, E. Dresser Rogers, and Sir Wilfrid Lawson at Radley's Hotel and informed them that whereas they would be satisfied with nothing less than manhood suffrage, they might be forced to accept a less comprehensive measure. Bright agreed that the workers were justified in seeking a broad concession, insisting, however, that he favoured nothing more than a household suffrage bill. Bright's view was shared by Ayrton, the member for the Tower Hamlets, a sign that Beales's hopes for an immediate union of all reformers was excessively optimistic. Two MPs, Taylor and Lawson, did none the less endorse the working-class formula, and Samuel Morley, the wealthy hosiery manufacturer and philanthropist, promised financial assistance even though he regarded demands of the League as immoderate.[41]

A resolution introduced by J. B. Leno was carried at a 16 March meeting, advising 'the working classes to depend on their own exertions to obtain their political enfranchisement'. Trade unionists were slow to realize that franchise reform did not mean the same thing to all its proponents and felt betrayed by the moderation of the middle-class Radical goals. Howell's motion to reprimand Bright for 'deserting the principle of manhood suffrage' – which he had never, in fact, supported – was only narrowly defeated. Beales cautioned the delegates not to hope for a comprehensive bill unless they were willing to work for it energetically and to enlist the trade unions in the agitation. With almost the whole of respectable society and much of the Liberal Party hostile to their intentions, the working men would have to rely on their own efforts to alleviate their political disability.[42] The adoption of the rules a week later showed that the League was no more receptive to the idea of an indiscriminate, universal enfranchisement than were middle-class democrats. The objective of the League was 'to procure the extension of the elective franchise to every resident and registered adult male person of sound mind and unconvicted of crime'.[43] These qualifications were intended to ensure that only responsible working men would obtain the vote. Hence the working-class conception of the rights of 'free-born Englishmen' did not extend to paupers, vagrants, and the lowest stratum of the poor. This reflected the largely urban, artisan composition of the League, true alike of the leaders and the rank and file. Its failure to strike roots among the urban proletariat and the agricultural labourers meant a relatively narrow base of support, a serious weakness in view of the initial reluctance of trade unions to affiliate. In time the promotion of outdoor agitation would result in somewhat wider participation.

The League proposed to operate through a network of branch associations and by means of public meetings, lectures, and the dissemination of propaganda, all co-ordinated through a central office in London. The initial formulation of principles made no mention of demonstrations or of more incendiary means of pressing their case. The League was to be a respectable organization, in the mould of the Anti-Corn Law League, promoting its views through education and persuasion, acting simultaneously on the people and the politicians and using the gentle pressure of the former to secure a timely concession from the latter.

Despite the warnings of realistic observers, like Edmond Beales, the Reform League was launched amid high expectations of early victory. The working-class participants were convinced that unity within the labour movement could be secured, that middle-class Radicals could be won over, and that the alliance formed between the two elements would force the Government to settle the issue. While the results of the next two years did not wholly disprove this contention, the obstacles that stood in the way of success were more formidable than they anticipated. Not only did the Second Reform Bill prove disappointing in scope; the alliance with Bright and the Radicals was slow to develop and was conditional upon the acceptance of less than a full measure of reform. Furthermore, the movement was plagued from the outset by internal conflicts that its managers could never wholly reconcile. That it managed to survive and devise an efficient mode of action was largely the result of a fortunate choice of officials. In Edmond Beales, the President, and George Howell, soon to become the Secretary, the Reform League found not merely dedicated workers, but the kind of men who were determined to maintain its course whatever storms and mishaps threatened to destroy it. While others became impatient, they realized that in restraint lay the only hope of victory, even if that victory would only be a partial one. Rather than risk the kind of confrontation with authority that might lead to violence, they proceeded cautiously, appealing to the workers to win their political heritage through peaceful agitation.

4

The Workers Demand the Vote

In its early months the Reform League found that it had more to fear from its supposed friends than its avowed enemies. Despite the election of the widely respected Beales as President, the feud between Potter's followers and the Junta prevented the League from securing the allegiance of all the London labour groups. The leaders identified with the London Trades Council and the International Working Men's Association outnumbered their *Bee-Hive* rivals on the organizing committee and the first Executive Council. Potter, Hartwell, Thomas Connolly, and Joseph Leicester – two trade unionist allies of Potter's – all participated in establishing the League, but Potter's supporters were not welcome at the early meetings and were excluded from the ruling circles when possible. By the end of 1865 Potter's position would become untenable, the personal conflicts heightened by the simultaneous squabbles within the London Trades Council. Domination by the Junta made Hartwell's position as Provisional Secretary uncomfortable, and at the first executive meeting he proposed the establishment of a sub-committee to consider the appointment of a general secretary. The question was referred to Montague Leverson, John Weston, and Howell, who agreed on Frederick Milne Edge, the candidate recommended by Mason Jones, Beales, and reputedly by Richard Cobden as well. Edge declined because of private business commitments, and Howell was asked to serve pending the selection of a permanent secretary.[1] It was subsequently suggested that the Reverend George Murphy and Howell serve jointly, but Howell persuaded the committee that divided responsibility would only lead to confusion. Murphy withdrew, and at the 24 May executive meeting Charles Bradlaugh nominated Howell as Permanent

Secretary, adding the proviso that he be paid for his services at a salary to be determined in the future. With the entire Potter clique absent, Howell was unanimously elected.[2]

Whether through lapse of memory or the desire to emphasize his indispensability, Howell depicted these events somewhat differently in his later recollections:

> Whilst I was still working at Messrs Dove's job at Islington early in 1865, a deputation waited upon me to urge me to undertake the Secretaryship of the Reform League then being formed. . . . I hesitated a good deal, as I could not well see how I could do the secretarial work of a political body and fulfil my duties to my employers as a foreman. . . . Then it was urged that promises of support had already been given so that it was intended to have a paid Secretary. . . . I was assured that I was the only man who could unite all parties, and I eventually consented to be proposed.[3]

It is improbable that any such group made overtures to Howell before 15 April, although it may well be that the London Trades Council were eager to replace Hartwell by a more congenial figure from the outset. Nor does it seem likely that Howell, so clearly identified with the Junta, would have been put forward as a candidate 'who could unite all parties'. On the other hand, there seems no reason to question Howell's memory of a deputation approaching him since his claims to the position were not sufficiently obvious to enable him to press his own case. The probable sequence was as follows: after Hartwell had withdrawn and Edge, the candidate of the middle-class founders, had declined the office, a small group, presumably including Odger, Cremer, and Applegarth, urged Howell, then serving as Secretary *pro tem.*, to seek it on a permanent basis. Scarcely acquainted with the man with whom he was to be intimately associated for over four years, Beales consented to rely on the recommendation of the labour leaders. He was at this time unaware that Howell was a partisan in the struggles against Potter.[4] If the Junta promoted his candidacy as a tactical measure, it was more than just an exercise in factional politics. Despite the limitations of his organizational experience – a deficiency shared by most of his working-class colleagues – Howell had proven himself an effective administrator and loyal collaborator, thereby earning the confidence of his associates.

As the nominee of the London Trades Council and International coterie, Howell immediately became the target of vituperative attacks in the *Bee-Hive*. When the Council's annual meeting became the scene of a renewed denunciation of Potter's independent labour policy, Hartwell retaliated editorially, accusing Cremer, Applegarth, and Howell of 'reckless misrepresentations of [Potter's] conduct'. He could not pretend to find such tactics on the part of Applegarth and Cremer remarkable, but Howell's conduct struck him as inexcusable:

The personal hostility of Mr Howell to Mr Potter is well known; it has existed for the last five or six years. But we think the position now held by Mr Howell, as Secretary of the Reform League, should have caused him, as a man of intelligence, to have seen the impolicy, however strong his opinions, of standing forth as an active and unscrupulous partisan. . . . His party feeling outruns his judgement, and the Council of the League made a grievous mistake when it selected a partisan like Mr Howell to be its Secretary.[5]

Hartwell was justified in complaining that the Secretary was something less than dispassionate in his political behaviour. On the other hand, given Howell's background, it was hardly possible for him to remain neutral amid these battles. There was a certain hypocrisy in Hartwell's plea for impartiality, using, as he did, the *Bee-Hive* as a weapon in the same conflict, even though it meant publicizing labour disunity before the uninitiated public.

When Hartwell began to intimate irregularities in Howell's election, Beales retorted that Hartwell would himself have been elected – with a stipend – had he not declined on the grounds of lack of time. Beales insisted that Howell's name was not proposed until Hartwell refused the office.[6] In December 1866, a month after the reorganization of the Executive Committee which saw the defeat of both Potter and Hartwell, the latter sought to expose the supposed deceit of his enemies in a series of highly polemical articles. Hartwell now claimed that he had only declined the secretaryship because he felt it should be held by a man of independent views – which he manifestly was not – and because payment for services had never been mentioned to him. He asserted that the 'Odger party' was aware before the 15 April meeting that Edge would refuse and had prepared 'a whip-up in consequence to get in Mr Howell without any time for opposition'. In other words, the Junta had staged the entire procedure, packing the meeting with their supporters and taking advantage of an occasion when Potter's friends would be absent. 'Under the circumstances,' Hartwell continued, 'Mr Howell was carried in by his 12 friends out of 15 [members present], and thus one of the most violent partisans on either side was pitchforked into that office.'[7]

Edge replied that his intended withdrawal was quite unknown to any League member until he actually announced it on 15 April. Only at that point, after several nominations and a lengthy discussion took place, was Howell elected. His appointment, moreover, was only *pro tem.*, since many members still hoped that Edge might so arrange his affairs as to enable him to take up the position. 'If there were any pre-arranged plan,' Edge wrote, 'for the running in of Mr Howell I was certainly ignorant of it; and I may be permitted to add that the entire proceedings of the meeting in question showed an utter absence of such pre-arrangement.'[8] Beales corroborated Edge's remarks, adding an impassioned, if rather futile appeal for unity.[9]

If Hartwell's carping attacks were a persistent irritant to Howell, they were certainly not the most serious obstacles to be overcome during the League's early months. In spite of the enthusiastic response of some middle-class Radicals, many others either disapproved of its platform or doubted its prospects. Beales and Mason Jones, its initial proponents, never envisaged the League as an exclusively working-class organization. The composition of both the organizing committee set up in March and the first Executive appointed in April indicated a determination to apportion the management of the League among both middle-class supporters and artisans, although the membership was to be predominantly working class. The honorary vice presidents were all bourgeois, their number increasing from eight at the beginning to over 120 by the summer of 1867.[10] This group included financial benefactors like Samuel Morley, William Hargreaves, and Samuel Pope, parliamentary advocates like Thomas Bayley Potter (Cobden's successor at Rochdale) and Peter A. Taylor, as well as Radicals who took part directly in League operations, such as Charles Bradlaugh, Lieut-Col L. S. Dickson, Josiah J. Merriman, Dr J. Baxter Langley, and E. Dresser Rogers.

The growing roster of celebrated names – itself a partial directory of mid-Victorian Radicals – could not conceal the fact that an even larger and perhaps more influential body of Radicals kept aloof.

John Bright, John Stuart Mill, and Goldwin Smith all found League policy unpalatable and refused invitations to become vice presidents.[11] Although he later overcame his misgivings, E. S. Beesly was at first reluctant to lend his name because 'there [was] no real effective desire for such a reform as you advocate'.[12] John Malcolm Ludlow turned down a bid for support on the grounds that 'the present agricultural population is too ignorant and too dependent upon their employers to have the vote'.[13] Howell claimed that Richard Cobden was 'favourable', but it appears doubtful that he did any more than encourage potential contributors, especially Hargreaves, T. B. Potter, and Frederick Pennington.[14]

After the open split at the Radley's Hotel meeting, the leaders of the Reform League were not hopeful about converting the delegates at the National Reform Union conference in Manchester on 15 and 16 May. Beales, Mason Jones, and Howell represented the League, while Cremer and Odger attended on behalf of the International. Howell spoke in favour of Merriman's manhood suffrage amendment, warning the largely middle-class audience that the London workers were pledged to 'the principle that would give all men, irrespective of their position in life, a vote for members of Parliament'. Lacking a vote himself, he added that he was unlikely to accept a measure that would continue to deprive him of his political rights. If they were prepared to advocate democratic principles for Americans, they should adopt them for home consumption as well. Beales tried to counter the defeat of Merriman's amendment by proposing the recognition of 'the constitutional right of every man to the suffrage as the true basis of all agitation for reform'. The restraint of this formula made it no more agreeable to the Reform Union leaders, who regarded household suffrage as the only sound basis of legislation. P. A. Taylor urged Beales to abandon his motion for the sake of unity, possible only if the working men settled for a lesser measure.[15] Unwilling to widen the all-too-apparent breach, Beales agreed to withdraw his compromise resolution, much to the dismay of Ernest Jones, who complained to Marx that 'Beales behaved *badly*' and Taylor 'scandalously'.[16] Jones was convinced that the conference had been 'rigged' by the middle-class leaders, but he assured Marx several days later that 'You overrate the importance of the National Reform Union if you suppose it has *much* power. It has a little, but very little. It will die

D

out, and our movement as it grows will gradually swallow it up without effort.'[17] Neither Taylor nor Jones was correct in his predictions. Unity was never achieved between the two groups, although after the Manchester conference the League vowed not to show hostility towards the Union.[18] Some semblance of mutual tolerance was maintained during the months between the defeat of the 1866 Liberal Bill and the passing of the 1867 Conservative one, and that mostly because Bright was able to mediate between the two camps, upholding Union principles while recognizing the greater impact of League agitation. Jones's estimation of Reform Union prospects failed to take into account its superior financial resources. Formed in Manchester in 1864, the Union had immediately fallen under the domination of Bright's followers. Under the presidency of George Wilson, the former chief of the Anti-Corn Law League, the Union reflected much the same political and social complexion as the earlier organization, a correspondence which explained its ability to tap middle-class donors for large subscriptions. Those manufacturers who contributed to both the Union and the League were invariably more generous to the more moderate organization. Samuel Morley, the League's principal backer, gave twice as much money to the Union. Middle-class reformers found it useful to encourage League agitation in order to frighten the Government, but they hesitated to espouse its principles and made sure their donations were not large enough to finance large-scale agitation. By controlling the purse strings, they were able to exert an important influence on the course of the League's operations. The Union may have been able to report only 150 branches to over 400 for the League in the early months of 1867, but its income exceeded anything to which the League aspired. With perhaps one-third the membership, the Union was none the less able to launch a £50,000 Guarantee Fund which boasted ten donors of at least £500.[19]

A more serious threat to the Reform League's future than either the schism within the labour movement or the coolness of middle-class patrons was the indifference of organized trade unionism. While the leaders were often prominent in trade unions themselves, they were unable for over a year and a half to win over the rank and file, who saw politics as less vital to their interests than industrial questions. Through propaganda and local organization the working-class politicians tried to overcome the trade union parochialism which stood in the way of any mass undertaking. With the failure of the Liberal Bill and the deliberate solicitation of working-class support by Bright, a joint effort by the League managers, by the Potter circle, and, within London, by Benjamin Lucraft ultimately broke down the reservations of the trade unions, paving the way for the demonstrations from July 1866 to May 1867.

Howell's plea to his fellow workers in June 1865 reflects the League's initial failure to attract mass support. After denouncing a system which withheld the vote from six million men, he decried the persistence of class legislation and discriminatory taxation. Trade unionists, he wrote, 'spend thousands of pounds annually to obtain some trifling advance in wages and some small reduction in time' all because their interests were ignored by Parliament. The implications of his argument were clear enough: as long as trade unions remained preoccupied with industrial issues, their gains would be marginal and excessively costly. Only through a unified campaign on the political and industrial fronts could they hope to satisfy their grievances.

Let us once be able to maintain by the force of intellect and truth our rights as workmen . . . and depend upon it we shall rise in the social scale. . . . Our own organizations prove our power of government, our self-restraint, our financial ability and economy, and our law-making capabilities *likewise*. They show more, they prove that we understand justice, and are earnest in the protection of every member, whether he be assailed by an employer, or a fellow workman and brother Unionist.[20]

Howell and his associates hoped that middle-class patronage would cloak the League's activities in respectability, but, on a more crucial level, they realized that survival depended on middle-class subsidies. The discord evident at Manchester hardly augured well for an immediate outpouring of money, and despite a £100 donation from T. B. Potter in May 1865, the League was desperately short of funds during its first months.[21] Beales himself paid the rent on the Adelphi Terrace office for a time and secured advances from a few affluent supporters to tide the League over until contributions became more regular.[22] Howell considered resignation when there were no funds to pay his salary, and it became necessary for several Executive Committee members to pledge a weekly sum towards his remuneration.[23] In order to compensate him further, the Howell family was given the back room of the Adelphi Terrace office, and they lived there free of charge from July 1865 until April 1868, when it was taken over by the Adelphi, the League's short-lived working men's social club. His initial wages of £1 16s per week were no more, and may have been less, than he had earned as a bricklaying foreman.

In July the newly constituted Finance Committee, headed by E. Dresser Rogers, received instructions to approach all those who had promised assistance, and by the 21st Howell could report P. A. Taylor's offer of £25, to be given on the condition that seven others matched it.[24] Samuel Morley had been informed by Mason Jones, whose enthusiasm waned rapidly, that the League had no future, and Howell had to persuade him that Jones's disenchantment was not universally shared. Morley sent in his £25, but it was not until the beginning of 1866 that the list of eight donors was completed. Morley's gift was the first of many: an additional £100 by April 1866 and three further donations of £250 each, not to mention the major share of the £1,900 special electoral fund in 1868, established the Nottingham philanthropist as the League's greatest benefactor.

Sensitive to these financial restrictions, Beales urged a modest programme of consolidation that would not strain the limited resources at their disposal. In the first phase of the League's history his guiding hand is recognizable, and his ability to mediate among the factions prevented the organization from foundering. As President, he wisely counselled against entanglements in fruitless contests during the July 1865 election. When J. Baxter Langley, a surgeon and a member of the Executive, decided to stand as a candidate in Greenwich, Beales warned that unless Langley polled well, a League endorsement would only diminish its influence. Odger and Cremer did persuade the Executive Committee to encourage working men in Greenwich to aid his candidacy, but no official endorsement was forthcoming. Langley ran a poor fourth in a field of five candidates, securing less than 200 votes. In two elections in which notable Radicals were running with Liberal blessings, prospects were more favourable. Thomas Hughes, the Christian Socialist barrister and author, was elected for Lambeth, his electoral committee having included members of the Junta.[25] Howell took time out from his official duties to help the noted defender of trade unionism. But, as Beales had anticipated, the Reform League made no significant impact during the election; Hughes's success hardly compensated for Langley's resounding defeat. The League did not reserve its endorsement for the leading reformers like Hughes and Mill: on 14 July the Permanent Committee voted to congratulate all the Liberal victors.[26] Such a gesture revealed the extent to which the working men identified their cause with the Liberal Party, relying as much on its generosity as on their own initiative for the fulfilment of their goals. The equation of Liberalism and reform survived even the disappointment of the 1866 Bill. Gladstone's public conversion to democratic principles in 1864 had consolidated a 'Lib-Lab' *entente* which was rooted in the artisan ideal of self-help. Liberalism seemed to represent a challenge to privilege and the concession of just rewards to the morally worthy. More than any other politician, Gladstone became the spokesman for these values. He did not have to struggle to earn the devotion of the masses; it was thrust upon him and, once secured, it could never be wholly relinquished.

As long as Palmerston remained in power the League entertained little hope of change, but immediately after his death Howell began to prod his Liberal friends. Now that the main opponent of reform had been removed, he pleaded with Bright that

no time should be lost by the Liberal Party in arranging their tactics, and organizing their forces, for a determined parliamentary campaign for Electoral Reform during the coming session. . . . If the Liberal Party through procrastination or supineness, or by apathy or indecision, neglect to take their stand upon the present vantage ground, as the representatives of the liberal and progressive spirit of the nation, they will properly forfeit the confidence and support of the toiling masses of their countrymen, and instead of occupying the foremost place in the councils of the nation, will sink into deserved insignificance and obscurity.[27]

He further argued that any government measure should be more comprehensive than the bills of the 1850s, 'inasmuch as the people have evidently progressed since that time'.[28] Howell hoped that this warning would be heeded, but the threat had little substance to it, since neither he nor the other League leaders could see any alternative to reliance on the Radical wing of the party. Bright was content at this stage to maintain contact with Howell, but he saw no need as yet to move closer to the League position, regarding with scepticism the idea that the working-class leaders might take an independent line.

While awaiting the introduction of a Liberal Bill, the League devoted its attention to establishing branches and arranging local meetings, responsibility for which devolved mainly upon Howell. Beales restrained impatient members who favoured extravagant demonstrations, and until the end of 1865 small – and often sparsely attended – meetings were the general rule. It was a prudent, if exceedingly cautious, policy: the League concentrated on building up its membership for the long struggle which lay ahead. After several months of improvisation the Executive Committee appointed an official group of lecturers, consisting of Howell, Odger, Cremer, and several others. By application to the Secretary, any branch could obtain a speaker who would address its members on the franchise, taxation, the land question, or the British Constitution, as well as help in promoting the League's programme.[29] Daily administrative chores restricted Howell's own travels to the London area, but the rapid proliferation of branches kept his evenings busy. These meetings were often held in public houses, which men like Howell, who had gained his oratorical experience through the temperance movement, deeply regretted. He explained apologetically that the League preferred not to use pubs, but found that temperance halls or public meeting-rooms were either closed to political groups or too expensive to rent.[30] In November the Reverend W. H. Bonner was hired for a provincial lecture tour, and for the next year and a half he acted more or less autonomously – sometimes too much so for Howell's liking – as a speaker and financial agent for the League especially in rural, dissenting communities.[31]

As the only full-time, paid functionary, it was Howell's task to co-ordinate the operations of the increasingly complex organization. He was responsible for carrying out all the instructions of the Executive Committee, for keeping the financial records, subject to the weekly scrutiny of the Finance Committee, and, most of all, for the enormous correspondence through which the League kept in touch with branches, potential contributors, newspapers, and politicians. Although insecure in his new authority and sensitive to the slightest questioning of his competence, he delighted in his work and quickly established himself as an adept administrator. The more confident he grew in his own capacity, the less he enjoyed delegating responsibility, preferring to supervise every bureaucratic detail himself.[32] Autonomous agents and dissident branches alike seemed to pose a threat to his authority and were abruptly rebuked at the first hint of insubordination. Nor was it merely his own self-esteem which was at stake: unruly branches, like the one in Paddington, could disrupt the League's operations and hurt its reputation.[33] If a branch complained of delays by the Secretary in answering inquiries or in sending membership cards, Howell immediately appealed to the Executive Committee to clear him of blame. The first of repeated probes into the finances by members who feared that officials might be feathering their own nests was effectively scotched through Rogers' intervention.

I beg to request [Howell wrote Rogers] as a favour that you will report on the state of our accounts at our next meeting, as Mr Geo. Brooke threw out an expression about 'cooking the accounts' at our last meeting. I can well trust to your impartial judgement as to whether I was justified in what I said about the books.

With reference to keeping the books correctly, I never expected that the little petty cash book you now hold would be my only cash book for the League. As it was, I continued to use it as I had begun. If however there is anything suspicious in the accounts, at once challenge explanation and so prevent a future rupture.[34]

Howell's book-keeping was somewhat rudimentary at first, but this was certainly not for the sake of concealment.

Much of his correspondence was concerned with local affairs and, especially at first, with the procedure for organizing new branches. In reply to one such query he advised that,

They first get a small committee of 10 or 12 who take up cards of membership from the central office. They then appoint a secretary and other officers, and we supply them with cards as a branch for sale in their district. We also supply the publications of the League. . . . The branch then remits one-third of their subscriptions to the central boards [sic] keeping two-thirds for local purposes. Thus every facility is afforded for their growth as their funds are not impoverished for central purposes.[35]

In conformity to new model principles he warned that 'we are obliged to go to work in a thorough business-like manner as a commercial firm would'.[36] Branch secretaries were encouraged to take advantage of the publications and lectures supplied by the London office, and if they proved co-operative, Howell was generally sympathetic to their difficulties. Branches were expected to defray the expenses of a deputation, but the central office, he assured one local functionary, was 'most lenient in this respect'.[37] On the other hand, his letters contain frequent reproaches to local secretaries for inefficient management of their funds, for failing to send delegates to Council meetings, and for general negligence.

More important than the prodding and advice was Howell's responsibility for the arrangement of deputations – involving by late 1866 an intricate scheduling problem – and the issuing of membership cards, over which he tried to retain strict control. A. D. Bell estimates that between April 1865 and July 1867 Howell arranged over 200 meetings, and that by May 1867 he had issued 65,000 membership cards.[38] In its first year – before Howell had any office help at all – the League distributed over 100,000 copies of addresses and circulars.[39] Whether soliciting for funds or requesting attendance at a meeting, the Secretary often sent out dozens of copies of the same letter or invitation, all in his own hand. Although he might record after a typical day, 'Wrote letters from 10 a.m. to 9 p.m.,' Howell did not find the quantity of work intimidating.[40] By the early months of 1866 he could hardly contain his delight in his new career, so much more satisfactory than the tedium and strain of the building trade:

. . . my health has been better this winter than it has been in any winter these eight years. This I may attribute to indoor employment, for I feel that if I had been exposed to all weathers my strength would still be unable to bear it. So far as home comforts are concerned, I have been fortunate, for we are living at our offices, and it enables me to do much more work with greater ease than I could if living some distance off. And I have worked hard to make the League what it is. . . . But we now see the results, for the League is held in high repute by all who *know* it, and they are not a few. My heart is in the work, so that I never feel weary of my task, although sometimes very fatigued in body & mind. It is my good fortune to be on good terms with very many great and good men, and I feel proud of my position.[41]

In November 1865 the Executive Committee decided to hold a demonstration the following month, a warning to Russell that the working men were in earnest. The question of collaboration with the Reform Union was again raised, and Howell told E. O. Greening, the well-known Co-operator, that 'open hostility is by no means desirable on our part. If it comes let it be from them, and with it the onus.'[42] On 24 November, the Executive Committee resolved 'that steps be taken at once to effect a common understanding', but private soundings indicated that joint rallies and deputations were inadvisable. After a crowded St Martin's Hall meeting, Russell received a Reform League delegation on 16

January and announced to the predominantly working-class group that his ministry intended to stand or fall with its Reform Bill.[43]

The deputation helped to convince the Government that working-class apathy on the reform question had evaporated. While this may well have strengthened the hand of the parliamentary reformers, it did not precipitate any legislative revolution. Behind the scenes further negotiations between League leaders and prominent Radicals followed the meeting with the Prime Minister. On 24 January Howell discussed the possibility of a rental qualification for lodgers with W. T. McCullagh Torrens, the MP for Finsbury, and several weeks later P. A. Taylor and T. B. Potter queried the Executive Committee as to their views on the proposed £6 rental franchise.[44]

The Representation of the People Bill which Gladstone introduced to the Commons on 12 March was, despite the growing agitation, a more modest measure than Russell's 1860 Bill. The government proposed to reduce the occupation qualification for the franchise from £10 rating to £7 rental in the boroughs and from £50 rental to £14 in the counties, in addition to extending the vote to the £10 lodgers. Not only did this scheme fly in the face of the workers' demand for manhood suffrage; it was also a far cry from Bright's goal of householder enfranchisement or at least a £5 or £6 qualification. But once Bright and the Radicals accepted the Bill, the League was subject to pressures from within and from middle-class friends to follow suit.

Internal divisions between the moderates and the militants came to the surface in the Executive Committee debates over the Liberal measure. The moderates, led by Beales, Howell, and Rogers, believed the League would be deprived of middle-class contributions if they repudiated the Bill. Intransigence at this point might protect League principles, but it would sow the seeds of bankruptcy. In the long run they felt that timely compromise would enable the League to survive and continue the battle for manhood suffrage. Convinced that men like Bright and Morley envisaged the Bill only as an introductory move, calculated to win enough Whig votes for passage, Beales and Howell felt that subsequent working-class pressure would prove instrumental in extending the legislation. At an unusually well-attended Executive session on 16 March, Dr Philip W. Perfitt, a Deist preacher, called on the League to reject the Bill 'in consequence of its not meeting the just expectations of the people'. No agreement could be reached at this meeting, but during the next few days the moderates canvassed the members, obtaining enough votes to pass Odger's conciliatory resolution endorsing the Bill 'whilst strictly adhering to the principle of Residential and Registered Manhood Suffrage as the only just, sound, permanent, and satisfactory basis of representation'.[45]

Howell realized that the League had placed itself in a vulnerable position, and his remarks at the time were faintly apologetic. He confessed to the Secretary of the Reform Union, with whom he maintained cordial relations, 'It was felt by all present that if the Government attempted to abate one jot from the stand they had taken, we should at once, without hesitation, oppose them. The Bill is small enough, goodness knows, and if it be tampered with in Committee it will become a contemptible farce, unworthy of the Liberal Party, an insult to the people.'[46] Despite the qualifications with which the League endorsed the Bill, the surrender was too much for an unregenerate Chartist like Ernest Jones, who resigned rather than sanction 'a measure which is a deliberate insult to the working class, and will deprive them of the little political power they possess'.[47] Urging him not to remove his name from their roster, Howell spelled out the League's predicament:

If the majority of the present electors were favourable to a large extension of political power to the people at present unrepresented, or were in any way inclined to support the principles of the League, then we could exert sufficient influence to produce a better measure. But as it is at present, we have to wrest from them the lever with which to obtain a better measure, and thereby destroy their exclusiveness.[48]

For the moment Jones would not yield, but after the defeat of the Liberal Bill he returned to the fold, as he promised he would do.[49]

The League's acquiescence did not at first markedly improve its financial situation, although £50 from Morley – his third donation – and contributions from William Hargreaves and A. W. Paulton helped to finance numerous meetings held in support of the Bill.[50] The *Commonwealth* reported ninety-eight reform meetings during the second week of April alone, and Howell complained that only the lack of funds prevented the continuation of meetings in such frequency.

The modest programme promoted by Beales and Howell during

the first year was challenged in April by Benjamin Lucraft, who initiated weekly outdoor meetings on Clerkenwell Green. Lucraft, a chairmaker and former temperance agitator, added a new dimension to League activity, reaching in these demonstrations the strata of working men unresponsive to the conventional branch meetings. Once he had taken the initiative, the Executive felt obliged to vote £4 to subsidize the Clerkenwell Green events.[51] Howell spoke at the fourth of these gatherings, saluting Gladstone and praising the Government for its 'determination and moral courage'.[52]

The optimism of the early months of 1866 was shattered on 10 May by the collapse of the banking house of Overend and Gurney. During the late spring and summer the country was plunged into an economic crisis, with food prices and unemployment mounting. Unwilling to recognize the danger signals, a coalition of Conservatives and Adullamites, determined to kill Gladstone's Bill, defeated the Government on Lord Dunkellin's amendment to substitute rateable value for rentable value in the borough franchise qualification. The overthrow of the Liberals extricated the League from the compromising and uncomfortable position in which the Bill had placed it and ended the internal divisions of recent months. The Executive felt that the Government had missed its opportunity, and the League was now justified in closing ranks behind its own more comprehensive platform.

Gladstone's inability to carry through even a minimal reform and the challenge to working-class self-esteem implicit in Lowe's anti-democratic speeches aroused the indignation of the working men. While Beales and Howell did their best to soften the impulse towards militancy, the reactionary policy of the anti-reformers heightened it. The Hyde Park riots of July 1866 reflected a new spirit in the movement, not merely bringing thousands of outraged workers into the streets, but hastening the attachment of organized trade unionism to the League. Equally significant was Bright's realization that a reform movement based on his moderate programme was no longer – if it ever had been – feasible. From the summer of 1866 he drew closer to the League, welcoming its mass agitation without assuming its leadership or adopting its principles. Only Bright had the stature to unite the divergent Radical forces, and if he did not, as Trevelyan implied, dominate the campaign of the ensuing months, he was its spearhead.[53] He sensed that the volatile mood of the public carried with it the danger of social explosion, but he also felt that it could be exploited profitably by someone with his popular appeal.

The first manifestation of the new temper among the League membership came, not unexpectedly, from Lucraft. His response to the defeat of the Liberal Bill was to 'escalate' his open-air demonstrations by moving them from Clerkenwell Green to Trafalgar Square. On the evening of 27 June he led a procession of 1,000 from Clerkenwell to the West End, where an estimated crowd of 10,000 congregated. Resolutions were passed criticizing Russell for not insisting upon a dissolution and 'viewing with alarm the advent of the Tories to power as being destructive to freedom at home and favourable to despotism abroad'.[54] Unwilling to allow Lucraft to outface them, the Executive decided to hold its own Trafalgar Square meeting on 2 July, and Howell was appointed to supervise arrangements.[55] This demonstration was the League's first real popular success, with an estimated 80,000 attending. Encouraged by the 2 July triumph, a special Executive meeting two days later voted to hold a national demonstration in Hyde Park on the 23rd. For the first time the League intended to invite provincial branches and other reform groups to take part.[56] The authorities became frightened by the spectre of revolution, and on 18 July Sir Richard Mayne, the Commissioner of Police, informed Beales that the proposed gathering would be prohibited. The League regarded the ban as an unwarranted interference with the right of public assembly, a threat which only strengthened their determination to persist. While the police had the right to exclude 'trespassers' from a royal park, there was no precedent for preventing a peaceful meeting. It was, in any case, doubtful whether the ruling could be imposed without recourse to force, a contingency too hazardous to contemplate. The lessons of Peterloo were imprinted on the Tory mind: no government should ever risk an armed confrontation with a peaceful crowd.

The League did not stand alone in its defiance of the official injunction: Bright constantly encouraged the resolve of the leaders against those who counselled submission. 'If a public meeting in a public park [he wrote Howell] is denied you, and if millions of intelligent and honest men are denied the franchise, on what foundation does our liberty rest, or is there in the country any liberty but the toleration of the ruling class?' The proposed demonstration constituted a public repudiation of the Conservative ministry, which, he added, was governing in defiance of the Constitution.[57] He was reluctant, however, to advertise these sentiments too widely, wiring Howell on the following day not to publish his letter. It did none the less appear – with the reference to the Tories excised – in *The Times* on the day of the demonstration.[58]

The risk of impending violence made Beales hesitate, but the majority of the Executive Committee were resolute, and on 21 July they voted to persevere despite the official ban.[59] On the morning of the 23rd a conference was held at the League offices, attended by members of the Executive, delegates from provincial branches, and representatives of the National Reform Union and the London Working Men's Association. At 6 p.m. the League officials set off for the Marble Arch in carriages, while groups of artisans proceeded on foot from different points in the city. They were greeted by the anticipated cordon of police guarding the park gates, and when permission to enter was denied, Beales led the procession to Trafalgar Square, where both he and Howell addressed the assembled crowd. Many of the demonstrators remained outside the railings along Park Lane, soon to be joined by a large Clerkenwell contingent. The police grew more alarmed as the mob increased, and they began to use their truncheons to restrain the surging mass. As the workers became more excited, the pressure of their numbers caused the park railings to give way, permitting access into the forbidden area. Under the direction of J. Baxter Langley, a noisy rally was held to denounce the conduct of the police. Flower-beds were trampled, stones were thrown, and a number of participants were arrested.[60]

The next day crowds again congregated in Hyde Park and resisted the efforts of the police to disperse them. Howell attended the Marlborough Street police court, where a group of demonstrators was charged with assault and disorderly conduct. Alarmed by the continued presence of working men in the park on the 24th and 25th, Spencer Walpole, the Home Secretary, negotiated a settlement with League officials, which promised the restoration of order if the police and soldiers were withdrawn. Howell explained to Walpole that the League had not selected Hyde Park as an act of provocation, but rather because it was the only suitable place in which they might hold a large demonstration. St Martin's Hall was too small, Exeter Hall was unavailable to the League, and use of

Trafalgar Square he regarded as, if anything, more of a public inconvenience than a park demonstration.[61]

While Walpole seemed convinced by this explanation, the officers assumed too hastily that the next Hyde Park demonstration, planned for 30 July, would be permitted. The Home Office at first vacillated and then denied its consent. If plans for a second confrontation with the authorities terrified respectable London, they did not disturb John Bright, who wrote reassuringly to Howell, 'I have no objection to act with you from any disagreement with your fundamental principles. I think you are doing a great service, and I wish you as much success as you can wish for.'[62] Mill, on the other hand, persuaded the Executive that another test of strength with the Government might provoke a serious collision, and the demonstration was switched to the Agricultural Hall. Here on 30 July the League held what the *Bee-Hive* hailed as 'the most numerous and imposing demonstration of popular feeling that was ever exhibited under a single roof'. An estimated 25,000 cheered as Mill, P. A. Taylor, Beales, and Bradlaugh denounced the retrogade Tory policy.[63]

These events gave the League some justification for the growing self-confidence that marked its conduct in the coming months. After the timidity of its first year the organization had revealed a new potency, forcing the authorities to recognize its ability to mobilize thousands of workers. With Hyde Park riots – 'the Sarajevo of Reform', as one recent historian has labelled them[64] – the working-class movement for political rights had come of age. No longer could politicians cite popular passivity as an excuse for inaction. While the incidents were correctly interpreted as a portent of further agitation, they were not the overture to social revolution. The eruption of violence had been largely accidental, the unfortunate result of government provocation and mob disorder. When the ministry coupled its resistance to political reform with a threat to the right of assembly, it seemed to the working men another instance of discrimination, corresponding to Robert Lowe's contemptuous dismissal of them as an irrational mob which had to be curbed. The Hyde Park riots confirmed that the workers would answer such a challenge with defiance. What had not yet been demonstrated was the discipline and capacity for a sustained national campaign, not only invoking the weapon of popular clamour, but also persuading public opinion of the justice of their demands. For the remaining months of 1866 the League concentrated on exploiting its sudden notoriety by expanding its activities throughout the country. Although the Executive Committee was soon reconstituted on a more efficient basis, the major share of responsibility continued to rest with Howell and Beales.

In February 1866 Potter and Hartwell, frustrated by their loss of influence in the League, had established the London Working Men's Association. The *Bee-Hive* maintained that the new body had not been 'formed antagonistic to the League', but its concern with industrial as well as political questions was properly seen as a challenge to the London Trades Council's predominance in metropolitan labour affairs.[65] Since the LWMA's political programme was virtually identical with that of the League, the two groups were able to collaborate in demonstrations on occasions when personal enmities could be pushed aside. With a membership that never rose above 600, the LWMA did not pose a serious threat to the League's management of the working-class reform movement. On the other hand, Potter's organization achieved a notable success in rallying trade union support in the 3 December demonstration and later convened the 1867 St Martin's Hall Conference, an important forerunner of the Trades Union Congress.

Despite its negligible membership, the LWMA had an effective mouthpiece in the *Bee-Hive*, whose outbursts against the League – and especially against Howell – appeared regularly. In response to the hostility of the *Bee-Hive* and most of the middle-class Press, the League managers began to look to the *Commonwealth* – especially once Odger became its editor in April 1866 – as the only reliable organ. In August a motion was introduced at the League Council to recognize it as the official newspaper of the League. Promoted by Cremer, Howell, Odger, and Leno, the plan provoked bitter dissension and had to be abandoned.[66] This rebuff to the ruling clique and the unwieldy size of the General Council prompted the reorganization of the Executive Committee in September. It was decided to elect fifteen members, who would serve for three months, by ballot from the General Council. The new committee, almost equally split between middle-class members and artisans, included most of the leading personalities, although Odger and his supporters won a majority of the working-class seats, leaving Potter with only one ally at the top.

Despite the League's refusal to sanction an official tie with the *Commonwealth*, the connections which evolved were certainly intimate, especially after Howell became Secretary of a reorganized board of directors.[67] While he denied any allegations of editorial responsibility for the newspaper, Howell admitted that he possessed 'no doubt some little influence with all connected with it'. But this influence did not, he claimed, prejudice the League's relations with the weekly, which were completely correct:

1st. The League is *not* responsible for *anything* inserted in the *Commonwealth*. 2nd. It is not the organ of the League any more than the *Star* is or any other paper that inserts our reports. 3rd. Its position with regard to the paper is this: it was started by League men at a time when we had but little chance with the newspaper press, and has from that time to the present steadfastly supported the League, its proprietors and writers being mostly on the Council of the League. But never have they in any way taken advantage of their position, either with regard to early or exclusive news. Nor has the paper ever received any money either directly or indirectly from the funds of the League.[68]

Despite these protestations, Howell clearly took a proprietary interest in its welfare. 'I fear,' he had lamented to Milne Edge a fortnight earlier, 'our paper must sink from want of capital to push it up. It is on the very brink of success, if we can but sustain it.'[69] It seems likely that Howell's responsibilities increased with the end of Arthur Miall's subsidies at the beginning of December.[70] Deprived of economic support, the *Commonwealth* found it harder to compete with the still-flourishing *Bee-Hive*, and the efforts of Applegarth, Howell, and Odger failed to sustain it beyond July 1867.[71]

Howell was in the middle of both the struggle to bar the LWMA from participation in the Hyde Park demonstration and the dispute over the *Commonwealth*. His loyalty to the London Trades Council coterie made Beales's task of conciliation more difficult, especially once Hartwell launched his attack on Howell in the *Bee-Hive* in December and January. While the articles contained grains of truth, their defamatory tone justifiably enraged the Secretary, who feared the effect such adverse publicity might have on his reputation. He complained to the Secretary of the League's Scottish department, 'I too wish that they had more work and less time to concoct stories which can only hurt the movement'.[72] As the articles became more abusive, Howell struck back in his correspondence, stressing his victimization by the *Bee-Hive*. 'I have personally opposed [Potter's] strike system for years,' he informed a supporter in Derby, 'and am hated by *his paper* for the course I have adopted. We want reform for all parties of the state, *not for the purpose of substituting one class rule for another*.'[73] Howell felt aggrieved at Beales's neutrality amid the raging conflict and occasional criticism of the Secretary's partisan zeal.

You sometimes accuse me [he wrote Beales] of temper in treating of these things. Well be it so. But I never mean to change *your* leadership for *George Potter's*, nor will I consent for the League to do so. No one feels more pride or gratification in working under you, Sir, than I do myself, and I will never change your high character and leadership for that of a trickster.[74]

The President himself became exasperated by the disruptive effect the scurrilous attacks were having on the movement and resented the need to refute Hartwell's misrepresentation of the facts. Howell worked hard behind the scenes to convince Beales that the *Bee-Hive* clique did not deserve even his toleration. He insisted that Hartwell had forfeited the confidence of the working men because of his financial unreliability, having failed to remit the League dues he had received and having 'lost or *destroyed*' the accounts for the Garibaldi Committee. In contrast, Howell declared that his own probity was indisputable: 'I challenge my enemies to examine my accounts from the first moment to the last. Nay, at Messrs Dove Brothers, the great Church Builders at Islington, whose situation I gave up at the earnest solicitation of members of our Council, I was spending from £90 to £100 per week and never had one of my [accounts] challenged.' Stung by the persistent attacks he had endured at the hands of Hartwell and Potter, he retaliated in kind: 'They live on *slander* and *falsehood*. They slandered good Mr Lincoln. They slandered Mr Gladstone. They have inserted the Trade slanders against Mr Bright. In fact, who have they not slandered? I leave them in contempt and disgust.'[75]

The *Bee-Hive* made Howell its main target not merely because of his partisanship, but also because he was increasingly assuming the dominant role in the management of League affairs. As Secretary, he sat on all the administrative committees, as well as on the *ad hoc* bodies appointed to plan demonstrations. As a result of difficulties with various League collectors over commissions, the solicitation of funds came more and more under his own direction. In addition, Howell's responsibility for the arrangement of lectures and deputations, involving intricate negotiations with provincial branches, made greater demands on his time in the autumn and winter of 1866 than ever before.

From its earliest months the League had sent lecturers into the provinces, the Reverend Mr Bonner and others spreading the reform gospel while raising money up and down the country. Once it had been decided to intensify the reform agitation, this makeshift system of deputations seemed insufficient. Langley devised a lecture programme which he intended to finance from an anticipated £10,000 fund and won executive approval for it in October. The lecturers were not only to deliver talks, but also to perform administrative functions on the spot that had formerly been left to the Secretary to carry on by mail. The Executive Committee had begun to realize – as Howell did not always himself – that a single full-time official could not cope with all the administrative details. However tireless a correspondent Howell was, his letters were not always an effective substitute for personal contact. The proliferation of branches increased his burdens, and their distance from London tended to prevent close supervision. Langley proposed that each lecturer should be responsible for his own expenses, but should not exact payment from the branches he visited. From the dues collected he might allow himself second class rail fare, a salary of £2 per week, 10s for incidental expenses, and a commission of twenty per cent, all subject to the Secretary's scrutiny. This relatively high remuneration prompted a raise in Howell's own salary to £2 10s, since it did not seem appropriate for the lecturers to earn more than the Secretary did.[76] The League decided to launch the programme with four full-time lecturers – Odger, Cremer, and two ex-Chartists, James Finlen and George Mantle – each enlisted for a period of at least four weeks.

The scheme was more easily designed than implemented; delays in arrangements and conflicts over expenses hampered its success. A dispute, for example, broke out between Cremer and Howell over the solicitation of money from Jeremiah J. Colman, the mustard manufacturer, for the £10,000 fund. Cremer resented the fact that Howell had written to Colman, regarding it as an attempt to deprive him of his commission. He accused Howell of 'trying to take the bread out of his mouth', but he withdrew these charges upon discovering that Howell had actually written to Colman, at Samuel Morley's suggestion, before Cremer had approached him.[77] Howell confided to Mantle, with whom his relations were far more amicable,

I can afford to pass unnoticed Mr Cremer's abuse, for who has he not abused? Did he not in your absence oppose your being on the Council?

I have always been in the habit of working to a straight line in my trade and I have not left my trade long enough to forget that line. Crooked and zigzag paths I have tried to eschew. I defy any man to prove any part of my conduct to be otherwise than straightforward and frank.

I have never deserted my friends for those who were in the habit of acting with me, never used the League for any private or personal advancement or profit, and I never will, or for the private interest of another. And if those who I once numbered as my friends have seen any cause for distrust, why not be manly enough to have it out face to face? My position as Secretary to this League has never been one of profit, but of hard work and personal abuse, and if I am now to be deserted by those to whom I have ever been true, the sooner they find another man to suit their purpose the better.[78]

No letter better illustrates Howell's neurotic sensitivity to criticism. Cremer was a reckless antagonist, quick to make accusations that could not be substantiated. But Howell's hysterical responses, his immediate appeals to Beales or Rogers or the Executive to clear him of any charges, indicate a deep insecurity which often threatened to undermine his relations with his colleagues. Easily offended by the slightest reproach, he lashed out blindly, discerning intrigues even among erstwhile friends. Ambitious, but unsure of himself, he was invariably on his guard and slow to forget an unintended slur or disparaging remark. Potter, Hartwell, and Cremer – each of whom earned his animosity – were all targets for his defensive recriminations, but so too at times were Odger and Mantle. In fact, Howell reacted in the same frightened and impulsive manner whether he were facing a real opponent or an imaginary one. It was perhaps unfortunate that an individual with these personality traits should have embarked on a career demanding discretion and amiability. Working-class politics was a raucous and unrestrained business, and Howell's position as Secretary, privy to the inner secrets of the League, made him vulnerable to attack from the 'outsiders' who resented his power. In an age in which corrupt trade union leaders were not uncommon, it was only to be expected that League members should be constantly on the lookout for any sign of embezzlement. No matter how much personal gratification Howell derived from his generally-recognized success as Secretary, he was never free of anxiety. It would be impossible to measure the anxiety that a man so self-assertive, so eager to please must have suffered in the abrasive *milieu* in which he operated. The shrill, combative tone of so many of his letters reflects an inability to ignore the affronts he continually perceived.

The lecture scheme was abandoned early in 1867 because of insufficient funds, but it was an effective method of promoting the reform cause as long as it could be sustained. In mid-December Mantle had been able to report that he had communicated with fifty towns and held sixteen public meetings during the previous month, many of them in 'places where the platform of the League had never before been advocated'.[79] But here, as in many other areas of activity, the League was held back by inadequate resources from mounting the kind of campaign for which its leaders were now prepared.

While Beales continued to arbitrate in the disputes which disrupted the League and to pacify Howell in moments of crisis, he too was in great demand as a speaker and frequently away from London. Howell tried to schedule the President's engagements so as to obtain the widest exposure during his tours, but many of the invitations that poured into the London office had to be rejected. Branch officials competed for the privilege of a Beales visit, and Howell was left to bear the brunt of their resentment when offers had to be turned down. With the growth of provincial branches, it became necessary to restrict Beales's visits to the larger towns, substituting men like Bonner, Mantle, or Odger for the smaller meetings. Howell understood the disappointment of neglected branches, but he was annoyed by their readiness to blame him when their expectations were not realized. He reproached one Nottingham official in characteristically petulant tones:

If I had nothing to do but run after Mr Beales all day long, I might then know the whole of his arrangements. But the fact is Mr Beales is so often out of town that I cannot at all times get to see or hear from him, and his engagements are so many that I have difficulty in getting them arranged. . . .

I *never disappoint* the branches though they may sometimes disappoint themselves. Let me tell you, Sir, that I never neglect my duty, much less do I toady to rich people. If my sympathies are anywhere they are with the struggling few, who are always fighting and never at rest.[80]

Howell's letters kept Beales informed of London office business, as well as explaining the details of his lecture schedule. It was a sensible division of labour, with Howell combining the duties of secretary, travel agent, and public relations man in order to free his superior from administrative trivialities. While he preferred not to leave the office for extended tours, concentrating on evening meetings in the metropolitan area, he did occasionally take part in demonstrations elsewhere, usually taking advantage of such trips for talks with potential local contributors.

At the same time Howell continued to promote new branches and to ply them with information about the League's activities. As long as his own integrity was not impugned, his letters were always conciliatory. Encouragement or gentle admonition on the part of the Secretary was a factor in preventing a breakdown in communication between London and the hinterland. The central office had constantly to strive against the backsliding of branches whose initial enthusiasm might be dispelled by incompetent local officials. By March 1867 Howell could boast of 427 branches, but many of these must have had the most ephemeral of existences.[81] In addition to providing incentives to activity, such as visits by League speakers, Howell was called upon to furnish advice as to the mode of operation. 'The best way to work the Branch to advantage,' he wrote one functionary, 'is to meet weekly and thereby create an interest in the movement, read our Council reports, or indeed anything bearing on the question.'[82] When another correspondent queried the stipulation of minimal dues of a penny per month – intended, of course, to apply to working-class members only – Howell replied,

Our rules does [sic] provide for 1d. monthly but there is scarcely a branch that does it now. They pay 1d. weekly which is little enough if a man be a reformer. However we must leave you to judge for yourselves as to the best way to get members. But let us recognize this fact that now is the time for work. We must play at agitating no longer.[83]

In January 1867 the malcontents on the General Council tried to engineer a revolt against the Executive, whose domination of the League was, if inevitable, none the less resented. The tactic chosen was the appointment of a Demonstration Committee, ostensibly to help the Secretary in planning an 11 February demonstration, but in fact to circumvent Executive control by creating a rival body.[84] The new committee met on the 5th and again on the 7th, and Howell, who attended these sessions, complained that the time was spent in 'cavilling and personal attacks'.[85] After a plea from Beales the General Council rescinded the resolution appointing the committee, confirming the Executive in office until after the February demonstration.[86] Howell, who would devote more attention to this event than to any other during his tenure, was relieved when the Council abandoned its attempt to circumscribe his power. He confessed to Beales,

I felt bound to work even harder than usual in consequence of [the] little dispute in reference to the Executive and Demonstration Committees. Each night this week I have been at my desk till nearly twelve o'clock to keep pace with my extra work. But I am happy to add that the work is progressing most favourably. Had the members who voted for the Demonstration Committee really known what had been done they would not have acted so hastily. And I feared if I opposed the motion too much my motive would have been misconstrued. As it was I was very much abused.[87]

This reassertion of executive authority did not protect Howell from continued attacks by disgruntled colleagues. In the same month Cremer accused him at a delegate meeting of withholding accounts, and Howell turned as usual to Dresser Rogers, insisting that 'it is for the Executive to clear me of that'.[88]

The expansion of activities from the summer of 1866 until the passing of the Reform Bill required more money than the League had at its disposal during its first year. The defeat of the Liberal Bill and Bright's advocacy helped to break down the obstacles to greater financial collaboration between middle-class donors and the working men. While Bright lent the movement his prestige and oratorical powers, affluent Radicals contributed to an extent unknown in the League's early days. If the money received was somewhat less than its managers wanted, it did at least enable the organization to break loose from the economic restraints under which it had laboured at first. Donations, which totalled only £477 from April 1865 to April 1866, jumped to £1,429 in the next twelve months. Morley's contributions testified to the change: in April 1866 he donated £50, but seven months later he sent in £250.[89]

As early as May the Executive decided to sponsor a £10,000 Lecture and General Purpose Fund, but nothing came of the plan until the autumn, when Howell began to solicit donations. Responsibility for their collection was divided between the Secretary, corresponding and cajoling from Adelphi Terrace, and agents operating on commission, like Edge and Cremer, who visited potential contributors. The intention was to raise half the sum through twenty gifts of £250 each, with the remainder being collected in smaller amounts. Six wealthy Radicals – Sir Wilfrid Lawson, Samuel Morley, A. W. Paulton, William Hargreaves, Frederick Pennington, and Thomas Thomasson – pledged the requisite sum. It was hoped that the new fund would enable the League to strike roots in the agricultural districts, where organization had been slow. Howell's expectations soared, since he imagined that resolutions and pledges would be translated into hard cash. 'Our movement goes on gloriously,' he rhapsodized to a Bradford supporter. 'If we had the money, our movement would become one of the greatest triumphs of modern days.'[90] But it became apparent almost at once that anticipated bounties were not forthcoming, and Howell was instructed to remind those who had promised donations to send in the money.[91] By 5 November he was bemoaning the fund's apparent failure in a letter to Morley:

I regret to say that we find it impossible to complete the list. I am therefore instructed to appeal to you for help, and to request that you will kindly aid us with such portion of that sum as you may deem advisable under the circumstances. . . . We act with the greatest economy, have but one permanent (paid) officer, myself at 36s. per week. Yet we find ourselves very much impeded in our usefulness for want of funds. The working men are taxing themselves very much, but we want to send out lecturers into the country districts, where political life still seems dead, so that before Parliament opens there can be no mistake as to the national character of our movement. . . . Do therefore come to our rescue. We have but few, *very few* wealthy friends to whom we can appeal, and first and foremost we have you.[92]

Morley, as usual, was as good as his word: he not only paid Howell £250 on 7 November, but permitted the use of his name in letters to others. Morley's generosity was not, however, imitated by the others: Lawson was the only other donor to fulfil his pledge. Thomasson sent in £100 and, several months later, Paulton £40, Hargreaves £50, and Pennington £100.[93] By the middle of the month Howell had revised his estimates: 'If we could get together say only £2,000,' he wrote P. A. Taylor, 'we could do a vast work.' Whatever sums did come in were appropriated for current debts and expenses – although they did help subsidize the lecturers in November and December – but the 'fresh start' for which Howell hoped never materialized.[94]

That the project collapsed was no fault of the Secretary's; indeed its failure did not redound to his discredit as the success of the 1868 Special Election Fund would do. On the other hand, the difficulty of arranging the 11 February demonstration – to coincide with the opening of Parliament – was greatly increased by the shortage of funds. To the responsibility of working out the details was added the constant search for money, both privately and through the branches. While the Executive spent an inordinate amount of time in planning it, the defeat of the Demonstration Committee proposal – a victory for Howell – meant that most of the burden fell on his shoulders. Following the participation of trade unions in the LWMA-led demonstration on 3 December, he invited William Allan and the Amalgamated Society of Engineers to join the February undertaking. Allan, the last of the Junta leaders to embrace League policy, not only agreed, but carried a resolution at a London Trades Council delegate meeting declaring 'our sympathy with, and adhesion to, the principles of the Reform League' and advising trade unionists 'to aid the forthcoming demonstration'.[95] Encouraged by the Council's belated change of heart, the League Executive voted Howell full powers to secure wide trade society co-operation. By early January he could report on communication with important union leaders, as well as with the International and temperance societies.[96]

If the success of the demonstration bore witness to Howell's administrative talents and capacity for hard work, the weeks of preparation provided outlets for his fears of failure. So much depended on him: if he could not execute the plans effectively, he might jeopardize not only his own career, but the reform movement itself. To make matters worse, the *Bee-Hive* kept up its attacks on him. The pressure mounted, and Howell's letters, dealing with a multitude of details, became increasingly frantic. He wanted to keep Beales in London, where 'all his cool courage and abilities' were needed, but the President's only daughter was dying, and he could offer little assistance.[97] The lecturers were ordered to wind up their tours and return to London to help the harassed Secretary. In January Mantle was requested 'to aid the Secretary in the office whenever he can find time to do so'. Howell was empowered to summon the Executive Committee 'at any hour of day or night', and it decided to meet Mondays, as well as Wednesdays and Fridays. By early February it was to meet almost daily. Odger, Finlen, and Samuel Brighty were hired at 7s per day to assist in carrying out the plans.[98] In imitation of Potter's methods, the League also held weekly delegate meetings to stimulate rank and file enthusiasm.

While the Executive attended to the procedure of the demonstration, Howell busied himself in correspondence with every League branch, with trade unions, and with possible speakers. Economy was the rule of the day: the Secretary was obliged to present a weekly statement of expenses, and the branches were warned to incur no expenses unless they had been cleared with Howell.[99] The Executive also voted to hire the Agricultural Hall, thereby rejecting by implication another outdoor challenge to the Government. Presumably the leaders wanted a show of strength, but were reluctant to risk alienating potential supporters on the eve of a new parliamentary session. As Howell explained to Bright, 'In the interest of peace and order, and to avoid any semblance of force, more particularly with regard to Hyde Park, our Council have decided to abstain from any outdoor meeting and to concentrate our forces in the Agricultural Hall, there to make one of the most imposing Demonstrations ever held.'[100] If the response of invited speakers and participating societies was moderately encouraging, the financial situation filled Howell with alarm. Large contributions tapered off at the end of 1866, and the League coffers were soon nearly empty. In mid-January the Executive authorized Howell to make the first direct financial appeal to the branches in the League's history.[101] His letter explained the new departure, adding that 'we now feel that the question must be pushed to the utmost, for if we do our work well victory is near'.[102] The impressive preparations and perhaps a few words from T. B. Potter or Samuel Morley elicited contributions of over £400 from a group of Bradford textile manufacturers, including Robert and Samuel Kell, Alfred Illingworth, and Titus Salt of Saltaire, which arrived just in time to pay most of the demonstration bills.[103]

The arrangements called for an intricate subdivision of London into ten districts, with each district further segmented into sub-districts. These were to be in the charge of a host of organizers, marshals, and sub-marshals.[104] Many of the demonstrators would themselves act as special constables to preserve order. The various sections of the procession were to converge on Trafalgar Square from different starting-points in London, continuing from there to the Agricultural Hall in Islington. Howell engaged ten bands and worked out arrangements for selling tickets and distributing banners, badges, ribbons, and rosettes. It was also left to him to organize a League deputation to Gladstone on the morning of the 11th, to be introduced by John Bright.

The months of preparation paid off handsomely, the demonstration taking place exactly according to schedule. A huge and orderly procession marched through London, with the Prince of Wales numbered among the spectators, to the Agricultural Hall, where a capacity crowd heard Ernest Jones, T. B. Potter, P. A. Taylor, and others hail their efforts to win political emancipation. Howell delighted in the praise he earned for its success, but he was still preoccupied with the financial crisis which had threatened to undermine their plans. It was with a great sense of relief that he was able to report several days later, 'We shall be able, *I think*, to meet all demands in the course of a fortnight but we shall be £500 to the bad from the Demonstration. A little prudence will set us right. But we must be solvent or our prestige is gone. Our credit is now good everywhere, we must keep it so.'[105]

Despite the Reform League's campaign, the Derby–Disraeli ministry had no intention of bringing in a bill in 1867. Their original scheme was exceedingly cautious: resolutions in the Commons, a Royal Commission, and perhaps a modest bill in 1868.[106] Political pressures both within his own party and from the Liberals denied Disraeli a leisurely resolution of the reform question, but the household suffrage measure which emerged in March was qualified by too many restrictions and safeguards to satisfy the Radicals. As an answer to the precautions the League had taken against any exhibition of working-class violence, the meagre concession seemed tantamount to treachery. Encouraged by their Radical allies, Howell and Beales had consistently assured their followers that moderation would pay off in the end. Only by adhering to a respectable course of action would the workers overcome the resistance to their enfranchisement, persuading the ruling classes that they were loyal citizens, whose continued exclusion from political rights was unwarranted. Now this argument, urged no less strenuously in the face of Disraeli's vacillations, began to seem less and less convincing. By late February the more militant elements within the League, restrained in late 1866 by the expectation of impending success, gained the upper hand, investing League pronouncements in the spring of 1867 with a new stridency.

One feature of the shift towards greater militancy was a readiness to endorse an independent labour policy, in defiance of both the League's moderate supporters and its professed enemies. Lucraft prodded the Executive into sponsoring weekly Trafalgar Square demonstrations in March and April. The exponents of this new attitude were Bradlaugh and Dickson, but they had the approval of working men like Lucraft, Cremer, and Mantle. Although Beales and Howell reluctantly went along with the Trafalgar Square meetings, the President insisted on suppressing those led by Lucraft on Clerkenwell Green. 'We must not hold them,' Howell warned, 'if we wish to hold the good opinion of our most earnest friends whose support we cannot afford to lose.'[107] His inclinations towards caution were reinforced by the demands of a new fund-raising campaign. In March and April he sent nearly one hundred letters to Liberal MPs and other Radical patrons, accompanied by an appeal from Beales and supporting statements from Bright and Morley. The results were not impressive, a £100 donation from Thomas Thomasson being the only large contribution during the spring and early summer.[108]

When plans for a Good Friday Hyde Park demonstration were jettisoned, William Osborne denounced the League for inactivity at an April delegate meeting, dismissing the organization as 'a dead body'. Beales tried to exonerate his fellow leaders, but Osborne pressed the attack so vehemently that the President threatened to leave. Although he was persuaded to remain, the delegates resolved to hold a Hyde Park demonstration on 6 May.[109] Overriding the wishes of Beales and Howell, the Executive Committee approved the proposal by a five to three vote and appointed Odger, Cremer, Lucraft, Mantle, and A. T. Bannister – presumably the five proponents of the plan – as an arrangements sub-committee.[110]

The League militants who championed the Hyde Park venture found the aspect of provocation most appealing. Bradlaugh warned that the working men were determined to hold the meeting whether or not the Government tried to stop it, vowing that they would not only demand admittance to the park, but enforce it if obstructed.[111] On 1 May Spencer Walpole issued an official ban and senselessly decided to inform the League of the prohibition at a delegate meeting that night. When three police officers presented the proclamation, Bradlaugh and Beales, who was now determined to see the crisis through, aroused the delegates to defy the prohibition.[112] Four MPs attended an executive session on 3 May and tried to persuade the League to reconsider its plans in order to prevent a collision. But the members were now intractable, convinced that the Government was threatening an illegal and, it was to be hoped, unenforceable act.[113] It was too late for the League to back down, even to the extent that it had been willing to yield in July 1866. As Howell informed Thomas Hughes, one of the MPs attending the meeting, 'Of one thing I feel certain, that is that there is *less danger of disturbance by our being present tomorrow,* than by our staying away. I trust that we shall do nothing to bring discredit upon our *friends* or our cause.'[114]

The authorities prepared for trouble, massing five thousand police and calling up troops from Aldershot, but by 4 May they had privately decided to capitulate. Several hundred thousand people gathered in Hyde Park, where the League had set up ten platforms, from which Beales, Howell, and most of the other League notables addressed the crowds. Despite the presence of police and soldiers, who merely looked menacing, there was no commotion. Unlike July 1866 the League showed its capacity for organizing a working-class agitation in defiance of parliamentary authority while keeping good order. The working men had been genuinely frightened by the threat of force – Howell even made contingent financial arrangements with his wife[115] – but the politicians were even more afraid to risk a clash with the people.

The League regarded 6 May as a 'great moral triumph', simultaneously enhancing its own prestige and revealing the workers' determination to the Government.[116] While Disraeli denied that he was yielding to external pressure, his acceptance of the lodger franchise provisions and of Hodgkinson's amendment removing the distinction between compound and personal ratepayers, shortly after the Hyde Park demonstration, seemed to contradict his denial. That the Bill was transformed from a limited franchise extension to a household suffrage measure, stripped of most of the guarantees which the Conservatives had originally been promised, was, at least in part, the result of the changes in the political climate which the working-class agitation had produced. If the League had no more influence in the original design of the Tory Bill than it had over its Liberal predecessor, it was effective in applying pressure during the critical months when the amendments were being considered. This intervention was probably not decisive, but it bolstered Disraeli's resolve to accept any reasonable amendment which would pacify the people and allow him to carry a creditable measure. Certainly he wanted to retain power and to outstrip Gladstone, but the fact that this could be accomplished only by passing reform legislation was a tribute to the impact which the popular agitation was finally exerting on Westminster politics.

It is as difficult to assess the ultimate influence of the Reform League on the passing of the Second Reform Bill as it is to determine the importance of the Anti-Corn Law League in securing repeal of the Corn Laws. In both cases the outcome depended on political decisions by statesmen, but the agitation helped to set the context within which these decisions had to be taken. It is certainly true that the League claimed much credit for wringing a reform bill from a reluctant Tory government. Moreover, Liberal friends fostered the League's sense of self-importance: Goldwin Smith, for example, told Howell:

It is impossible to doubt that the popular movement so effectively and, at the same time, so legally and so peacefully conducted by the two combined associations [Reform League and Reform Union] has been the main instrument in turning the present holders of power from the opponents of the limited Reform Bill of last session into the advocates of ·household suffrage. . . .[117]

One can argue that the Bill owed little, except perhaps in its modification, to popular pressure, but, on the other hand, neither the Tory nor the Liberal Government had been eager to take up the reform question. It is clear that a more important motive for Disraeli was the desire to 'dish the Whigs' and to consolidate his position as leader, but it is doubtful that parliamentary opinion would have accepted reform as inevitable without popular pressure.

If the Reform League rarely anticipated political developments or made the most of its opportunities, it was none the less able to exploit its numbers to advantage, creating an atmosphere in which the concession of a franchise measure came to seem the logical course of action for the Government. Under the direction of Beales and Howell, the cautious and deferential elements retained control – at least until the spring of 1867 – thus enabling the League to carry on an orderly agitation, never allowing the disruptive potential of the working-class movement to rise to the surface. By their own moderation these leaders helped to avoid social upheaval; they also ensured that the Reform Act of 1867 would be an initial instalment, rather than a full measure, of democracy.

5

The Reform League and the Liberal Party

With the enactment of franchise reform in the summer of 1867, the sense of urgency which had held the League together through the months of agitation could no longer be maintained. The urban workers had been appeased, and a decline in the level of activity followed immediately, especially among provincial branches, which tended either to dissolve or to fuse with local Liberal associations. Realizing the League's potential effectiveness in the context of the revised electoral system, Howell and other leaders wanted to reverse its decline by linking the League closely, but informally, with the Liberal Party. The events of 1865–7 strengthened their belief that a 'Lib-Lab' alliance was necessary to secure those political and social reforms, such as the ballot and trade union rights, that still awaited parliamentary action. This view was contested by the more militant forces in the League, increasingly vocal from the spring of 1867, who pressed for a more self-consciously working-class movement. While Howell hoped to attain limited, but practicable goals by means of private negotiations and bourgeois subsidies, others, less concerned with financial considerations, wanted to end working-class reliance on middle-class benevolence.

Although Howell's policy may well have been more representative of artisan opinion, he was constantly harassed by his disruptive opponents. Once the survival of the organization itself came into question, Howell's concerns became more personal: convinced that factions were tearing the League apart, he looked to the security of his own future. Thus he became ever more subservient to the designs of Liberal politicians in order to earn their trust and, it was to be hoped, their favours. The Liberal leaders, seeking victory in 1868 with the support of the newly enfranchised working men, were to discover in the League, which Howell delivered to them, an inexpensive, ready-made election agency. The 1868 compact was not an attempt to subvert the reform movement. From its origins the League had deliberately chosen – although not without some internal dissent – to identify itself with the Liberal Party, despite Gladstone's indifference to many Radical demands. Howell never concealed his own affinities with Liberalism and tried to deter the League from any course of action that might offend middle-class supporters. More than anyone else the Secretary was acutely aware that without their contributions the League's existence would be exceedingly precarious.

The electoral alliance was triggered by two related factors. In the first place, the League was divided on questions of finance and Fenianism. With Beales and Rogers eager for the chance to retire, the management of affairs fell to Howell more and more. At the same time other members of the Executive bridled under the Secretary's domination, and his authority became less effective as it grew in scope. 'I am fast losing my control over the getting in of funds,' he complained in September 1867, 'thanks to the Executive Committee led by Cremer and others.'[1] Secondly, the passing of the 1867 Act had halted middle-class generosity, unleashing a new financial crisis. Radicals did not mind subsidizing agitation for parliamentary reform, but they had little desire to promote an effective working-class political movement. Lacking adequate resources, the League would simply disintegrate without having either completed its programme or guaranteed the professional future of its officers. Howell therefore welcomed the prospect of a financial arrangement with the Liberals as a means of continuing the organization – and his own job – while serving the party most tolerant of the League's aspirations. What he failed to realize was that the Liberals needed the working men at least as much as the working men needed the Liberals. His pliability in the hands of clever politicians led him to barter away League support too cheaply in an agreement which afforded advantages to the party and, to some extent, himself as well, but not to the labour movement.[2]

In the early months of 1867 the League had begun to consider the appropriate course of action to be followed once the reform issue had been resolved. Howell took up the question with financial supporters, who counselled against dissolving the organization.[3]

The Executive Committee decided in June that the League could be effectively used for registration and election purposes. Given a large, disorganized electorate, it was essential to mobilize new voters in support of 'candidates pledged to advanced Liberal principles'. To further these objectives a new fund drive was launched, aimed especially at Radicals who, without adopting the workers' programme, were eager to gather them into the Liberal camp in order to strengthen the progressive wing of the party. James Acland, a Vice-President of the League and a professional election agent, was engaged as an adviser to the executive, and a sub-committee consisting of Joseph Guedalla, A. T. Bannister, Odger, and Cremer was appointed to investigate the constituencies in which approved politicians might be returned.[4] For the time being at least, the League officials were interested merely in opportunities for advanced Liberals, not necessarily men of working-class origin.

It was this policy of restraint which commended itself to prominent Radicals, such as Bright, who applauded the decision to keep the League in operation, and Morley, who permitted the use of his name in the solicitation of donations.[5] Morley encouraged Howell to list his annual pledges of £250 for 1867 and 1868 as contributions to the fund, and during the next few months William Hargreaves, Sir Wilfrid Lawson, and Isaac Holden followed Morley's example. None the less the large donors were rare, and the meagre contributions of a number of Liberal MPs ensured that this fund drive would be no more successful than earlier ones.

Howell and Beales hoped that the new projects would revitalize the League, but the loss of momentum in the second half of 1867 was not entirely reversible. Whatever Liberal bounties might be expected in the future, financial difficulties threatened to paralyse the League even before the current scheme began to bear fruit. In early August Howell warned that the bank balance was so low that it would be impossible to meet the expenses of the Hyde Park demonstration, and J. J. Merriman was obliged to lend £35 for current expenses. A month later it became necessary to resort to another appeal to the branches for a renewal of what was now termed 'your annual subscriptions'. Howell's letter underlined the most serious problem facing the organization: the inevitable disintegration of many branches in the wake of the Reform Act. He implored them 'to keep up regular meetings, if not so often as during the past two years, yet sufficiently often to sustain the interest of your members and keep them in active work'.[6]

While the League was weakened by the decay of its branches, the effectiveness of the Executive was undermined by discord among its members. 'We are passing through the critical ordeal of such bodies,' Howell lamented to Merriman. 'Now that the enemy is to some extent beaten, or at bay, we can find time to fight each other.'[7] The trouble, in fact, dated back to the spring, but by September the earlier dispute over tactics had grown into a full-scale assault on the leaders themselves, an attempt to discredit the officers by hints of corruption. In September Cremer charged Guedalla, a wealthy merchant and a Vice-President, with having asserted publicly that Beales was in the habit of appropriating League money for his own expenses without the authorization of the Finance Committee.[8] The honesty of the President had never before been questioned, and the accusation shook the League to its foundations. Guedalla denied any such allegation, but Mantle added to the crisis by claiming that other rumours of dishonesty had gained currency. Since he was responsible for the keeping of accounts, Howell called for an investigation by an impartial committee, which was duly appointed by 13 September.[9] Although it was the Secretary himself who demanded the inquiry, he despaired of the situation which had rendered it necessary. He complained to George Jackson that 'we are torn to pieces by factions, miserable cables [sic], and coteries, whose only genius is destruction'.[10]

Rogers, the Chairman of the Finance Committee, was unprepared for the new crisis and feared the implications of an investigation. Howell assured him that 'the Accounts are carried out just as they were when you last saw them', and he added,

I quite agree with you as to the impolitic course about to be taken. It will *imply* a want of confidence in the accounts. My only explanation is this. Some of them think that by harassing me with suspicion that they will cause me to resign. They know full well my touchiness on the question of accounts and therefore know how much they can pain me with innuendo and insinuation. I leave in the hands of yourself and other members of the Finance Committee to protect *me from their insults* if you find me worthy of your confidence as I have proven myself in the past.[11]

Rogers examined the accounts and, finding them satisfactory, assured his colleagues on 18 September that their fears were unwarranted. The charges, however, were raised once again at the next Executive meeting, where Mantle implied that Howell had tried to place his friends on the committee for 'personal and dishonest intentions'.[12] Howell warned Merriman that they were 'either drifting or steering for the breakers. I fear we are too near to recede. At least we shall suffer severely in either case, if we go on or strive to go back. I say dissolve. We can now do so with honour. I fear for the future.'[13]

There was, in fact, remarkably little to incriminate the Secretary. The Finance Committee had ceased to meet regularly, and Howell had been obliged to advance money on his own authority to deputations. He also encouraged William Malthouse of Walworth to stand for election, but such an overture hardly constituted dishonesty. Howell had clearly become panicky, his apprehensions stemming not from guilt, but rather from helplessness in the face of reckless charges. If he were to be maligned publicly, it would matter little whether or not the allegations had been substantiated. He was torn between the wish for a speedy dissolution of the League, which might avoid a protracted battle, and a full-scale confrontation. Rogers pleaded with him to ignore his accusers, but Howell insisted upon clearing his name.

I quite understand [he told Rogers] how you or others not implicated can be quiet and philosophic when charges like those of Friday night are made. But I can also see that you or the others would lose your temper if the accusations were made against you.

If the accusations had been first made on Friday night, and there and then refuted (as I certainly did refute them) then I could afford to laugh and to scorn the gentlemen – heaven save the mark – who concocted and spread the story. But to find that these slanderers had made their own lies the subject of public-house talk for the purpose of injuring Mr Beales's character and my own, I admit did upset my temper. . . . Had it not been for Cremer's hot temper this scandal might have gone the round of every lodger in London before I could have repudiated it. I ask you how it would have been possible to wipe out the calumny? They take care to keep out of the clutches of law and know your hands are tied and you are rendered powerless. . . .

You say if any scandal arise I shall suffer; this I deny. If I suffer it will imply some wrong. I shall place the books in the hands of Mr Morley and other large subscribers for their examination and shall be satisfied with their verdict. Do not think that I shall allow myself to be treated as a child, for I shall appeal beyond the Executive, beyond the Council, to the whole of our branches and subscribers everywhere. A turf bully [Mantle] will not frighten me, nor any or all of his associates. If they are determined to annoy and insult me at every turn, I will prove how futile will be their combined efforts.[14]

Howell's fears of an explosive climax were exaggerated: the more cool-headed Executive members, like Rogers and Beales, prevailed at the 27 September meeting, and crisis passed amid expressions of regret. For Howell it was all rather anti-climactic, but at least he emerged with his reputation intact. A remarkably vivid letter to his wife the next day testified to the terror with which he had awaited the meeting:

The terrible conflict of last night is over and I still survive. Did you not dream on Thursday night that I lay wounded and that you hurried home to wipe the cold dying sweat from my clammy brow and close my eyelids in peace? Well it is over and I am not much hurt. I dreamt on Thursday that I had a couple of great black beetles sucking my blood. I simply took them off and crushed them under my feet.[15]

Once the storm had blown over, Howell could concentrate on the rewards rather than the penalties of political office. With an eye to the advancement of his own career, he thanked Rogers for his advocacy, urging him 'to write a letter to our great friend Mr Morley and tell him what you think of our accounts. In the future it will do me some good when seeking another situation.'[16]

The dispute over finances was a contrived emergency; that over Fenianism, in which the League became embroiled during the last months of 1867, reflected an ideological, rather than a personal, split, with far more serious implications for the future of the League. As an insurrectionary movement seeking to overthrow British rule in the name of Irish freedom, Fenianism struck some of the same chords of sympathy among English workers that nationalist movements in Italy and Poland had earlier in the decade. But the fact that its 'outrages' were being perpetrated on English soil, coupled with the competitive threat that Irish immigrants posed to underemployed urban labourers, also aroused anti-Irish sentiments.

Within the League a conflict suddenly flared up at a 23 October meeting when Howell read a letter from Beales, in which the President took it upon himself to dissociate the League from Fenian terrorism, condemning its 'violent, sanguinary, and greatly irritating, but abortive proceedings, exciting a spirit of animosity and hostility here tending only to retard the political and social advance of their own country'.[17] Lucraft, who argued that the Irish 'were fully justified in using physical force to redress their wrongs', tried to prevent the letter from being published. Odger supported him and declared that if he were an Irishman, he too would be a Fenian.[18]

Howell and other moderates regarded Fenianism as a divisive distraction from agitation for further political reform. As he remarked several months later,

> This Fenian madness is warping every good effort we make, and will I fear produce an anti-Irish feeling. I do wish that every good Irishman would wash his hands of it and that the English people could see that it is being used for improper and unconstitutional purposes by the Government or those in power. We are making good and peaceful progress, and in another two years we should be able to carry good measures for Ireland, but now I fear for it.[19]

His optimism about the prospects for reform was in contrast to the sense of political alienation among those who encouraged Fenianism. Once again the moderate forces retained control, and the League went on record denouncing the movement, although not specifically by name. The solution was a compromise. While the Council agreed – after the Executive voted to do so by a majority of one – to publish Odger's speech urging clemency for the Fenian prisoners, it 'emphatically and indignantly repudiated any sympathy with assassination, or secret organizations for political objectives'.[20] The triumph of the moderates saved the League from almost certain self-destruction, but the legacy of animosity weakened the forces for cohesion in the Council. By increasing the mutual distrust between the officers and the extremists, the Fenian controversy spurred Howell to greater autonomy in his management of affairs, the implications of which were to become evident in his handling of the Special Fund.

Once the immediate threat to his authority had been overcome, Howell was remarkably sanguine about his personal situation in spite of tensions within the organization. He confided to his diary on the eve of 1868,

> This is my very first year of real comfort when I felt able to buy a few

things and not really pinch for it. Yet I have not lived extravagant [*sic*] but very moderately and carefully. Never felt that I should live fast or spend on gaiety. . . . After reviewing the entire year I feel satisfied and hope that during the coming year I shall be able to lay by more cash. I promise equal care, and only hope that we shall all have good health to carry out our desires. I must now try to get a little house through the Building Society.[21]

From his 1867 League salary of £149 he had managed not only to save £6, but also to buy Mrs Howell a piano and to pay for French lessons for himself.[22] In the winter months activity slackened enough for him to resume his course of studies, and on 3 January, for example, he was able to record, 'In evening spent 1½ hours at French, 1 hour at Adam Smith, and one hour at Machiavelli's *Prince.*'[23]

The League's prospects, on the other hand, offered no cause for complacency even after the Fenian conflict had been papered over. The financial outlook remained bleak, and, once the Registration and Election Fund failed, contributions dwindled rapidly. One of the persistent problems had been the chaotic system of collection which the League employed. In order to eliminate the proliferation of paid agents the Executive had designated Cremer and the officers as the sole authorized collectors.[24] While this introduced some order into the process, it did little to solve the main problem – the shortage of money that became more acute with the passing months.

In September the Executive had begun to plan an ambitious series of political and educational lectures. As usual Howell did most of the work, devoting much of his time in the autumn to arranging speakers and halls. He approached the eminent, ranging from Gladstone to Louis Blanc, but the lack of funds and the refusal of many of those invited limited the programme to five lectures between November 1867 and February 1868. With the possible exception of Ernest Jones, the speakers were irreproachably respectable: A. J. Mundella, W. E. Forster, Henry Fawcett, and James Stansfeld. The lack of public enthusiasm for the lectures made it necessary to abandon this project, like earlier projects begun so hopefully. Howell wrote sadly to Ernest Jones, 'We have been so badly supported as to funds that we are obliged to defer any more lectures for the present. The London people do not pay for lectures like they will in the provinces.'[25]

Indeed, as Howell was shortly to discover, money could be obtained only in return for specific services to the donor, not in order to promote League propaganda. No longer relying simply on importunate letters, Howell began to seek out potential subscribers, spending long afternoons in the lobby of the House of Commons and the waiting-rooms of Pall Mall clubs. Interviews with P. A. Taylor, A. W. Paulton, and John Holms yielded small contributions,[26] but other attempts were less successful. Samuel Pope, the wealthy honorary secretary of the United Kingdom Alliance and prospective candidate for Bolton, proved an elusive customer. Howell's diary entry for 3 February underlines his predicament: 'Tried to see Pope . . . Arranged with Cremer to canvass Pope . . . Waited in Westminster Hall with Cremer to catch Pope . . . Wrote special letter to Pope and others for subscriptions.'[27] When found, Pope donated £5, but the previous year he had given £25.[28]

Early in February Howell travelled to Bradford, whose Nonconformist manufacturers were noted for their sympathy to political reform and their antipathy to trade unionism. The Bradford group – including the Kell brothers, Alfred Illingworth, and Titus Salt – had been responsible for a large contribution the previous year, and Howell hoped to tap this source again. He was, however, soon disabused of any such expectation. 'My private impression,' he wrote, 'is that the manufacturing class are rather afraid of the power the people now have.' Interviews with Robert Kell, Illingworth, and Salt convinced him that these men were 'all closefisted and not inclined to give'. The Bradford Radicals stipulated fusion with the Reform Union as a condition of support, even though Howell explained that such a step was not practicable.[29] While his appeal was not wholly fruitless – Salt donated £100 in April – Howell was discouraged by the apparent indifference of middle-class Radicals to the fate of the League. 'It does seem strange,' he remarked to Robert Kell, 'that after doing such good service for two years, and being capable of much more service for some time to come, we should be in such crippled circumstances for a few hundred pounds.'[30] Moreover, as he emphasized in another letter, it was in the interest of the respectable to uphold the League: 'The greater the element of our middle classes in these movements the less violent and more progressive will be the results.'[31]

The disappointing response from Bradford indicated to Howell the need to try a new approach. In November 1867 he had entered into correspondence with James Stansfeld, the Radical MP for Halifax and a close associate of George Grenfell Glyn, the Liberal Chief Whip, about the possibility of launching a Pioneer Club, 'where men of the working, middle, and upper classes can meet together and talk over in a free and friendly way' political and social questions.[32] Although little progress was made at first, by mid-February Howell was able to inform Stansfeld that he had found about thirty supporters for the project.[33] During the course of early talks the two men came to trust one another, and Howell began to regard Stansfeld as the sort of Radical to whom the League might turn for assistance. Immediately upon his return from Bradford Howell visited him and received promises of help in obtaining £500 for the League. The contrast with his reception in Bradford could not have been more striking, and Howell was soon extolling the member for Halifax as 'one of the best of our public men'.[34]

Throughout the spring plans were hatched for the Adelphi Club, as the Pioneer came to be called. After several alternative sites had been canvassed, Howell was requested to give up the back room of the League office as quarters for the club, for which he was to receive an additional £21 a year as compensation. By the time it was launched in June the initial investment had exceeded the receipts in donations from Morley and others, but there were about three hundred members at the outset, of whom some twenty per cent, including Stansfeld, Mill, Hughes, and Fawcett, represented the middle class. Mill contributed a set of his writings for the library, which also contained all the leading newspapers and periodicals. With the addition of carpets and armchairs and all manner of refreshment, every effort was made to 'combine the luxuries and advantages of West End Clubs, with an economy adapted to the means of Working Men'.[35] By the beginning of 1869 the club was deeply in debt, having failed to wean enough working men from their accustomed haunts to keep it solvent, and the League soon disclaimed any responsibility for it. When the League dissolved later in the spring, the Adelphi disappeared along with it. Only a handful of politicians thought the club worth their patronage, and despite Howell's encouragement of trade unionists to take advantage of the chance to meet men 'who can very materially aid them with introductions to members of Parliament and other leading men',[36] the workers too kept aloof. If the club attracted the sentimental proponents of social harmony, electoral and financial

advantage was to prove a more effective cement between the
Liberal Party and the Reform League.

Throughout its history the League was prepared to endorse particular political candidates, but it found it more difficult to articulate
a general electoral policy. In December 1867 the Council had
unanimously called for the election of 'a number of working men
proportionate to the other interests and classes at present represented in Parliament'.[37] A month later the Executive proposed to work
for the return of 'advanced Radical Reformers'.[38] While these objectives were not mutually exclusive, they were also not necessarily
complementary, and the League was never clear about spelling out
its priorities. Soon to become a candidate himself, Howell was none
the less sceptical as to the advisability of nominating men of working-
class origin. 'As to working men representatives as a rule,' he
wrote, 'our time is not yet come. We want *good men* no matter
whence they come or what they are.'[39] It was not that he desired to
rule them out entirely: 'If we can get some good working men in,'
he informed George Jackson, 'we shall do great good.' He was,
however, quick to add, 'But we must be cautious. They must be
picked men of high character and good general intelligence.'[40]

In the absence of a systematic League electoral policy, it was, in
fact, the steadfast Liberalism of its Secretary which prevailed
during the General Election of 1868. His sense of working-class
solidarity eroded by the rifts within the Executive, Howell had no
doubt that the only reasonable course for the organization was to
make itself politically useful to the party of Gladstone. Certainly
financial inducements assured Howell's commitment, but these
merely reinforced his convictions about political necessity. Even
before the arrangements for the Special Fund had been negotiated,
he told Titus Salt that he regarded the disbanding of the League
before the election as 'a national misfortune for the Liberal Party'.[41]
His practical loyalties were consistent with the gradualist tendency
of his reform ideas. While professing his Radicalism in a speech at
the League's Pimlico branch, he maintained that 'we in England
can only permanently succeed by compromises; we shall only
attain the desired goal by very slow stages'.[42] No more than Beales
was he in favour of an indiscriminate approval of all who ran under
the Liberal banner. In all fairness to the integrity of his conviction,
if not of his practice, Howell favoured only those who might

generally be accounted reformers, the politicians who followed the precepts of Bright and Mill, if not quite those of the League itself. As he declared to Jackson,

We must go in for the best men we can get to come forward, but better have *new* liberals than old Whigs. *I hate the Whigs*. They have ever been our enemies and are now. . . . We must fight the next election tooth and nail and *if the Whig is doubtful* I personally should prefer a Tory. But of course this is a delicate matter and one which requires care in the working out, but we must tell the professing Liberals that their programme must be a good and bold one and their pledges must be kept or they will not do for us.[43]

The Executive had voted in July 1867 to find out which boroughs might be likely to elect League-supported candidates, but it was not until the following May that a sub-committee was named to plan for the coming election. A new Executive Committee, rendered more amenable by the removal of Lucraft, was willing to delegate responsibility for electoral matters to the six-man group and, even more, to the Secretary. After Morley's abortive Bristol by-election contest in May, six Executive members – including Howell and Samuel Brighty, an experienced temperance agitator – were dispatched to Bristol to deal with the workers in preparation for the General Election.[44] Howell deplored the defeat of the League's most loyal patron, comparing it to the rejection of Burke by his Bristol constituents in 1780.[45] But after ten days in the city in July he was hopeful that the path had been cleared for a Morley victory in the autumn, '*if the old Whig Party act at all fair*'.[46] A report to the candidate followed a second visit in August:

Cremer and myself . . . have visited a number of the leading working men, and met them in a delegate meeting. . . . We find the Registration going on well in both associations. But as we feared the Working Men's Association have no funds except the shillings of its working-class members. . . . Branches are being formed weekly and a good healthy feeling seems to prevail. . . . The Temperance people have called a meeting and some of them are for pressing the question of the Permissive Bill at all hazards. This we must try to avoid. I have done something towards throwing oil on their troubled waters.[47]

In addition to assisting Morley, the Executive sent Thomas Mottershead to the Tower Hamlets to prepare the ground for

Beale's race and Odger to Northampton, where Bradlaugh's entry was creating an embarrassing predicament for the League. The noted Secularist had attended a meeting of the election sub-committee on 24 June to declare his intention to stand as a candidate. Soliciting League support, he insisted that his candidacy was not in opposition to the Liberal, Charles Gilpin, but rather to the Whig, Lord Henley. Without waiting for the Council to act, Bradlaugh announced that he had received its endorsement. The Executive refused to decide the matter until Odger was able to report on the attitude of the League's Northampton branch.[48] Despite local enthusiasm for Bradlaugh, the Executive endorsed only Gilpin, suggesting that the two other aspirants submit their claims to a preliminary poll of the Liberal electors. Bradlaugh was further urged to withdraw if the majority were against him, rather than split the Liberal vote.[49] The real obstacle to a settlement was the refusal of Gilpin, a patron of the Adelphi Club, to break his compact with his Whig colleague.[50] The Northampton branch was annoyed by London's invidious method of working against Bradlaugh while pretending to be governed only by local senti-ments, and Howell was obliged to reassure them:

I trust the tenor of the resolution will preserve us from a breach with our Northampton Branch. Everything we have done has been with the simple view of getting the Liberal electors in public meeting to select their candidates, of seeing fair play to all parties, and has certainly not been done with any desire to interfere with your local efforts and decisions.[51]

Such protests notwithstanding, it was Henley rather than Bradlaugh who stood in the way of a democratic selection. Howell and Cremer decided to visit the city themselves 'to talk over matters *quietly* and *confidentially*',[52] but they failed to achieve their aim – to compel Bradlaugh's withdrawal. Glyn confided his mis-givings to Gladstone: 'Bradlaugh will do harm . . . B is not amen-able to the League – or I think I cd. manage him.'[53] In September Bradlaugh brought his case to the Council, but he obtained no satisfaction in his questioning of the machinations of Howell and Cremer in Northampton.[54] Rather than risk public repudiation by the League, he postponed his attack until after the election.

The problem of reconciling entrenched interests and the new Radical forces, which Howell and Glyn both appreciated, was by no means limited to a few constituencies like Northampton. Glyn understood that 'the old local party managers do not realize the altered state of matters & if they do they are extremely slow to coalesce with the new men'.[55] On the other hand, the hostility of the Whig magnates to Gladstone, which had curtailed the usual sources of election funds, forced the Liberals to rely on the new men themselves. Through the mediation of Goldwin Smith and Stansfeld, Howell and Cremer were brought into contact with W. P. Adam and Glyn's secretary, H. Scudamore Stanhope. By 6 August Cremer was able to report to the Executive that a Special Fund of £1,000 would be raised to finance deputations to various boroughs in order to assess Liberal prospects. Based on a list compiled by James Acland, the boroughs identified were those which had hitherto returned one or more Conservative members.[56] Plans for the fund were unfolded in early August. Glyn, who put up little or none of the money himself, insisted on maximum secrecy, lest a compact with the artisans enrage the Whig section of the party. Howell and Cremer, who operated almost completely autonomously, responsible to the Executive in only the most tenuous sense, worked through Stansfeld and Morley. The latter, grateful for League assistance in Bristol, provided most of the £1,900 which was ultimately raised.[57]

During the first phase of activity from early August to mid-September fifteen working-class organizers, under Howell's direction, were assigned in pairs to sixty-five boroughs. Howell's instructions to his deputies were specific: 'Get all the information you can as to who are candidates, what their politics, how they stand, either locally or otherwise, what associations there are in towns, where they meet, and on what nights, names and addresses of secretaries, etc.'[58] Once this information had been amassed, the agents were expected to establish or strengthen working-class political organizations, either as League branches or as Liberal associations, and to resolve personal difficulties which might impede efforts on behalf of Liberal candidates. All this work demanded tact to avoid offending local interests by appearing to dictate policy. As Howell explained,

Our desire is to inquire as to whether we can give some little aid to local officers by operating upon the working-class vote through their Trade Societies or other Associations. We think we can, and are willing to do all in our power to assist to return advanced Liberals to the next Parliament. *Quite understand that we do not intend interfering with local action in any way*. If we can supplement local effort we will.[59]

When the agents sent in their appraisals, Howell compiled them and transmitted the information to Morley and Stanhope. The volume of election reports provided vital data on the dominant local interests, the prevalence of corruption, the state of working-class organization, and the type of candidate suitable for a particular constituency. Howell summarized its general conclusions in a preliminary statement to Stansfeld:

. . . in *most* cases our opinion is that the only thing to be done is to lay the foundation for a thorough organization of the Liberal Party in which organization the working men shall be consulted and called into active political life. One great cause of failure in the past has been the ignoring of the working-class voter. This must not now be. They are a power and must be' consulted, and subjected to discipline. We find no difficulty with them when treated fairly. . . . We are of opinion, 1st, that the next contest will be most severe, that all that wealth and influence can do will be done to turn the scale in favour of the Tory Party. They will have but little regard either to decency or truth or honesty. 2nd, that the Liberal cause has had an immense impetus but found the Party not sufficiently organized to use and control it. That this can now be done, the fruits of which will last for many years. 3rd, We find amongst the working men far more enthusiasm for our League than we had expected and are assured that we can render greater assistance during the coming contest.[60]

The Liberal Whips were delighted with the results of the League investigation. Glyn commented to Gladstone, 'They are so sound and so sensible & in most places their great object is to unite the two sections of the party *for you* & not put up their own or any extreme men.'[61] Howell urged Stansfeld to tell Morley how pleased the party was with his efforts.[62] Although Morley was willing to continue his subsidies, he would have preferred to share the financial burden with others. He proposed to send out a 'strictly private' appeal to a few dozen 'safe friends', but Glyn and Stansfeld vetoed the plan, fearing that it might create unwelcome publicity for the compact.[63] Stansfeld insisted that 'some arrangement would have to be made' with Morley, who yielded in the face of Howell's pleas and the Whips' inflexibility.[64] Having supplied most of the initial

£1,000 for the preliminary inquiry, Morley was obliged to provide the additional £900 for constituency work.

The second phase of the enterprise involved concerted efforts to aid certain designated Liberal candidates. Howell and Cremer were assigned direct responsibility for several constituencies – Blackburn, Brighton, Northampton, Rye, Sheffield, Shoreham, Stafford, and Stoke – which Glyn thought required special attention.[65] In addition, Howell was given delicate tasks like 'setting things all right with the railway men' in Swindon[66] or promoting the re-election of Bernhard Samuelson for Banbury, even though he was forced to admit that the nominee 'is not quite up to our mark' on trade union questions.[67] Howell's absences from London in August and September enabled his critics on the General Council to censure him for leaving the office without their knowledge or consent. Discussions about the Secretary's supposed negligence indicated that most Council members were in the dark about his electoral activities. With many of the Executive members away on special assignments, however, it was difficult to call them to task for disregarding official duties.

The League's avowed interest in 'advanced Radical Reformers' and the Liberal Party's design for victory often coincided. In Sheffield, for example, A. J. Mundella was challenging the anti-Gladstonian, anti-trade unionist Radical independent, John Arthur Roebuck with the quiet encouragement of the Liberal managers. The party was afraid to dissociate itself openly from Roebuck, the incumbent, preferring to work through Goldwin Smith and the League agents. As early as June Howell told the Secretary of the Trades Council to 'try your very best to return [Mundella]. He is just the right man for Sheffield and will be a great accession to the cause of labour in the House of Commons.'[68] Mundella, who had the support of the Sheffield trades, was distressed by Gladstone's publicly-avowed neutrality and unwilling to trust entirely to the efforts of local labour groups. He implored Howell to furnish all possible aid, 'as I am a strong radical and they tell me that the moderates are afraid of me'.[69] Howell sent down Brighty and John Hales, taking precautions at the same time against offending the local leaders. 'We feel deeply interested in your election,' he wrote William Dronfield. 'It is in fact a national contest and not a mere local one. Both these men [Brighty and Hales] are trustworthy and I trust you will deal frankly with them. We do not

see [sic] to *interfere with you* but to *aid you if we can*.'[70] Despite
these assurances Howell told the two agents to take the initiative
into their own hands, and he was soon able to boast that 'in
Sheffield our delegates have done what the local agents could not
do, viz. unite the numerous trades into one committee for electoral
purposes'.[71]

Not every candidate was as willing as Mundella to identify himself with the Reform League, some obviously afraid that there
might be strings attached to such an alliance. Since the approved
candidates were prescribed by the managers in Parliament Street,
Howell could hardly have stipulated conditions even if he had
wanted to. He could thus, in good conscience, reassure William
Rathbone, the nominee for Liverpool, 'You are not supposed to
endorse *anything, only tell us how to serve you*. We think we can give
great aid. If you think we cannot, there the matter I suppose will
end. But in no case would you be mixed up with our movement
either in Liverpool or here.'[72]

Complications arose not over constituencies like Liverpool or
Sheffield, but rather over those in which Liberal and Reform
League interests to some extent diverged. In Brighton – one of
Glyn's 'special' constituencies – Henry Fawcett and James White,
the two sitting Liberal members, ran in tandem, and the candidacy
of William Conningham, a League Vice-President, was unwelcome
to the party and, consequently, to Howell. He explained to the
Secretary of the Brighton branch that 'we can better spare a politician, even one as good and advanced as Mr Conningham, than we
can one who understands the questions of capital and labour, and
whose sympathies are with the mass of toilers rather than with the
employers', i.e. Fawcett.[73] Howell's efforts ensured that Brighton
members remained faithful to the Liberals. Conningham, finishing
a poor fifth at the poll, resigned from the League after the election.[74]
In Halifax a Whig–Liberal alliance existed between Edward
Ackroyd and James Stansfeld, the architect of the Special Fund.
E. O. Greening, an ally of the League, entered the race with the
encouragement of Mill, Ernest Jones, and the local branch. But
Stansfeld was no more willing to break his electoral compact than
Gilpin had been in Northampton. Despite Howell's assurances to
one League functionary that 'we shall never be disloyal to our
Branches,' his loyalty to Stansfeld precluded any endorsement of
Greening.[75]

Although a few prominent League members – Beales, J. Baxter Langley, Cremer, and Howell himself – were encouraged in their candidacies, the general pattern is clear: through his compliance with the provisions of the Special Fund, Howell mortgaged the interests of the Reform League to the purposes of the Liberal Party. The aim of the party strategists was to defeat as many Tories as possible, and this led them to oppose any candidate who threatened to divide the Liberal vote. The fact that such a policy implied a reliance on entrenched Whig interests in many boroughs and the exclusion of working-class candidates was not regarded as an excessive price for victory. Howell could hardly have anticipated that his support on behalf of designated Liberals would rapidly degenerate into acquiescence in any candidacy – Whig or Radical – which had official sponsorship. But once he had committed himself to an alliance with the party on its own terms, he had surrendered the one advantage he possessed: control of the still-formidable League apparatus. The nature of the victory indicated that League involvement had been effective. Howell's agents had visited eighty-five boroughs which had previously returned Tory members, and their activities had been instrumental in at least thirty of the forty-nine seats gained from the Conservatives. If the actual League candidates were all defeated, Howell could console himself with the success of stalwart friends of the League, such as Morley, Lawson, and Samuel Plimsoll.

In retrospect, it was not the actual acceptance of Liberal money that seems objectionable: Social Democratic Federation candidates received money from Maltman Barry, a Conservative agent, in 1885, and even Keir Hardie obtained a subsidy from mysterious sources in his 1888 Mid-Lanark contest.[76] Nor can one accuse Howell of yielding to bribery, although he did receive commissions and salary supplements of over £120, as well as partial payment of his Aylesbury campaign expenses.[77] If his motives were, in part, personal, he was looking to long-term advantages rather than to quick profits. Howell's mistake was to sacrifice the independence of the League without obtaining any real concessions from his Liberal partners. His policy was perfectly consistent with the principles he had long expressed. He believed that the survival of the League depended on Liberal favour, and his own inclinations on this subject were fortified by the artful persuasion of Radicals like Morley and Stansfeld, to whom he deferred so readily. Howell was not

alone in denying the alternative of the political self-reliance of the
workers, championed by the League militants. Like most trade
union leaders of his generation, he regarded such a notion as precipitate and imprudent. The labour movement was neither ready
nor willing to strike out on its own as a political force. The Reform
League could play an auxiliary role, but it lacked the means and the
resolve to wage an independent campaign. But if Howell correctly
assessed the temper of his fellow artisans, he allowed himself to be
deceived by Radical professions. The very success of the electoral
arrangement enabled the government that took office at the end of
1868 to discount the claims of the working men who had contributed to its victory. Moreover, the alliance with Liberalism, rather
than strengthening the League, led to its rapid demise.

Within the League itself the repercussions of the election agreement started as soon as Howell presented his report. For most
members it provided the first clue as to the character of the Special
Fund. Noting that it derived from the need to work for the return of
advanced Radical Reformers, which required 'a large outlay, much
larger than the funds of the League permitted', Howell's statement
made no mention of its source, naming Morley simply as the
treasurer of the Fund.[78] The appended report of the Finance Committee asserted that 'under some restrictions [the Fund] was made
available, so far as possible, after meeting other expenses, to assist
in defraying expenses of Members of the League as Candidates'.[79]
While Howell's statement had been deliberately vague and mislead-
ing, that of the Finance Committee was an outright misrepresentation. The only members who derived benefit from the Fund,
besides Beales, were Howell and Odger, neither of whom was re-
imbursed for election expenses until several months after the
report had been issued.

These explanations were intended to forestall the recriminations
of disappointed candidates, like Bradlaugh or Col Dickson, and
indignant members whose suspicion had been aroused by the
secrecy surrounding the Fund. A revolt had been quelled in
August, but it was impossible to stifle inquiry once the election had
taken place. As a portent of the impending outcry, the Executive
carried a motion reprimanding Howell for his absence at its meeting
on 18 November.[80] The Secretary upbraided his critics the following week, insisting that he had been absent from meetings only five

times during his tenure and had been, in fact, merely late to the session in question. At the same time Bradlaugh opened fire at a Council meeting, demanding to know the names of the contributors and the nature of the expenditure. As a conciliatory gesture, Cremer proposed that the accounts be opened for a fortnight to Council members, although the ban on publication of the details would not be lifted.[81] Bradlaugh had wrongly assumed that the money had been used to promote the election of other League members, while he had been excluded. Since an insinuation of this nature reflected an ignorance of the actual circumstances, Howell felt that he could disregard Bradlaugh's fulminations. He was satisfied that 'no evil will result therefrom except perhaps to Mr Bradlaugh himself'.[82] The source of grievance was all too clear: 'He thought [Howell told Glyn] that we could give him money for his election, but we kept to our arrangement and would not swerve for men even of our own Council.'[83]

Odger, who had kept silent while receiving pay from the Fund during constituency investigations, was a more troublesome antagonist. He resented his exclusion from the race in Chelsea with League complicity, and on 2 December he accused the Liberal managers of sending Joseph D'A. Samuda, an opponent of trade unionism, into the Tower Hamlets as a rival to Beales. He further demanded an inquiry into the cause of the President's defeat and into the circumstances of the visit which Howell and Cremer paid to Northampton in August. Cremer countered by raising the question of whether Odger had received money and the promise of assistance in finding another seat from the Bass family as an inducement to withdraw from the race in Stafford.[84]

Howell protested to Beales that the provisions of the Fund had placed him in an invidious position. Having acted with propriety, obeying the instructions of his patrons, he now found his honour impugned by those who imagined themselves cheated of the spoils:

All over the country the matter is being reproduced to our disadvantage. And the whole secret lies here. A special fund was raised for the purpose of trying to oust certain *Tories* from certain seats. The names of the boroughs were given to us and our work pointed out. This we adhered to. We made no exception except in your case of the Tower Hamlets. You know the names of all who have had to do with the matter just as much as we do. Everything is fair and honourable, but the names are not to be made public, and it will be an act of dishonour of any man to do so.

If Mr Bradlaugh or Col Dickson want money to fight with, let them get it or conform to the arrangements and fight against Tories.[85]

The President rallied to the defence of his subordinate, and at the 9 December meeting Howell and Cremer were absolved of any wrong during their Northampton visit. None the less, criticism of Howell's policy was implicit in the Executive declaration that 'League candidates are not to be kept out of the field in the future merely because other candidates have been in the field before'.[86] Angry and self-righteous, Howell objected to the underlying inference of the resolution: without directly accusing the Secretary, his critics insinuated that he had betrayed the League, deliberately sabotaging the plan to promote working-class candidacies. Always easily wounded, Howell was never so touchy as when the castigation was, in some measure, deserved. In another letter to Beales he grumbled,

I consider the conduct of some members of our Executive Committee altogether inexplicable and calculated to injure the Reform League and also to do me, personally, immense injury. Why was not the Balance Sheet allowed to be read last night? I had it quite prepared....You must know that the position I occupy will be affected by these delays and insinuations.[87]

What rankled even more was that his Liberal friends seemed impervious to the problem of confronting his assailants with his hands tied by the bonds of secrecy. The Executive Committee ordered him to write to Glyn about Samuda's entry, but the Liberal Whip was in no hurry to rescue Howell from his predicament. A second appeal, protesting that 'every delay seems to confirm these men in their accusations and they taunt us with not having your denial', elicited the appropriate response from Glyn, disavowing any connection either with Samuda or the Tower Hamlets contest.[88] Howell was already preparing the ground for a direct financial link with the Liberal managers, independent of the surveillance of a body like the League. 'I have never had so much badgering over anything in my life as over this work,' he wrote Glyn. 'In any work for the future I would see to it that I dealt only with those who found the money and let all account vouchers be rendered to them.'[89] The nature of the 'work for the future' was intimated in his next letter:

I shall be very glad at the first opportunity you have to talk over the project mentioned some time since and which you said you would be glad to chat over with me at an early date. Now is a good time to begin to get the Liberal Party organised. It can be done quietly and cheaply and at the same time efficiently, if it be done with care.[90]

After Beales had refuted the charges about the Fund and Morley had written that its expenditure had been 'satisfactory to the subscribers who have provided the money',[91] the Executive Committee approved the balance sheet provisionally, reserving the right to discuss 'the propriety and authority of certain parts of the expenditure' in the future.[92] Although his method of accounting furnished a partial breakdown of the £1,972 7s 9d into categories of expense, Howell was as reticent about naming recipients as he had been about the donors. Baxter Langley tried to restore harmony by attesting that Howell and Cremer had been 'fully authorized' by the Finance Committee to make appropriations from the Fund, but R. A. Cooper insisted on the right to inspect payment vouchers. The Secretary yielded, allowing Bradlaugh, Langley, and others to scrutinize the mysterious documents. After this ordeal was over, he and Cremer felt secure enough to submit demands to the Executive Committee: Cremer claimed £90 commission on the last £900 of the Special Fund, and Howell asked the League to absorb his remaining Aylesbury election debts of £136 16s. Both requests were approved.[93]

The immediate crisis had now passed, but the atmosphere was too charged with discord for the League to survive much longer. The final bitter struggle destroyed whatever unity remained, and, in any case, Beales and Howell were now convinced that the organization had outlived its usefulness. The constant strife and financial hardship in the period since the passing of the Reform Bill had sapped the League's vitality and undermined rank and file confidence in the leadership. In the face of internal division Howell had assumed greater authority, but he had been unable to carry many of his colleagues along in his policy of alliance with Liberalism. The Reform League was the first organization to mobilize the new political consciousness of the Victorian artisan class, but, like its early socialist successors, it failed to resolve the conflict between the yearning for bourgeois acceptance and the maintenance of proletarian militancy. Those, like Howell, who looked to middle-class Radicals as the agents of amelioration now wanted to discard the

League and to concentrate on winning recognition from the Liberal Party. The opposing faction in the organization, including Cooper and Odger, hoped to renovate it as a more militant, republican body.

On 20 January Cremer proposed that the League conclude its affairs instead of 'perpetuating a state of chronic political agitation'.[94] The militants argued that it should not be disbanded until its original programme of manhood suffrage and the ballot had been achieved. For several weeks discussion continued, but Beales decided to resolve the issue by refusing to take further responsibility for the lease on the office and by declaring his intention to give up the presidency.[95] Beales's announcement was promptly followed by Howell's own letter of resignation, which gave two reasons for his retirement. In the first place, with the removal of Beales, 'we have not the same guarantees, either for support or management, which have hitherto characterized our movement'. Second, he continued, 'The League having been, from its commencement, an essentially agitating body, with a programme demanding only the Parliamentary enfranchisement of the People, it has practically accomplished its work, so far at least as the public mind is at present disposed to go.'

He looked forward to the imminent concession of the ballot and to progress in the areas of education, taxation, and land tenure, but agitation for these reforms, he felt, would require either an organization constituted on a broader basis or several distinct bodies. Of crucial importance, at least in the political realm, was the improvement of local organization. The hope for advancement in the years to come did not rest with a more articulate and militant association of working men, but rather with the more enlightened party. 'My profound faith in our great liberal leader, Mr Gladstone,' he added, 'makes me feel all the more secure as to our future. He evidently regards hustings pledges as promises to be faithfully kept and redeemed.'[96]

After pleas from Beales, Howell, and even Odger at a special 12 March Executive meeting, the members decided to dissolve the League, agreeing that it had 'accomplished, substantially, the objects of its original programme'. A Vigilance Committee was appointed with authority to summon together reformers in the event of future political crisis, and the concluding meeting was held a week later.[97] For the remainder of the year Howell carried on alone trying to raise money to pay the £675 of outstanding debts. Contributions from Bright, Glyn, Titus Salt, Thomas Thomasson, and A. W. Paulton helped him liquidate the League's obligations, but by the end of 1869 a £200 debt remained.[98]

By the time the Reform League was properly buried, Howell had found new professional opportunities. Even if the last months of its existence had been marred by the attempts to discredit him, Howell could look back over his tenure with some pride. As he wrote in his letter of resignation, 'During the whole of this time, now four most eventful years, I have had the management of the administrative department, and . . . this also has been conducted upon the most business-like principles of efficiency and economy.'[99] His colleagues might have found fault with his choice of business associates, but Howell's administrative competence and diligence had been beyond reproach. Entering the League as a bricklayer, with only the most meagre knowledge of finance and bureaucracy, he had managed in four years to find his vocation in organizational politics. Once the League was dissolved, he could not consider returning to the building trade. As he remarked to his friend Charles Bartlett some months later, 'I feel that I have some abilities which would be more usefully employed for the country than in laying bricks, not that I dislike work or my trade, but I can be more useful in other ways.'[100] His professional experience and his contacts with men of influence had opened a new world which he was determined to exploit to the best advantage.

6

The Business of Politics

Despite Reform League support for the principle of labour representation, the provisions of the 1868 electoral compact with the
Liberal Party served to deter working-class candidacies. Several
well-known personalities in labour politics, including Odger and
Hartwell, withdrew from contests under pressure, and ultimately
only three working men actually went to the polls: William
Newton in the Tower Hamlets, Cremer at Warwick, and Howell
himself at Aylesbury. Long before he had become Secretary of the
League, Howell had begun to nurse parliamentary ambitions, and
in view of his extensive knowledge of constituencies, it was surprising that he should have made his first attempt in one wholly unsuited
to a candidate of his background. Aylesbury was a large two-member
borough, encompassing over 100 square miles of Buckinghamshire.
It was almost completely agricultural, with only a small
town and several villages inside its borders. During the previous
decade it had come under the political influence of the Rothschilds,
who owned enormous estates in the region. Nathaniel Mayer de
Rothschild, son of the first Jewish Member of Parliament, had been
elected for the borough in 1865 and served in the Commons until
his elevation to the peerage twenty years later. He was to be succeeded at Aylesbury, by then virtually a family political property,
first by his brother-in-law and subsequently by his son. The other
Member, first returned in 1859, was another local landowner,
Samuel George Smith, a Conservative banker. With the traditional
landed influence still predominant, the agricultural workers and
small tradesmen were unlikely to respond to the appeal of an urban
trade unionist like Howell.

His decision to contest Aylesbury arose out of a visit to the
borough at the end of September by Thomas Mottershead, employed at the time as one of the League's itinerant constituency

agents. When J. Baxter Langley, who was scheduled to speak in the town, was forced to cancel his engagement, Howell agreed to substitute for him. Addressing a meeting of workers at the Corn Exchange on 8 October, he pronounced what was to become the major theme of his campaign. Rothschild and Smith, by forming a compact to exclude a third candidate, were, for all practical purposes, attempting to disfranchise the voters. Howell argued that this alliance was especially insidious because a high proportion of the new voters were probably Liberals. Rather than sanction the undemocratic arrangements of the incumbents, the Reform League determined to bring forward another Liberal to run alongside Rothschild. Mottershead had evidently prepared the ground for the Corn Exchange meeting: immediately after Howell's speech a resolution was carried declaring him 'eminently qualified to represent them in Parliament' and pledging the support of the working men.[1]

Howell apparently decided to try his luck only after sentiment among Aylesbury electors had been tested. Rather than seek a constituency in which he might have some hope of victory, he stumbled, almost inadvertently, upon a borough in which defeat was inevitable. Glyn found Howell's action inexplicable and told Gladstone, 'I much regret now I did not put one or two of [the working men] forward *earlier*, but though they constantly sent to me & helped me, the men, Howell and Cremer, who I should like to see in the House never expressed any wish to become candidates.'[2] Howell's campaign speeches emphasized his original motive in seeking the nomination: a desire to afford the voters an opportunity to return two Liberal members. It was pointless, he maintained, for Aylesbury electors to send one member to Westminster to vote for particular measures and another to vote against them.[3] His own ambitions were a secondary consideration; he would not have stood for election had a local Liberal candidate emerged. Challenging the Conservative, and not Rothschild, he insisted that he would withdraw if his candidacy endangered the Liberal member's seat. He further proposed a coalition with Rothschild – a more rational, Liberal alliance which would enable the electors to cast both their votes for candidates of the same party.[4]

At the same time he sought to strike a balance between an inflammatory appeal to the agricultural workers and a conciliatory approach which might earn middle-class approval. Howell's election address was an exemplar of studied moderation, indistinguishable from that of any other advanced Liberal. Denouncing the compact to return the sitting members unopposed as 'a gross violation of the spirit of our Electoral Laws, and unjust to the great body of electors', he outlined the most Gladstonian of legislative programmes. Pledging himself to work for the further amendment of the Reform Act, the disestablishment of the Irish Church, the reform of the land tenure system, the development of national un-sectarian education, the promotion of arbitration in trade disputes, and the equalization of poor rates, he also subscribed to Gladstonian financial precepts, advocating strenuous efforts 'to economize our National Expenditure and to reduce the heavy burden of Taxation'. No mention was made of the need for trade union reform or of the desirability of 'socialist' welfare measures. Instead Howell vaguely promised to 'aid every progressive movement for the advancement of Civil and Religious Liberty and for the general prosperity of the United Kingdom'. It was impossible, however, to evade the fact of his working-class origins, and he decided to depict his candidacy as a challenge to the Liberalism of the voters:

I seek your suffrages to defend a right, the right of *the great mass of the people* to a voice in the making of our laws; to support a policy – the policy of the Liberal Party, whose recognized leader is Mr Gladstone; and to promote a principle – the principle that other interests in the State, besides land and capital, should have their representatives in the British Parliament – the interest of the Wage-receiving classes, and of the entire industry of the Nation, whether Agricultural or Manufacturing.[5]

The Conservative reaction to Howell's entry into the race could hardly be expected to be indulgent. The Tory *Bucks Herald* wrote disparagingly of his initial speech, ' . . . it is only necessary for well-constituted minds to hear the violent processes which the reign of the [Reform] League proposes to introduce to make them shudder at and recoil from their programme'.[6] Howell's next major meeting, at the County Hall on 17 October, was disrupted by Tory hecklers, many of them local farmers fresh from market bargaining and probably none too sober. He had at first been received with ap-plause, but the clamour of the hecklers was soon so pronounced that even the forcible ejection of a few of their number failed to make the candidate's words audible. As one local paper described the scene,

The knot of turbulent Conservatives, not liking to see the meeting going on so prosperously, redoubled their efforts to drown his voice, till the speaker desisted, and a general scramble ensued, from the efforts of the Liberals to turn out the uproarious disturbers of the meeting. The scene which followed was both amusing and disgraceful. All appeared to enjoy it, while the majority felt that the few promoters of the uproar were a disgrace to Englishmen, as indeed they were. From this point little was heard of Mr Howell's speech.[7]

Far more serious was the use of coercion as an electoral weapon by local Tory notables, a common practice as long as traditional influences remained strong and voters were still deprived of the protection of the ballot.[8] The incidents of which Howell complained cannot be proven, but they were typical of political contests at the time, underlined again and again in the Reform League election reports. The Vicar of Haddenham threatened to take glebe land away from his cottagers if they voted for *either* Howell *or* Rothschild.[9] A Tory landlord ordered his tenants to vote as he did or risk the consequences.[10] As long as there was no stigma attached to intimidation, Howell's plea to voters to resist coercion was futile.

Conservative tactics did not make Rothschild more receptive to Howell's call for coalition. Far from a progressive himself, this heir to a great European fortune doubtlessly felt a greater affinity for his Tory 'opponent' than for the working-class upstart. Howell's workers charged, in fact, that Rothschild's agents had been soliciting support for the Tory candidate, urging constituents to split their votes between Rothschild and Smith.[11] Rothschild denied the allegation, insisting that 'if I had thought we could have carried two Liberals, you can be sure I should have done my utmost to win the other seat'.[12] He used the supposed Conservative preponderance as an excuse for refusing to coalesce with Howell when a deputation led by J. B. Leno, Howell's election agent, visited his headquarters. Rothschild's agent argued that since the Tories could actually win both seats, an alliance with Howell would only endanger an already precarious seat. The Rothschild camp continued to brave Leno's threat that 'plumpers' (electors casting both votes for the same candidate) would be used in Howell's behalf.[13]

Howell was encouraged by expressions of solidarity he received from prominent Liberals. John Stuart Mill wrote that it would give him 'much pleasure to see Mr Howell returned to Parliament'.[14]

The MP for Plymouth, Walter Morrison, donated £50 towards his campaign expenses and announced that there was 'no man whom I would more gladly see in the House of Commons as the representative of the most advanced section of the Liberal Party'.[15] Yet these sentiments could not compensate for the hostility with which Howell's candidacy was greeted by the Tories and the barely concealed contempt on Rothschild's part. Howell hoped his Liberal connections would apply pressure, but Morrison and Glyn failed to persuade Rothschild to come to terms with the working-class candidate. In fact, the family's traditional donations to party funds may well have prevented Glyn from intervening too zealously, lest he risk causing offence.[16] As he explained to Gladstone,

Howell has no chance at Aylesbury *but* I am very much disappointed at the line Rothschild has taken. He has refused today to coalesce or act & in strong terms – I have done all I can – Howell is a true man and has been of great use to me. He has unfortunately chosen the wrong place and went to A[ylesbury] against my advice – a stranger cannot win there & Rothschild's treatment has done harm & will create a bad feeling. The upper part of our party are so jealous & sensitive just now. I have written to Howell – Morley, Goschen, Forster & others have all written to me in his favour today. The League are very angry but they have waited too long.[17]

At first there was a slightly obsequious quality in Howell's campaign pronouncements, but soon a stridency emerged, especially after it became clear that Rothschild would not give in to his appeals. He changed his tone more than his content, but it was still unlikely to increase his middle-class support. In a speech to the villagers of Aston Clinton he stated that it was 'impossible that the interests of the working and trading classes of this country can be properly cared for as long as the whole of our legislation is in the hands of the capitalists and large landed proprietors'.[18] Another tactic was to emphasize Rothschild's Judaism, calling the religious issue to public attention without appearing to resort to bigotry. Neither Disraeli [*sic*] nor Rothschild, he asserted, would have been able to enter Parliament had the Liberal Party not removed the disability against Jews.[19] At the raucous 16 November nomination meeting he accused his opponents of labelling him an 'infidel' because of his stance on the Irish Church and raised the religious question in his peculiarly illogical rejoinder:

I am not an infidel. I believe as truthfully and honestly, and have from my youth up, the principles of *our common Christianity*, as any of these Tory gentlemen. Allow me to say with all deference – I do not wish to say a word against Mr Rothschild – but why do they not make it a *question of religion against him*? They say I am going to bring back the Pope – why do they not say that *he is going to bring back Judaism*?[20]

In view of the disadvantages which Howell could not overcome, his electoral achievement was impressive. Running a strong third, he received 942 votes to 1,772 for Rothschild and 1,468 for Smith.[21] Hampered by lack of funds and a local reputation, opposed by the forces of wealth and influence, Howell had ready excuses for his defeat. 'I could have got in easily,' he told one friend,

if the Liberal member had done his duty but they all dread working men being in the House. I had to fight against the Farmers, Employers, 'Gentlemen', Parsons, and a large number of shops tradespeople!!!! Well, they had to spend no end of money to keep me out as it was. My election cost about £400 – theirs about £4,500 each!!![22]

This financial disparity was particularly serious since Aylesbury was classed with the counties for electioneering purposes, thus enabling candidates to hire cabs to bring voters to the polls. In this respect, as in so many others, Howell's wealthy rivals were at a considerable advantage.[23] In a letter to Walter Morrison, one of the few large contributors to his funds, Howell reiterated his belief that Rothschild was the real culprit: 'The clannish caste of the Rothschild family refused coalition and did all they could against my being returned. Bribery, treating, and coercion were used.'[24]

Howell's reproach was, indeed, justified. The *Bucks Advertiser* concluded that with a majority of the electorate voting exclusively on the Liberal side (plumpers for either Howell or Rothschild and those who split their votes between the two), Rothschild would have improved his position in the poll had he collaborated with Howell. By a united effort, the *Advertiser* claimed, both seats might have been secured for the Liberals: 'so far from its being true that Mr Rothschild held his seat by the forbearance of his opponents, the majority of 304 conclusively shows that Mr Smith can never be returned again without the help, open or tacit, of Mr Rothschild'.[25] Yet, to blame Howell's defeat on Rothschild's conduct or on the preponderance of wealth was to disregard a crucial factor: the prejudice against a working-class candidate, especially one who lacked local roots. As the *Bucks Chronicle* noted, 'The main objection to Mr Howell's return, in many minds, was the certainty that in the event of his election, he would although sitting as the member for Aylesbury be under the influence and subject to the dictation of the Reform League.'[26] Morrison shared Howell's disappointment, but he told him frankly,

I never thought you would win. You were far too late in the field. And no doubt unfair means were used. . . . I know nothing whatever of the borough of Aylesbury, but I wondered much at your challenging an agricultural borough. Independent of all unfair practices, there is a tendency for them to go with a neighbour. They distrust a stranger be he who he may.[27]

It was, ironically enough, the failure of the Aylesbury Liberals to elect Howell which reinforced his dependence on Liberal patrons in London. A victory might have enabled him to assert his independence: as the sole artisan MP, his prestige would have made the party managers anxious to retain his loyalty. Instead, he was reduced to further subservience, clinging to the handouts of politicians. Howell, not the Liberal leaders, hastened to acknowledge a sense of obligation. Once again beholden to Samuel Morley – this time for a £50 election contribution – he wrote, 'My gratitude shall be shown by my future devotion to the same good work, not perhaps in precisely the same way as in the past, but by recognizing the great steps we have made in the reform cause, and by using present advantages in the best manner.'[28]

Henceforth Howell's own zeal for further reform was subordinated to financial considerations. For the next few years he took his cue from the Liberals, at least as long as they were willing to foot the bills. 'Some of our friends abuse the middle class,' he remarked to a Bristol acquaintance, 'but *they* find the money and therefore should not be too much abused.'[29]

In February 1869 Howell approached Glyn about the new 'project' that he had mentioned in December. The Liberal Whip resented Cremer's attempt to exact payment for their election work, but he expressed interest in Howell's proposal for constituency organizational work. Howell intimated that £1,000 might be required for the first year's effort.[30] Despite Glyn's resistance to such claims, Howell helped Cremer draft a letter to the Chief Whip seeking a reward for the 'essential service' which the two men had undertaken in the Liberal interest. The letter recapitulated their struggle to maintain secrecy in the operation of the Special Fund and their difficulties, especially in the Northampton, Hackney, and Chelsea elections.

So far as we are concerned [the appeal continued] we were the least paid of all who went *out*, as our expenses were much heavier, whilst our pay was just the same in amount as any of our co-workers, however humble his abilities or inadequate his work. Circumstances therefore compel us to ask you to consider our claims, as our Election contests and extra expenses have placed us considerably behind.[31]

Stansfeld convinced Howell that it was inadvisable to demand recompense for past services, promising instead that he would try to secure £200 to permit Howell to launch his organizational work.[32] Cremer preferred an immediate settlement of accounts, but Howell accepted Stansfeld's reassurances: 'If I can but get everything cleared up [he replied] as to my contest and just get a start in business as already suggested, I feel sure that I shall some day have the honour and pleasure of supporting you with my vote and perhaps voice in the House of Commons.'[33]

In the weeks that followed, while the League was dismantled, Howell devised his scheme for a private Liberal Registration and Election Agency. He proposed to deal with the problems of registering new working-class voters, insuring that they be furnished with the necessary information and forms. He would devote himself to integrating them into active political life, a process which would have an enormous impact on subsequent elections.

For this work I feel assured [he informed Stansfeld] I have peculiar facilities. I have a most extensive knowledge of all kinds of working-men's associations, both social and political, and am known personally to most of their officers. I can without difficulty have access to all their meetings and address them in reference to this important subject.

In addition, he would be prepared to undertake practical election work in any designated constituency, providing that he would not be asked to assist any candidate 'whose support could not be relied on by the Liberal Party on all great questions of national policy'. Finally, he would strive to lessen the cost of elections through effective management of local campaigns, taking care that limited funds not be squandered.

The great thing [he concluded] will be to give me a fair start for the first year. If I can get £500, I shall be able to do some good service. Of this it will cost £60 for rent and housekeeper, £12 coal and gas, furniture for office £40. . . . I feel quite certain that I can earn my salary and do valuable work. I am anxious to get into the matter *now* as Cremer, [Thomas] Connolly, and others are wanting to start something of the kind with me as their Secretary. An Association will not do for this kind of work.[34]

It was by no means certain that an association would not 'do', but Howell was determined to avoid sharing any prospective bounties with former colleagues.

By the beginning of June the arrangements were completed, and on the 12th Howell received a first instalment of £50 from Stansfeld, delegated to serve as treasurer. According to the agreement, Glyn and Morley were each to contribute £200, with Stansfeld himself providing the other £100 to make up the £500 grant.[35] Howell gratefully vowed to Morley that

it will be my constant endeavour to use that money judiciously and economically, so that those who contributed it shall feel satisfied of its being usefully applied. All the work I do will not be apparent, for I intend working quietly and unobtrusively, so that local men shall not be offended with my efforts. It is not for agitation, but organization, and I will do my best to produce good and useful results.[36]

Howell's actual salary was calculated at £3 3s per week, but by the beginning of November office expenses and extensive travel, especially in southern England and the Midlands, had raised his costs to nearly £250, £100 more than he had already received from Stansfeld.[37]

During his first six months of activity Howell sent out nearly 20,000 circulars and corresponded widely with working men throughout the country, offering information on registration, lectures, and rules for setting up Liberal associations. He also travelled to some two dozen towns to establish new political bodies or to revive old Reform League branches as Liberal registration societies. With the encouragement of his patrons, he volunteered his services as a paid lecturer for the National Education League, an affiliation he felt would 'increase my influence with the working men of this country'.[38] In June, upon hearing of the illness of the aged incumbent, F. F. H. Berkeley, Howell hurried to Bristol to assess working-class opinion in case a by-election should ensue.[39] When the appointment of W. H. Gladstone, the Prime Minister's son, as a Lord of the Treasury occasioned a by-election in Whitby in November, Howell spent a week there addressing shipwrights and carpenters, visiting trade societies, and canvassing voters.[40]

Although he was kept busy and well remunerated for his services, the results were barely perceptible, and Howell grew dissatisfied within a matter of months. Organizational work was extremely slow, hampered by widespread indifference among the new voters. In early November he suggested to Stansfeld a change in the original scheme:

. . . as I am now working I do nothing to bring in money for future work, so that when my present resources are dried up, I shall have nothing to fall back upon. . . . My remedy therefore is this – that the gentlemen who have been generous enough to give me this start should consent that I shall have the remainder of the money to purchase a little business which will give me ample time for political work and enable me to do all I am doing – only spreading it over a longer period – and at the same time enable me to do it as efficiently and as well whilst I shall have something to fall back upon for a living without entirely living upon political movements.

For I feel it will take a long time to get sufficient employment as a political agent to keep me, especially with my notions of Parliamentary Agency. Besides which I own I don't like trusting entirely to politics for one's bread. It lessens a man's influence and independence. I want to preserve both. I don't want to be a *mere political hack* open to every engagement, if it only brings in money. . . . I want to be independent amongst my own class and I can if this be done. For I cannot always lend myself to all the *foolish movements of working men.* [My italics.][41]

Stansfeld demurred at first and had the temerity to offer Howell a job as a bricklayer in his brewery.[42] But within the next few months Howell's cajoling convinced him that it would be more expedient to end the financial agreement. By the middle of 1870 Stansfeld and Morley paid Howell the remaining £350, with which he bought six worker's cottages on Verulam Street, near Gray's Inn Road.[43] In the search for a steady income the working-class Radical set himself up as a slum landlord. The rents from this capitalist enterprise did furnish a small return, but it was, in fact, hardly a profitable investment. Within a year and a half he had unloaded the properties on Thomas Brassey, then interested in the possibility of rehabilitating the neighbourhood. The money he received from the wealthy railway contractor helped to finance the purchase of the house next to his own (secured in 1868 with a building society loan) on Faunce Street in Kennington.[44]

Although Howell continued to confer with Glyn about working-class organization, he soon felt it preferable to end his direct connection with the Liberals. The implications of his contract had been to give Glyn a veto on positions he might have wanted to accept, thus creating a source of conflict between 'money on the one hand, loyalty on the other'.[45] However much he might disdain 'the foolish movements of working men', Howell recognized the risk he incurred by divorcing himself from labour politics. Rather than continue as a private agent, he decided – after receiving the £350 – to amalgamate his political activities with those of the newly-formed Labour Representation League. If he had profitably regained his independence, he none the less found himself again in search of a livelihood to supplement his receipts from his Verulam Street tenants. Throughout the early 1870s, even after his appointment as Secretary of the Parliamentary Committee of the Trades Union Congress, he was invariably on the lookout for new opportunities in either labour politics or abortive business ventures. Neither the generosity of the Liberals – at least at the outset – nor his decision to leave their employ prevented him from subsequently denouncing their ingratitude in failing to provide for his welfare.

Despite Howell's suspicion of attempts to reconstitute the Reform League, he had become involved early in 1869 in establishing the Labour Representation League, which was soon to duplicate many of its features. He had been disturbed by the Liberal Party's reluctance to promote labour candidacies, and it was this policy that became the principal object of the new organization. The League arose out of a proposal for a Working Men's Parliamentary Association formulated by William Allan, Applegarth, Howell, Lloyd Jones, William Newton, and Odger in January 1869. While this group showed no immediate signs of life, rival bodies were springing up in other quarters. At the initiative of Richard Marsden Latham, a Radical London barrister, the competing groups were brought together, but it took several meetings to iron out the inherent conflicts. Latham patiently mediated among the factions,

managing to secure enough concessions from all parties to launch
the League on 11 August with an agreed programme. With Latham
as President, Allan as Treasurer, and Jones as Secretary, a thirty-
two-man Executive Committee was appointed to include all the
prominent leaders of the London labour movement.[46]

The prospectus issued in August promised to mobilize 'the
strength of the operative classes as an electoral power, so that when
necessary it may be brought to bear with effect on any important
political, social, or industrial question'. Rejecting the concept of an
independent labour party, it sought rather to operate as a pressure
group within the existing party system, a restriction which made
the new League no less vulnerable to the magnetism of the Liberals
than the Reform League had been. No matter how compromised
in practice, its stated goals did represent an enlargement of the
boundaries of political aspiration. The League's main object, the
manifesto announced,

will be to procure the return to Parliament of qualified working men:
persons who by character and ability command the confidence of their
class, and who are competent to deal satisfactorily with questions of
general interest, as well as with those in which they are specially
interested.

This was a response to the demand of the more militant elements
within the labour movement for effective parliamentary representation. The extension of the suffrage had been an important advance
in political terms, but the external pressure of the newly enfranchised could not compensate for the lack of working-class members.
Few aspired to depose the ruling classes: rather they wanted the
addition of a group of working-class MPs who might speak directly
for the interest of labour. This was an aim that men, like Howell,
who aspired to parliamentary seats themselves could endorse without altering their political convictions. Beyond its strictly electoral
objectives, the League intended to furnish the machinery for promoting 'all such political, industrial, and social questions as involved the well-being of the working classes', serving, in effect, as
a general legislative watchdog for the people.[47]

Although the rules provided for a network of provincial branches,
the League remained throughout its life little more than it had been
at the start: a tenuous coalition of London labour interests. Those
provincial groups with which it collaborated electorally tended to

be independent associations, frequently tied to the Liberal Party, and League expansion was impeded by provisions for individual affiliation, excluding corporate bodies like trade unions.[48] Moreover, the programme bore the imprint of its troubled birth: while attempting to be comprehensive, it was merely vague, an unsatisfactory compromise between those committed to independent labour action and those who wanted to strengthen ties with the Radicals. During the ten years of its existence it continued to lose members, the militants breaking off into more extreme republican groups, such as the Land and Labour League, and others discovering more productive avenues for their talents within the institutions of trade unionism. Its functions as the guardian of social and industrial interests were appropriated by the Parliamentary Committee of the TUC, and its attempts to attract middle-class members were in vain. In the end, the League concerned itself chiefly with the modest objective of working-class candidacies, both in parliamentary and School Board elections, but even here its success was vitiated by its indecision about contesting seats against Liberal nominees.

The League endorsed Odger's challenge to the Whig alderman, Sir Sydney Waterlow, in Southwark in 1869, but Odger came in second, splitting the Liberal vote and handing a victory to the Tory.[49] On the other hand, despite assurances to the contrary from Glyn, the League was compelled to stand by while Sir John Lubbock, the official Liberal, displaced Applegarth, the workingmen's nominee, in the 1870 Maidstone by-election. Applegarth withdrew, as Howell was to do the following year in Norwich, rather than provoke Liberal wrath by opposing an inoffensive middle-class candidate.[50] The League tried to make clear that its conception of labour representation did not imply a direct challenge to the Liberals in every constituency. The moderate group – Howell, Applegarth, Potter and others – were anxious to devise some sort of arrangement whereby the party chiefs would support working men in a few select boroughs, in return for which the League would aid official party candidates in the majority of contests. This was, in fact, almost a resurrection of Howell's 1868 electoral policy with one significant modification: the Liberals were now expected to look with favour upon the advent of a small band of labour MPs. A series of unpublicized meetings was held, first with Beales, Mill, and Sir Charles Dilke, and then with Glyn and the Reform Club executive, but it proved impossible to reach any definitive settlement.[51]

The failure to reach an accord with the Liberals not only placed obstacles in the path of Howell's own career, but it also diminished the likelihood of Liberal concessions on trade unionism and other questions demanding legislative reform. Howell was convinced that any widening of the gulf between the workers and the Gladstonians would only endanger the Party's electoral prospects. Stansfeld regarded Howell's misgivings as merely a sign of frustrated ambition, although his offer of a bricklaying job could hardly have been expected to afford much consolation. Other Liberals were somewhat more receptive to Howell's prognosis: William Rathbone, a somewhat reluctant beneficiary of Reform League aid in 1868, recorded,

I had a long talk the other evening with Howell, one of the leaders of the Trades Unions and working men – a very good fellow. He says the Liberal Party are losing ground much [*sic*], for many reasons. Some of their economics are considered harsh and partial . . . everywhere there is less of geniality and *bonhomie* in the treatment of the working classes by the Liberals than by the Conservatives.[52]

It was true that Howell could never quite distinguish between his genuine fears for the future of reform and for his own career. Taking pride in his ability to discern the fallacies in Forster's Education Bill, he inquired of his friend Bartlett,

Is it therefore unreasonable that I should feel some ambition to get in the House where I can use my own brains and not place it in the hands of others to use for me? Many of these fellows get our brains and never acknowledge their obligations either by work or deed.[53]

Another letter to Bartlett, who had emigrated to America, reflected his disillusionment at this time: 'Our Liberal Party [he wrote] is very generous. If I waited till some offer came from them, not of gratuity but of service, I think I should find old age creeping on and still unremembered. But I have never asked and never will.'[54]

Developments in France soon impelled the League to identify itself with the more extreme elements in the labour movement, thus destroying the possibility of an operative alliance with the Liberals. The League's immediate reaction to the Franco-Prussian War was one of antipathy, regarding it as a dynastic conflict and 'a wicked outrage against every civilizing principle'. The working men were chiefly concerned to prevent their leaders from involving them in the 'fratricidal slaughter'.[55] But once the hostilities ended, the League and other labour groups rallied to the French cause, protesting Prussian territorial ambitions and demanding that England avoid 'all entanglements of prejudice' in the event that the French people instituted a republic.[56] With the support of the Positivists and, to some extent, of Marx, the articulate labour leaders became at once anti-German and increasingly bellicose. 'Don't wonder if I go to the front,' Howell warned Bartlett, 'for I am getting desperately choleric, nay even martial in my thought and bearing. There's no knowing what a wild enthusiasm may bring forth, and I have no very great regard for life and never had.'[57] Despite the unbending pacifism of the Workmen's Peace Association, a remonstrance to Gladstone in January, signed by Howell, Applegarth, Odger, Potter, and the Positivist leaders, called upon the Government to insist that Prussia either make reasonable terms with France or face armed English intervention.[58] The advent of the Commune, however, destroyed the pro-French united front. Howell and other labour leaders formed a Working Men's Auxiliary Committee in February to collect relief for distressed French workers, but they were unsympathetic to the principles of the Paris revolutionaries.[59] While Howell lamented the 'reactionary and cruel' tactics of the National Assembly, he rapidly discarded his unaccustomed militancy, shifting his attention to the affairs of the new TUC Parliamentary Committee and the vestry of St Mary's, Newington, to both of which he was elected in the spring of 1871.[60]

During the latter part of 1871 the Labour Representation League began to toy with the idea of an independent party. A conference in Birmingham in December 1872 called upon workers to contest elections 'irrespective of old party ties', but no practical steps were taken except to recommend the creation of a national fund to subsidize working-class candidates.[61] Shortly after Henry Broadhurst's appointment as Secretary, the League issued a circular urging working men 'to organize in [their] several constituencies, not as mere consenting parties to the doings of local wirepullers, but as a great Labour party'.[62] Yet, in spite of repeated pleas, it was impossible to implement these proposals without a great deal of money; the most that could be done was to stimulate local action and to furnish information, speakers, and suitable candidates. During the

1874 campaign the League sent workers and provided limited financial assistance to labour nominees.[63]

While Howell urged the League's council to take steps to keep the popular feeling in favour of labour representation alive, the organization rapidly declined in strength and prestige once the election was over.[64] It was never able effectively to mobilize working-class opinion as the Reform League had done, and the deaths in rapid succession of Latham, Allan, and Newton deprived it of badly-needed unifying leadership. After the refusal of Samuel Morley and Thomas Burt, the presidency was offered to F. W. Campin, whose election in May 1876 prompted Howell's resignation from the council.[65] The League lingered on until 1878, increasingly Liberal in its pronouncements, coming to life again only briefly over the Eastern Question.[66] From its inception until 1876 Howell played an active part in its affairs and received its endorsement in Norwich in 1871 and 1875 and in Aylesbury in 1874, but it remained for him throughout these years an organization of secondary importance both for his career and the course of the labour movement.

Complaining that 'politics would starve the devil both as to cold and hunger', Howell now determined to seek his fortune in the world of business.[67] His first project, reflecting his own hardship in acquiring a house in 1868, was intended as both a profitable and philanthropic venture: to put his knowledge of the building trades to good use in the Adelphi Permanent Building Society, which was formed, with Howell as Secretary, in August 1870. It planned to lend money to working men at a low rate of interest to facilitate the purchase of their own homes, the money to be repaid in easy instalments over a period of fourteen years. A board of directors, including Applegarth, Latham, and Leno, was selected and by September Howell was optimistic about its prospects.[68]

> I think I told you [he wrote Bartlett] that I was working away at a Building Society. I have been so far successful. A good list of names for Arbitrators, a good board of Directors, a good banker, good solicitors, and good Trustees. I have written a good prospectus, which with a few good verbal emendations has been unanimously adopted. . . .
> I have also taken another Secretaryship [of the People's Garden Company] which will in time pay me if it proceeds. This will enable me to pay a clerk to do the drudgery. But how to live whilst these two are

being developed is the problem to me. For the next two years I reckon hard work, little pay, no thanks, and quite possibly failure. But get over that and I count on success.[69]

Although Howell was able to list a number of eminent men as Arbitrators and Trustees, there were notable refusals. Samuel Morley and the Earl of Carnarvon, for example, would have nothing to do with the Society. Howell implored Applegarth to approach Auberon Herbert, Carnarvon's Radical brother: 'Explain to him how we are incessantly at work for no pay whatever and that in this we hope to be able to do good to our fellows and at the same time get some little pay for work done.'[70] By January he was bemoaning the fact that 'my Building Society has not started yet. One delay has caused another until I feel sick but must not give up for I have sacrificed too much for it.'[71] The main difficulty was the Society's inability to attract investors, and by May Howell was obliged to divert prospective borrowers to other societies. He blamed the inauspicious beginnings on the timidity of his directors:

Adelphi Building Society had done nothing because I have been cursed with a lot of theoretical directors who do nothing and will not let me do anything. However I am about to reconstitute the Board and send Applegarth, Greening, [James] Hole, and [E. B.] Saunders away. I will get businessmen – greengrocers and tallow chandlers are better for business than theoretical reformers who know no business. *A Man* should combine both. I have never received a penny from it after 14 months' work.[72]

It was Howell himself who was largely to blame. He lacked business experience and had no conception of how to constitute the Society on a sound financial basis. Finally, on the verge of collapse, the Adelphi was reorganized at the end of 1871. Howell was no longer Secretary, but he retained a directorship. His loss in salary and shares of £200 was made up by June 1872, thus averting the expected disaster.[73]

In August 1870 Howell had also been appointed Secretary of the People's Garden Company, an investment society whose object was

to secure for the People pure air, fine music, and healthy recreation; for which purpose they propose to purchase land to be laid out as gardens and recreation ground where the Shareholders and Members with their families may obtain rational amusements of an elevating character.[74]

He hoped that, if the Company were to prosper, this position would afford him £100 a year, but this again proved to be wishful thinking.[75] By January the familiar pattern was repeating itself. 'The Gardens Company lingers,' Howell wrote, 'as we cannot get it capital fast enough to make a real start.'[76] Disgusted by its stagnation, Howell resigned as Secretary, without receiving the anticipated salary. He was obliged to settle for £25 in shares as compensation.[77]

Undaunted by these failures, Howell unveiled his plan for the Metropolitan Dwelling House Improvement Company. Once again investment was involved, this time in slum properties. As with his other business schemes, this was not an original conception. Rather he was copying an increasingly common – and profitable – practice of the time, the employment of private capital to provide housing for the poor, either through restoration of slums or new construction. His intention was

chiefly to buy existing property in crowded districts, and put the same in substantial repair, paying special attention to the drainage, water supply and ventilation. The Company will thoroughly cleanse and purify the interior of those dwellings, and render them more healthy, convenient, and comfortable for those whose earnings will not allow them to pay much in the shape of rent.[78]

Since such properties tended to be owned by men unwilling to repair them, they promised a sound investment to those who would put up the money for their restoration on the expectation of increased rental values in the future. Howell discussed it with Octavia Hill and with Thomas Brassey, who agreed to serve as Chairman and to contribute an initial £1,000.[79] Once again Howell's expectations ran ahead of the actual developments. He wrote confidently to Beales that he planned

to do something to improve the homes of our poorest and in this movement my previous knowledge and skill [will] be of great service. I have been in want of some permanent income for a long time, and I hope this will secure it and at the same time do much good. [80]

Although Brassey was attracted by the prospect of urban renewal as a philanthropic venture, he had second thoughts about lending his name to what he regarded as an unpromising investment scheme. Instead of sponsoring the company, Brassey offered to pay Howell £60 a year to find properties for him to buy and rehabilitate himself. Howell reluctantly agreed, and Brassey's first acquisition was the Verulam Street cottages.[81]

Howell had not at this time abandoned his efforts to wrest some position from the Liberal managers. He pressed Beales to intercede in his behalf for an appointment as an assistant commissioner in a government inquiry into benefit and building societies.[82] Beales was soon able to report that Glyn would consider his application.

I am glad that [Glyn] remembers me favourably [he replied] and hope that his memory will not soon grow dim again. Mr Glyn should remember not merely good offices rendered, but the abstention of [sic] adverse criticism upon many points of the government promise and performance. I of course could not do anything which would run the risk of a Liberal defeat, but upon some questions they have really invited it, and if we had been hasty in taking up the cudgels, I think considerable dissatisfaction would have been the result. I wonder if Mr Stansfeld ever remembers how some of us have worked for him, now that he is reconstituting his office. Surely there would be a chance of some good appointment when my qualification would be given a fair test.[83]

Howell refused the secretaryship of the Working Men's Club and Institute Union, since it was offered with the proviso that he sever his connection with politics. This, he felt, 'would be cutting the locks of Samson, leaving me shorn of whatever strength I might possess'.[84] He did, however, plant the seeds of a new career in journalism. In July and August 1871 he sent Goldwin Smith, by now having left Cornell University for Toronto, four articles on 'The Social Life of English Workmen', which Smith was able to place in a Canadian newspaper. These were followed by articles on Mill and on the Nottingham TUC (1872) for the New York World.[85] Finally, he began to contribute regularly to the Bee-Hive, an association which would last as long as the paper survived.

In 1867 Thomas Hare, the leading proponent of proportional representation, had invited Reform League leaders to collaborate with him in discussions on the redistribution of seats and the organization of constituencies. The meetings, held in February and March 1868, led to the formation of the Representative Reform Association. Howell was named Secretary of the new body, which opened offices and began to publicize its programme in the summer of 1868.[86] In view of parliamentary coolness to its proposals, little headway was made, and Howell soon realized that 'the Representative Reform Association cannot be pushed on [sic] the same as the Reform League was, or the same as the Land Tenure Reform Association can be, for it can only be advanced by quiet arguments, by means of publications & speeches occasionally'.[87] For the next few years activity was confined to corresponding with foreign societies and disseminating information.

The driving force behind the Association was Walter Morrison, who largely financed its programme. He hired Howell, performing secretarial duties without pay until 1872, at a salary of £100 a year to serve as general factotum in the campaign to popularize proportional representation. During the next two years Howell took time out from his other work to solicit contributions, to explain Morrison's proposed bill to trade union and co-operative conferences, and to manage the business side of the organization. Predictably, Morrison had no success in promoting his reform and soon tired of the lonely and expensive enterprise. By November 1874 he announced his intention of giving up the Association, regretfully concluding that his ideas were too advanced for the country.[88] Howell too deplored its demise, 'apart altogether', he wrote, 'from personal gain – and the salary to me for the three years has been a great gain'. Howell observed that progress had been made in educating the public, at least in regard to the value of equal electoral districts, adding that the rest of Morrison's programme 'has to be gradually pressed upon thinking men of all parties'.[89]

In the summer of 1869 Howell was drawn into the new, predominantly middle-class Land Tenure Reform Association. Led by John Stuart Mill, its object was to abolish primogeniture and to remove all impediments to the free transfer of property. The Executive Committee, which included Dilke, Fawcett, P. A. Taylor, John Morley, and more moderate labour leaders, reflected its inherent respectability, distinguishing it from the land nationalizers in the Land and Labour League. Hoping to attract all the working-class reformers, Mill appointed Howell as the organization's financial agent and, in some sense, as emissary to the labour movement.[90] Howell, who deprecated the republican Land and Labour League as 'a body which goes in for the most wild theories as to the land and Social and Political questions generally',[91] was unable to entice the extremists into Mill's group. By April 1870 Mill felt obliged to invigorate his programme, adding provisions for a taxation on the unearned increment on rentable land and for the nationalization of waste land.[92] The Association survived until the mid-1870s, but it never attracted a mass following, and even the moderate working-class adherents, like Howell, were soon too deeply engaged in the struggle for trade union law reform to pay it much attention.

The National Education League was probably the most important of the middle-class Radical organizations which appealed to London labour leaders. Howell participated in preliminary discussions in August 1869 and attended the League's inaugural conference in Birmingham two months later.[93] Immediately appointed to the Executive Committee, he cast himself as spokesman for his fellow workers, affirming their commitment to 'compulsory, free, and secular education'. He assured the delegates that 'the working classes of this country are anxious for, and demand, a complete national system of education, which shall reach all classes'.[94] Howell was obliged to limit his attendance at subsequent meetings, as he explained to the League Secretary, since he could not afford to attend 'except on very special occasions – such occasions will arise when every member should be prepared to make almost any sacrifice'.[95] He was unable – or at least unwilling – to make that sacrifice often, but he was prepared to speak and organize for the League, as long as there was some remuneration for his efforts. Howell was adept at combining trips for the League with other political activities, thus making it possible to claim payment from two sources. After his Liberal registration work had ended in 1870, he began to lecture more frequently for the League, travelling in February and March to Blackburn, Halifax, Manchester, Birkenhead, York, Scarborough, Hull, and Great Grimsby at a salary of £2 10s per week.[96] When his Liberal Party subsidies expired, Howell claimed that only his employment by the National Education League enabled him 'to keep matters going'.[97] In fact, these lecturing engagements brought him nearly £100 in 1870.[98]

The Liberation Society was no less eager than the National Education League to enlist the newly enfranchised working men in its ranks. Founded in 1844 to 'liberate' religion from state control, the Society had acquired great wealth and prestige in its years of agitation. Relying largely on the donations of Nonconformist businessmen, it was able to spend over £24,000 between 1865 and 1870 to further its goals, in striking contrast to the penny-pinching of the

Reform League and the Labour Representation League during the same period.[99] The Society was slow to proselytize among the workers, and it was not until July 1871 that its Executive Committee decided to establish a separate body 'composed of those who have influence with the working classes'.[100] A group met with Howell, Potter, Latham, Daniel Guile, and Joseph Leicester, all of whom suggested the formation of a small committee distinct from, although subsidized by, the Society. The working men insisted that wider latitude be granted to speakers at working-class meetings than was customarily allowed to Society lecturers. The result was the formation of the Working Men's Committee for Promoting the Separation of Church and State, with the power to adopt its own methods of action and the promise of financial support by the parent body. The Executive further stipulated that

the primary aim of the Committee shall be the creation of opinion in favour of disestablishment and the use of electoral power for that purpose; but when it is considered desirable that it should take action in regard to parliamentary proceedings, the policy to be pursued shall be agreed upon between the Committee and the Society.[101]

By the end of the month the new group had been constituted, with Howell as Chairman and Potter as Secretary. The Society agreed to advance its offshoot £10 at the beginning of each month to cover operating costs, any additional expenses to be paid at the end of the month upon the presentation of vouchers.[102] Howell disapproved of these makeshift financial arrangements, but what rankled most was the Society's evident unwillingness to compensate members adequately for their services. He vented his irritation in a letter to Potter:

I really was under the impression that most of the preliminary arrangements as to finance had been arranged between you and Mr Carvell Williams previous to the formation of the Committee. I certainly expected that the question of rent for the office and pay for office work had been mutually agreed upon. . . . Did he really expect that we should create a movement involving a great amount of work, all of which was to be done by anyone? If you can undertake such extra work without extra help and extra pay, be it so. But the thing is preposterous. . . .
So far as I am concerned, it will be much the best that I never go out at all. I really cannot afford to do so, and the chairman had better keep free from money. I will do all I can for the movement, but money out of

pocket I cannot afford. . . . Is it not wonderful how some men of what is called the middle class expect us to more than equal their contributions, not by work only, but by petty expenditure caused by that very work. More than ten per cent of my income, in addition to labour, has been devoted to this kind of work for more than 20 years. I wonder how many can say the same.[103]

Whatever Howell's own misgivings, the Committee issued a manifesto in October setting forth its views and appealing to the people to take up the disestablishment question. The statement declared that the Church of England had failed in its religious mission, that its enormous revenues created a disparity between Anglican and Nonconformist clergy which bore no relation to the religious preference of the people. In addition, it argued that

the Establishment is a source of national weakness, because it divides the nation into two hostile parties. It prevents good men uniting, as they otherwise might unite, in works of philanthropy and in movements for social reform. It thus carries a mischievous sectarianism into almost all the affairs of life.[104]

During the next few months Howell and Potter reiterated this message at working-class meetings throughout the country. Distinguishing their motives from the purely religious objections of the Nonconformists, they charged the Anglican clergy with obstructing every measure of reform intended for the benefit of the working classes.[105]

In February 1872 the Liberation Society agreed to sponsor twenty additional provincial meetings and in June extended its patronage of the working men's group until 1873. A Finance subcommittee expressed satisfaction with the programme that had been undertaken, at a cost to the Society thus far of only £170. The meetings, most of them addressed by Howell and Potter, had been well attended, and their speeches were 'of a character well calculated to advance the Society's purpose'. In several towns workingmen's committees had been set up, but these do not seem to have been very energetic.[106] By the end of the year the Committee wanted to extend the agitation, but the cautious Executive refused to sanction additional expenditure, and activity ceased by the middle of 1873.[107]

Howell discovered yet another opportunity to combine his devotion to social reform with his desire for money in the Plimsoll movement. In January 1873 Samuel Plimsoll had published *Our Seamen – An Appeal*, a sensational exposé of what he called 'coffin ships' – merchant vessels that were undermanned, overloaded, and generally unseaworthy. He appealed to the Leeds TUC for assistance in his campaign on behalf of the merchant seamen and encouraged Howell to form the broadly-based Plimsoll & Seamen's Fund Committee in March, with the Earl of Shaftesbury as Chairman and Thomas Hughes as Vice-Chairman. Plimsoll himself was so effective a publicizer that within a few weeks the flood of invitations to speak became almost unmanageable. Howell, as Secretary, and Lloyd Jones took on many of the engagements that Plimsoll could not fulfil, addressing enthusiastic crowds in Whitby, Hartlepool, Manchester, and Birmingham. But the Committee soon realized that the impulsive Plimsoll, whose reckless accusations provoked several libel suits, was not only its principal asset, but also a constant burden. In addition to substituting for 'the Sailors' Friend' at provincial rallies, Howell was obliged to resolve the crises which Plimsoll's escapades created. Furthermore, it fell to the Secretary, already fully employed in his TUC duties, to marshal evidence for the Royal Commission on Unseaworthy Ships, as well as to carry on the administrative chores involved in raising more than £13,000. Howell was, however, never one to shirk extra responsibilities, if he were well compensated for his efforts. In the two years of this committee's operations he was paid £656, a supplement to his earnings that raised his income to a level he had never before enjoyed.[108]

Despite his unfortunate experience in Aylesbury in 1868, Howell neither abandoned his parliamentary ambitions, nor tried to find an industrial or a London seat. In January 1871 the Labour Representation League invited him to contest a vacated seat at Norwich, to which he agreed at once. Thomas Hughes immediately went to Norwich to sell the candidate to the local Liberals, and Howell issued an extremely circumspect election address. Deliberately appealing to the middle class as well as to the labour interest, he pledged himself to work for 'all movements tending to the development of intellectual and moral progress, and the expansion of material wealth so as to secure the participation of all in the general prosperity of the community without prejudice to any interest and without injury to any class'. He stressed the need for a reduction in taxation, state education for all children, the protection of trade union funds, the use of surplus labour on uncultivated land, and the amendment of the land laws. While promoting 'such legislation as will enable England's workmen to live in England without sinking into the degraded condition of a pauper surplus', he concluded, 'I shall seek to do so with scrupulous regard for the legitimate interests of all other classes of the Community, as I am firmly convinced that the peace and safety of the nation can be best secured by an equitable and careful adjustment of the claims of all.'[109]

While he received tentative promises of support from Glyn and Stansfeld, he encountered little enthusiasm for his candidacy in Norwich itself, where, he wrote, 'the Whigs and Tories are horrified'.[110] During a visit to the town on 23–24 January several attempts were made to induce him to withdraw. After J. J. Colman, of the great local mustard family, decided to stand, Howell recognized that it would be futile to persist. Insisting that he would have supported him against anyone but Colman, Glyn urged Howell to retire and offered to pay his election expenses.[111] Howell agreed, justifying his course in a letter to R. A. Cooper, a former Reform League associate who had refused to endorse him against Colman:

I felt before I consented to stand that I could not well fight Mr Colman, but his hesitancy led me to doubt whether he would consent to stand at this juncture. Some of our men were averse to my withdrawal at first, for say they, we might be always withdrawing without gaining a single advantage. But we cannot afford to spend £200 except with a good chance of winning. I bow to the fates and retire for the *first*, and I hope the last, time.[112]

The obligation to withdraw rather than split the Liberal vote irritated Howell and other labour politicians, but they saw no way out of the predicament. While the Liberals professed their support for working-class candidates, in practice they repeatedly barred them from available constituencies. Without a ready source of money the Labour Representation League simply could not afford to sponsor independent candidates, and the trade unions, some of which had the funds, were unwilling to intervene in electoral politics. Howell expressed his sense of grievance in a letter to Samuel Morley: 'We have to win our spurs. My chief fear, however, is that we shall find ourselves, by force of circumstances, fighting our own party. We cannot always be put off by the cry of letting in a Tory.'[113]

The 1874 election in Aylesbury was, much to Howell's dismay, a recapitulation of the contest six years before. Once again the same three candidates stood, and once again Rothschild, despite the security of his seat, refused to coalesce with the labour nominee. Howell appealed for help to Joseph Arch, Sir William Harcourt, Rathbone, Goldwin Smith, Earl Russell, and the Prime Minister, but little was done to dissuade Rothschild from his obstinacy or effectively to assist Howell.[114] 'I am left to fight this contest,' he lamented, 'against a Tory without help of any kind, which is not fair from the Liberal Party, for I have been a consistent and I trust honest Liberal for about 23 years.'[115]

Gladstone was, in fact, willing to issue an exceedingly guarded endorsement, emphasizing his belief that some spokesmen of the working classes should find their way into the House of Commons. While he believed Howell to be as worthy a representative of labour as could be found, he would not presume to judge the expediency of his becoming a candidate.[116] The reaction of the local Press had altered somewhat since 1868, with the Liberal *Bucks Advertiser* now supporting Howell, although without much enthusiasm:

We frankly confess that Mr Howell is not a candidate to our liking. He would go into Parliament as the avowed representative of labour, and we strongly object to any particular class or interest being advocated in Parliament to the prejudice of the nation at large. Between Mr Howell and Mr Smith the electors have at best a choice of evils, but Mr Howell, we believe, would be the lesser evil.[117]

The Tory *Bucks Herald* never faltered in its hostility, calling Howell 'a candidate who represents some of the worst features of the revolutionary Radicalism of the day'.[118]

The campaign itself hardly differed from the course of the preceding one. Howell stressed the need for land reform, the extension of the county franchise, and the repeal of the income tax – all of which were calculated to increase his popularity among agricultural workers – and played down trade union questions. Once again his speeches were interrupted by disorderly Tory hecklers, who occasionally tried to drag him from the platform.[119] He did, none the less, increase his poll, receiving 1,144 votes against 1,761 for Rothschild and 1,624 for Smith. Howell, who claimed that he had to fight against 'a combination of wealth, parsondom, and beer', was hurt by the disproportionate expenditure of his rivals, the suddenness of the election, and the inadequacy of his organization.[120] Yet, as in 1868, it was primarily Rothschild's compact with Smith which militated against his success. Howell received contributions from a number of Liberal politicians, including Dilke, Mundella, and Plimsoll, but most of his expenses were covered by a £600 donation from Samuel Morley.[121]

In May 1875 J. H. Tillett was unseated as one of the members for Norwich, and Howell decided to contest the seat. He solicited the support of Colman and Cooper, issued an election manifesto, and addressed a working men's meeting in Norwich on 17 June.[122] The forces of labour were mobilized in his behalf: a laudatory editorial appeared in the *Bee-Hive*, and a local chapter of the Labour Representation League was organized.[123] This time Howell vowed that he would 'not move for any candidate', but the election writ was postponed pending an inquiry into corrupt practices in the constituency, and his candidacy never materialized.[124]

The years between 1869 and 1875 revealed to Howell the rigours of a political career. His principal aim throughout the period was to carve out a position of financial security, based, in some way or other, upon his experience in the labour movement. With the exception of his Trades Union Congress office, Howell found it impossible to obtain both financial independence and security of tenure. For much of this period he earned a considerable amount of money, but most of the organizations which supported him tended to be of short duration. His energies were dissipated in innumerable projects, none of which developed into adequate vehicles for his talents and ambition. The means of entry into the House of Commons eluded him, and his business ventures, however auspicious they appeared at first, all ended in failure. Without the initial subsidies from the Liberal managers and the subsequent bounties from Brassey, Morrison, and Plimsoll, these years would have been lean as well as unproductive. Howell was gradually learning that industry and political loyalty did not inevitably lead to success: the road to bourgeois respectability was paved with obstacles which he might, in the end, be unable to overcome.

7

The Rise of the
Trades Union Congress

While 1867 brought important political advantages to the working classes, it was also the occasion of the worst setback to the progress of trade unionism since the prosecution of the Tolpuddle Martyrs. In January the Court of the Queen's Bench decided in the case of Hornby *v.* Close that unions, if not actually criminal in nature, operated sufficiently in restraint of trade as to be illegal. If their status had never been formally guaranteed, unions had enjoyed the protection of the Friendly Societies Act since 1855, and the right to organize had been generally recognized. Now this precarious security was undermined, and trade societies found themselves without safeguard for their funds in case of defaulting officials. Several months earlier the outbreak of violence in Sheffield had aroused widespread anti-unionist indignation, giving rise to a demand, endorsed by the workers themselves, for a public inquiry. In response to these conflicting pressures the Conservative ministry set up a Royal Commission to investigate the Sheffield outrages and to examine more generally the workings of trade unions.

Working in rivalry with George Potter and his London Working Men's Association, the Junta leaders and their political allies immediately constituted themselves as the Conference of Amalgamated Trades. Their object was to marshal evidence in defence of unionism before the Commission in order to secure full legal protection for the societies and their funds. The selection of Frederic Harrison and Thomas Hughes as commissioners assured not merely that the working men would obtain a fair hearing, but that their cause would be energetically championed. Robert Applegarth, the chief witness for the unions, emphasized provident benefits and denied any secrecy or recourse to coercion in their operations.

Rather than fomenting strikes, these societies were interested in craft standards and protection for their members, restraining as much as possible aggressive tendencies among workers. William Allan, Coulson, and Howell were among the witnesses, and the questioning – largely stage-managed by Harrison – elicited responses which underlined the moderate and responsible conduct of the amalgamated unions. Appearing before the Commission on 2 April 1867, Howell described his own experience in the Operative Bricklayers' Society. With most of the examination conducted by Harrison, who had arranged for his appearance, he discussed the achievements of union activity, not merely in raising wages and shortening hours, but also in creating an atmosphere of moral restraint which curbed drunkenness.[1]

After months of testimony the findings of the Royal Commission were published, and the results vindicated the efforts of the Junta and their supporters. Even the Majority Report – predictably cool to trade unions – felt that they merited some official recognition, while the Minority Report, written by Harrison, went much further, advocating the removal of all discriminatory restrictions against workers' combinations. Attempts by sympathetic MPs to introduce reforming legislation failed, and it was not until February 1871 that Gladstone's Government presented its own proposals. Although the Liberal Bill provided full statutory recognition and financial security, its third clause rendered trade unionists liable to criminal penalties for vague offences like 'intimidation' and 'obstruction', thus curtailing the possibility of peaceful picketing. The Junta ironically deserved some of the blame for the Bill's liabilities, as well as much of the credit for its concessions. The campaign of Applegarth and his associates to depict trade unions as conciliatory societies, promoting welfare and eschewing violence, had been almost too successful. Their opponents could argue that the professed moderation of trade union policy obviated the necessity of sanctioning the right to strike.

Throughout the course of the Commission's deliberations the Conference of Amalgamated Trades, fearful that Potter or less responsible provincial leaders might encourage militant tactics or encroach on its independence, had tried to retain full control of the unions' defence, working closely with the Positivists in their attempt to promote legislation. When the Manchester and Salford Trades Council sponsored the first national Trades Union

Congress in June 1868, the Junta decided to ignore the historic gathering.[2] The same hostility to outside interference led them to boycott the second TUC convened in Birmingham in August 1869. This time, however, they made sure their interests were effectively represented by Odger and Howell, who served as unofficial agents of the Junta at the Birmingham meetings.

The Birmingham TUC was the occasion for a renewal of hostilities between Howell and Coulson, provoking a final breach between the two rivals and leading to Howell's angry resignation from the London Order of the Operative Bricklayers' Society. Although he had been in Manchester and Rochdale on Reform League business during the 1868 Congress and may have met with delegates, Howell certainly took no part in its sessions. By 1869 both the political situation and Howell's outlook had changed. He was now a member of several groups, like the Labour Representation League, which took part in the Birmingham gathering. It seems likely that Applegarth and Allan urged him to attend the Congress, and Howell, eager to extend his contacts and prove his dependability, was determined to do so.

On 20 July Howell informed the OBS Executive Council of the forthcoming Congress and offered his services as the union's representative. 'As one of the subjects to be discussed is the representation of labour in the House of Commons,' Howell wrote, 'I feel that I ought to be present to represent our society as the only member of our society and trade who stood the contest of the general election.'[3] At the same time he sent virtually identical letters to his own No. 4 (Paddington) Lodge and to the No. 13 Lodge, of which his friend Charles Shearman was a leading member. Since Coulson adhered to the decision of the Conference of Amalgamated Trades to boycott the Congress, he resented the prospect of Howell's posing as the Bricklayers' delegate. If Coulson was not going to participate, he certainly did not wish to provide Howell with the chance to further his own career. The Executive Council met and thanked 'Br Howell for his kind offer' but concluded that there was 'no necessity to send a delegate.'[4]

Despite this curt dismissal, William Fordham of the Paddington Lodge tentatively agreed to sponsor Howell as branch representative if the Council persisted in its refusal. When Fordham expressed doubts about the possibility of subsidizing the trip, Howell eagerly jumped at half a loaf, informing Fordham that he was willing to pay all of his own expenses except rail fare.[5] When Coulson discovered that a special Paddington Lodge meeting had been called for 31 July to confirm Fordham's offer, he decided to attend. The members had not been informed in advance of the subject of the meeting, and Fordham explained at once that the officers proposed the appointment of Howell as delegate since the Executive Council refused to send him. Angered by the attempted defiance of his authority, Coulson pointed out to the members the irregularity of their proceedings. After heated debate the motion in favour of Howell's appointment was withdrawn.

Howell and Fordham were not to be outwitted so easily, and the setback to their plans proved temporary. At the next ordinary meeting of the branch, with only seventeen members present, Howell appealed once again, offering to attend the Congress entirely at his own expense. The members, easily swayed by their more articulate leaders, agreed to nominate Howell to represent the Paddington Lodge.[6] Such a designation did nothing to resolve the controversy, since newspapers, indifferent to fine distinctions, listed Howell as delegate of the London Bricklayers in spite of Coulson's disclaimer. The Executive Council hastened to inform the Birmingham Congress that 'Mr G. Howell does not represent our society and that we will not be responsible for anyone who may attend in the name of the society.' In addition, Coulson reprimanded the Paddington Lodge for insubordination:

Such informal action is not consistent with unionism or our general laws, and therefore not creditable to any member who was a party to the appointment, for every rule and authority was set aside for personal consideration, and no end of mischief might have been created if the Executive had not taken the proper precautions.[7]

Fordham refused to yield, evading Coulson's inquiries and upbraiding him for his 'formal and inquisitorial' manner.[8] Goaded beyond endurance, Coulson retorted that

it is your duty to reply to all questions that the Executive Council desires to know, with the facts known to you, and not as you have done, send your opinions in such an evasive way. . . . Your letters have been read to the Council, and my 'inquisitorial' letters also have been read and endorsed by the Executive. I beg to remind you that myself and the whole of the Executive Council are elected by votes from the whole of the Lodges, and we are responsible to the body for what we do, and every officer is bound to furnish us with anything we require of the doings at a Lodge.[9]

That an exchange of such bitterness damaged Coulson's cause more than that of his opponents was due to the simultaneous occurrence of the Markley affair. The settlement which Howell negotiated in 1863 had proved to be merely a truce in Coulson's aggressive campaign to extend the authority of the London Order into Manchester territory. The northern society was rapidly losing ground to its rival throughout the decade, and by 1868 – despite a larger total membership – George Houseley, the Manchester Secretary, could report only 93 branches to London's 96 and a significantly smaller treasury.[10] When the Manchester bricklayers struck in April 1869 against the hourly wage and compulsory arbitration, Henry Markley, a disreputable agitator and member of the London Order, who had himself challenged Coulson for the secretaryship in 1866, applied to Coulson for permission to open a London-affiliated lodge.[11] Despite the open threat to the Manchester society, Coulson and the Executive Council endorsed Markley's scheme. In the meantime, Markley had arranged to supply employers with blackleg labour, his lodge serving as a profitable channel for transmitting London workers to replace the Manchester strikers. Coulson was doubly culpable: not only had he sanctioned the affiliation of Markley's lodge, but, unknown to the Executive Council, he also accepted £20 from Markley with which to subsidize London workers willing to serve as blacklegs.[12]

Trapped in a war on two fronts, the desperate Houseley appealed to the London Trades Council to arbitrate the dispute. At a meeting in Sheffield in July the Council deputies – Allan, Odger, and Guile of the Ironfounders – negotiated an agreement between the two societies. Houseley won his principal objective – the withdrawal of the blacklegs – but only at a humiliating price. Unable any longer to stop London encroachment, he was obliged to accept Coulson's assertion of the right to open branches anywhere he deemed advantageous. Houseley further agreed to submit the strike to arbitration.[13] Battered by the assault of his rivals and of the employers, the Manchester leader moved reluctantly towards the principles of the amalgamated policy, the policy which the London Order had adopted after the 1859–61 dispute. Markley, however, impeded a resolution of the conflict, refusing to withdraw his blacklegs or to accept the decision of the arbitrators, and Coulson was forced to repudiate him and dissolve his lodge.[14]

The sordid details provided Howell with an opportunity to even the score with Coulson, whose complicity in the Markley affair soon began to have repercussions. Although the General Secretary denied supplying workers for the Manchester employers and urged his members to comply with the provisions of the arbitration settlement, this new conciliatory attitude did little to allay suspicions. After several of the London branches had demanded an investigation, Coulson tried to use a September general meeting to justify his conduct. He minimized his involvement with Markley, admitting, however, that he had received £20 and sent seventeen men to Manchester. Howell attended this meeting in order to direct the attack on Coulson, whose position was sufficiently compromised to make him apologize and plead for mercy. At Howell's instigation William Fordham moved and carried a resolution censuring Coulson for working with Markley and undermining the Manchester strike.[15]

Despite his public humiliation, Coulson could not be supplanted. In July 1870 Howell made his final bid for the secretaryship, canvassing support among several disaffected lodges.

I attribute the falling off in our Society [he wrote one branch] chiefly to the neglect, want of energy, and incompetence of the General Secretary of our Society. The chief qualities he seems to exhibit are a species of cunning, often found in a person of low capacity, and the ability to abuse and slander those who are opposed to his ruinous policy.[16]

But he was no more successful in this contest than in his previous attempt, and a year later he withdrew from the London Order altogether. Hostile to Coulson's authoritarian tactics and frustrated by his own impotence, Howell explained to Fordham,

I am thoroughly dissatisfied with the way our Society is conducted, and cannot see without deep regret that as a Society we are sinking very low. Our numbers have gone down from about 6,500 to a few hundreds only. The Society takes but little part in any public question, and would not even have been represented at some of the Congresses or Conferences had I not been there to do so.[17]

Howell's assessment of the London Order was wrong – it continued to grow in strength through the 1870s and 1880s, while the

Manchester union declined, wasting its funds in ineffective strikes – but he realized that he had no future in it under the existing leadership.

Even more than the inaugural meeting at Manchester in 1868, Birmingham really established the Trades Union Congress. Concerning themselves with political as well as trade questions, the delegates, representing some forty societies, charted the course of future activity: the discussion of issues relevant to the labour movement and the promotion of parliamentary legislation. The forceful resolutions contrasted with the more timid proceedings of the previous year, and the presence of men like Howell and Odger prevented the TUC from dissipating its energies in provincial squabbles. Although he defended the policy of his absent London friends, Howell's active, self-assured participation in the proceedings enhanced his own reputation among the delegates. He was more successful in imposing his personality on the Congress than Potter, who had tried to cultivate the provincial union leaders, and, within the next two years, was to eclipse him as the dominant London figure in TUC affairs.

The Junta had been able to secure the postponement of the third annual Congress, scheduled for London in 1870, but once the terms of the Liberal Bill became known, the Conference of Amalgamated Trades finally acknowledged the need to identify itself with a wider movement. At a preliminary meeting summoned by the London Trades Council on 1 March 1871 Applegarth presented the Conference report on the Trades Union Bill, and five days later the third Trades Union Congress opened at the Portland Rooms, near Tottenham Court Road. Attended by delegates from forty-nine societies, including, for the first time, the large amalgamated unions, the London Congress was the most nationally representative gathering to date. At its first session Potter was elected Chairman of the Congress and, at the suggestion of Allan, Howell was named Secretary. After the preliminary business had been settled, the Congress turned its attention to the proposed legislation. Most of the Bill was approved, but the delegates rejected its criminal provisions 'as derogatory to the character of trade unionists and unnecessary for the protection of any interest connected with the industry of the country'.[18] It was resolved that the entire Congress should form a deputation to H. A. Bruce, the Home Secretary, and

Howell was instructed to prepare a report on the Bill and to summarize unionist objections at the meeting.[19] Mundella introduced the delegation to the Home Secretary, who defended his Bill but promised to look into specific labour grievances. Howell's statement expressed the general fear that magistrates would be liable to construe the disputed clause in a prejudicial manner. Bruce informed his audience that the Bill was not so designed and refused to prejudge its consequences. Howell replied that 'at least the deputation was entitled to anticipate eventualities', but Bruce refused to give ground.[20]

Angered by such ministerial inflexibility, the delegates 'refused to sanction any Bill that in its provisions presupposes criminal intentions or tendencies on the part of English working men as a class'. In the most significant action of the entire session the Congress elected a five-man committee – consisting of Howell, Potter, Lloyd Jones, Alexander MacDonald of the Miners, and Joseph Leicester of the Flint Glass Makers – to watch over the progress of the Bill and to secure the rejection of the objectionable clause. In addition, the group was empowered to convene another Congress 'if they deem such to be necessary'.[21] In this way the Congress established the first Parliamentary Committee, but without really assuring its own self-perpetuation. The TUC was still regarded by many as a temporary body, with the Parliamentary Committee as its agent for the attainment of immediate goals. Once again TUC discussions had ranged freely from pressing industrial matters to issues of only peripheral importance to the trade union world, revealing in its debates more cohesion than initial meetings had promised.

The Parliamentary Committee, with Potter as Chairman and Howell as Secretary, met almost immediately after the Congress ended. On 14 March it drafted a letter embodying the critical resolutions which was sent to every Member of Parliament. A further statement of protest was issued at a meeting at the end of the month.[22] The Government's response to this mounting agitation was to remove the criminal clauses from the measure, incorporating them in a separate Criminal Law Amendment Bill. Although this stimulated wider support for the Trades Union Bill, it merely enacted the obnoxious provisions in another form, and the working-class agitation continued unabated. The Parliamentary Committee resorted to massive lobbying of MPs, a course of action which appealed strongly to its Secretary, who was accustomed to private negotiations with politicians. In letters and visits to sympathetic members, Howell and his colleagues reiterated their complaints against the discriminatory legislation, intensifying their campaign when the House of Lords amended the Bill to make it even more stringent.[23] Howell, who in the course of his tenure was to develop his skill in parliamentary lobbying into an art, met with Henry Winterbotham, the Under Secretary at the Home Office, and with Hughes, Mundella, and Samuel Morley over the issue of the Lords' amendments.[24] Much to the dismay of the trade unionists, the amendments were upheld in the Commons despite ministerial opposition.

At the beginning of September the Conference of Amalgamated Trades dissolved itself, leaving the future management of labour agitation entirely to the Parliamentary Committee. Although it had only belatedly recognized the value of a national organization and had, therefore, contributed little to the formation of the T U C, the Conference had achieved its primary objective – the legal protection of trade unionism. But just as the Parliamentary Committee was inheriting control of the movement, it was coming under attack from one of its erstwhile friends, Professor Beesly. Always close to Applegarth, who now left the forefront of labour politics, Beesly had become increasingly disenchanted with the new leadership, and especially with Howell. His place as architect of labour policy was taken by another Positivist, Henry Crompton, to whom Howell's methods seemed less objectionable. From 1867 on Beesly had urged the working men to assume a more independent line, warning them against placing their faith in the Liberal Party. As long as the union leaders relied upon the efficacy of private arrangements for Radical concessions, he argued, they would achieve only marginal benefits. Beesly believed that Howell's involvement with the Liberals during the 1868 election and after had undermined the trade union cause, reassuring the party leaders against the risk that working-class support would be withdrawn.[25]

By 1871 Howell was, as has been noted earlier, somewhat less sanguine about Liberal benevolence than he had been a year or so earlier. His personal rewards for placing the services of the Reform League at the disposal of the party leaders in 1868 had not met his expectations, and the promises of comprehensive legislation had been thwarted by anti-union sentiment in the Commons. None the less, by tying their sails to the Liberal mast in 1868, Howell and his associates had made a subsequent separation more difficult, even if there had been a practicable alternative of massive working-class pressure. Indeed, it was felt that just because of their political loyalty,

they had a claim upon the Government then in power, while they had no such claim upon the Tory or Conservative Party. We had worked incessantly in most of the constituencies during the General Election of 1868 to place the Liberals in office with a swinging majority. . . . Therefore we claimed, in return for our work, the fulfilment of promises given . . . .[26]

It was only in periods of frustration that Howell envisaged an independent labour party, but this reflected a momentary sense of despair rather than any fundamental disenchantment with Radicalism. He still longed to coalesce with its more progressive forces and to enter Parliament under its auspices. One such moment of disillusion followed the passing of the Criminal Law Amendment Act, when he informed William Hicking that 'we must make our platform broad and catholic so as to embrace all subjects of importance to our class. In fact we must create a Working Class Party, for Whig, Tory, and Middle-Class Radicals ignore our wants and requirements'.[27] This *cri de coeur* had a double meaning: 'our wants and requirements' were not only those of the trade union world, but also of Howell himself. In fact, his personal aspirations and his ambitions for trade unionism coincided; for both salvation seemed to lie in acceptance by Liberal opinion and respectable society. Working-class exclusiveness was no more desirable in trade policy than in discriminatory legislation. It was only when he felt thwarted that Howell found his proletarian spirit aroused; it fed on defeat, not on victory.

In a *Bee-Hive* article in July 1871 Beesly gave vent publicly to his dissatisfaction with the policy of the labour leadership. Ignoring the feathers he was about to ruffle, he wrote:

I cannot help thinking that the interests of the trade societies have suffered by the bad management of their own leaders. If some of these would think a little less about getting into Parliament themselves, and a little more about organizing an effective pressure upon the representatives of large constituencies, the result might be different.[28]

The barb found its intended target, and an indignant Howell soon denounced Beesly's 'dastardly attack' as 'cowardly' and without 'the slightest foundation in fact'.[29]

When the fourth annual Trades Union Congress opened in Nottingham in January 1872, Howell read a Parliamentary Committee report which emphasized the need for resolute action. The Committee felt compelled 'to recommend the repeal of the Criminal Law Amendment Act, as no amount of modification or amendment can correct sufficiently its mischievous provisions or obliterate its implied stigma on the trades unionists'.[30] After Mundella and Auberon Herbert offered their advice on the legislative course to be followed, Howell and several others argued vehemently for complete repeal, and a resolution embodying these sentiments was carried. To give practical effect to their demands, the Congress recommended the withdrawal of support by working men from any candidate who refused to commit himself to vote for repeal.[31]

Almost as important as the formulation of a legislative programme was the determination to regulate Congress proceedings. A Standing Orders Committee was appointed on the second day to introduce greater coherence in the daily conduct of business and to eliminate some of the procedural confusion of previous sessions. The Parliamentary Committee was also instructed to prepare permanent standing orders and to submit them for the approval of the next Congress. Howell had been paid two guineas for his services at the London Congress and would receive the same amount at the conclusion of the Nottingham meeting, but otherwise the Committee had not been remunerated for its efforts. Now for the first time the delegates acknowledged the need for regular sources of income to enable the Secretary and his colleagues to broaden the scope of their activities. They empowered the officers to raise funds by levies or voluntary subscriptions, which would help to 'maintain the action of the Committee' and provide the Secretary with some compensation for his services.[32]

Removed from the Junta's home territory, the delegates at Nottingham revealed a marked anti-London bias in their choice of candidates for an enlarged Parliamentary Committee. Those initially nominated included eight provincial leaders plus Howell, although Potter's name was subsequently added to the list. In the actual election the original slate was carried, with Howell only just scraping by in ninth place. Potter was defeated, a victim, paradoxically, of the resentment among provincial unionists of the Junta's formerly exclusive policy. Allan, who had been serving as Treasurer since 1871, was appointed a member by virtue of his position, the London clique's sole representative on the Committee. Meeting on 13 January, the new body elected Alexander MacDonald, who had come third in the voting, behind two members of the Nottingham Trades Council, as Chairman in place of Potter; Howell retained the Secretaryship.[33] The delegates gave the Committee a mandate to take 'any action that might be necessary to secure the repeal of the penal clauses of the Criminal Law Amendment Act, the Truck Act, the getting of a proper Compensation Act, and to watch over the interests of labour generally in the proceedings of Parliament'.[34] In contrast to the situation in 1871, it was no longer left to the Parliamentary Committee to determine whether another Congress should be summoned. The men elected at Nottingham, despite their inevitable autonomy, were clearly accountable to the 1873 Congress for their conduct, an indication of the growing self-awareness of the T U C.

Despite the evident intention of the Congress to make the Parliamentary Committee more effective by enlarging it, the new group immediately fell under the domination of Howell and MacDonald. Previous and subsequent committees would include greater London representation, but the prevalence of provincial members on this one ensured that the few accessible leaders would retain control of affairs. At its first meeting in Nottingham on 13 January the Committee, after electing officers, decided to leave the 'ordinary parliamentary work' in the hands of the London members acting in concert with MacDonald and any others whose duty might bring them to London.[35] Although Howell, in particular, sought to stifle any provincial initiative which threatened his ascendancy, the majority of the members were only too willing to defer to the authority of their officers. Howell resented all criticism of his conduct, but he did at least formally inform his associates of the Committee's work. Content to rely on perfunctory communications, the members rarely required extensive explanations, thus encouraging Howell and MacDonald to persist in their elaborate schemes of private lobbying. What disturbed the Secretary most was the occasional recourse of some members to *ex post facto* admonitions instead of prior vigilance. When John Kane of the Ironworkers, for example, objected to the tenor of MacDonald's remarks at a deputation to the Home Office, Howell replied with unconcealed irritation:

You surely do not expect that we should write out every speech we make and send slips round first before we speak them. I did not get a reply even to a circular from more than two persons of the entire committee. No member has been or will be summoned from the provinces without your receiving a letter as well, nor indeed will any step be taken without your knowledge and consent. But you never sent back one word as to the memorial, although I sent a copy to you and also the cases. Not one instruction of the Congress has been or will be set aside.[36]

In fact both sides were to blame. Committee members tended to be negligent in their duties, rarely bothering to appear at meetings. Average attendance between January and June was three out of ten, and sometimes only Howell and MacDonald turned up. Allan was frequently ill, and both he and Thomas Halliday of the Miners were preoccupied with their own union business which kept them away from London for long periods. On the other hand, Howell and MacDonald, eager to evade the interference of their colleagues, rarely deemed it essential to summon provincial members. When they failed to obtain the 'rubber stamp' approval they desired, they were generally able to bully the others into compliance.

Immediately after he returned to London, Howell took steps to implement the Nottingham resolutions. He gathered information and sent reports to the *Bee-Hive* in anticipation of the resumption of Parliament. When MacDonald arrived in London on 13 February, the two officers went to the House of Commons to interview members, spending much of the next three days there. On the 15th they sought out W. V. Harcourt, the Liberal MP for Oxford, and tried to elicit his support for repeal, although even at this stage they were receptive to his alternative proposals for modification. Harcourt informed them that he had personally opposed the Lords' amendments and would work for their elimination. Interviews with Hughes, Mundella, Rathbone, and others proved disappointing. Hughes, for example, refused even to concede the trade unions' grievances and offered no support. While Beesly was criticizing the leaders for their modest objectives, Hughes rebuked them for being too ambitious. Mundella also urged caution, advising Howell to settle for the simple repeal of the Lords' amendments rather than of the Act itself.

On 16 February Howell and MacDonald saw Harcourt again, reviewing with him the Act and the cases which had arisen as a result of its operation. Harcourt encouraged them to press for merely the removal of practical grievances, insisting that no one in the House would respond favourably to proposals for total repeal. The two officers replied that although they remained opposed to the Act, they felt obliged to acquiesce in any change that would eliminate the clauses under which workers were being convicted. Harcourt suggested a resolution in the Commons in order to prompt the Home Secretary to bring in an amending Bill, and Howell promised to furnish him with a complete list of cases tried under the Act. Howell spent most of the next week examining provincial newspapers at the British Museum in preparation for his index of cases. He also drafted a petition to the Home Secretary urging complete repeal and submitted it to Mac-Donald, Crompton, and Lloyd Jones for criticism before it was approved at a three-man Parliamentary Committee meeting on 26 February.[37]

Howell consulted Crompton both on the content of the petition and the proposed line of discussion at the forthcoming meeting with Bruce. Crompton advised him to extract a precise definition of coercion, arguing that if the Home Secretary included moral as well as physical coercion in his interpretation of the law, he should be charged with directly attacking the civil liberty of the citizen.[38] Crompton's arguments for repeal were incorporated into the petition, but at the Home Office deputation on 21 March Howell and MacDonald indicated their willingness to settle for a simple elimination of the Lords' additions to the original Bill. Howell did insist on greater clarity in its provisions, appealing to Bruce to clear up the misunderstandings which had led to prosecution for 'besetting' when a worker had merely been present at the scene of a dispute. MacDonald argued that the Committee had no desire to embarrass the Government, on whose generosity it relied.[39] If, as Howell asserted, Crompton recognized the impossibility of immediate repeal and offered suggestions for an amending Bill, it is clear that he still had misgivings about the way in which TUC officials were proceeding. In his 'Memorandum' Howell noted that Crompton approved their having enlisted Harcourt's aid, but Crompton's own letter a few days after the deputation casts doubt on this interpretation:

> Don't go and get one of these bigwigs [Crompton wrote] to conduct your cause. They are not be be trusted. They are all aiming at place or advancement and will not take up your cause heartily but will in all probability sell you by . . . denouncing unionism in general.[40]

In April further progress was delayed pending an appeal of the conviction of George Turk for distributing handbills encouraging a strike of Hammersmith engineers. The prosecution then decided that it wished to drop charges, and the conviction was quashed. By its mismanagement of the affair the Hammersmith committee and its defence counsel, Liberal MP Henry James, lost the opportunity for a test case against the Act. Howell and MacDonald decided to act quickly and obtained an interview with Harcourt and Mundella at the House on 29 April. James joined the discussions, disavowing any knowledge of the intent to make the Turk incident a test case. He expressed his disapproval of the harsh sentence originally imposed and his opposition to the criminal clauses which had permitted it. The TUC officers then requested his aid in changing the law, and James promised to co-operate with Harcourt in working for its alteration. He persuaded the others that it would be better to introduce an amending Bill than to follow Harcourt's earlier suggestion of a resolution calling for action by the Home Secretary. On 6 May a rough draft of the Bill was completed, embodying the provisions worked out by Howell and MacDonald in consultation with the Liberals. The next day Howell again saw Harcourt, who had not yet seen a completed draft. Eager to ensure Howell's fidelity and, through him, that of the Trades Union Congress, Harcourt advised the Secretary that he need not concede as much as he had in the Bill. The penalty for 'words' as constituting coercion was first changed to 'threats', and then, on a further suggestion from Harcourt, the clause was simplified to specify simply 'acts calculated to intimidate'.[41] The Bill sought to eliminate the clause affecting picketing, re-enacting those aspects which the sponsors deemed essential, but without the vagueness which allowed judges to seize the chance to obtain convictions. Harcourt, James, Mundella, Rathbone – who had abandoned a similar, although more restricted Bill of his own – and George Melly were to handle the measure in the House.

Howell was delighted with the outcome. Despite his initial qualms at not being able to secure repeal, he was convinced that the amending Bill would prove effective in protecting workmen against indiscriminate prosecution. Susceptible as always to the flattery of his calculating Liberal patrons, he felt he had done the movement a service while impressing politicians with his own capability. This apparent double triumph raised his self-esteem, as a letter to Bartlett revealed:

[The Bill] is in my opinion a really good Bill. It has been drawn with very great care, every word has been weighed by us most carefully, and I find that I win respect from such men as Vernon Harcourt and Henry James by the way in which I meet them even in the domain of law, and discuss some of its abstruse principles. This is not boastful, but what I have seen and felt from very close contact with both the men.[42]

His own vanity and the persuasive powers of politicians had convinced him that his tactics were beyond reproach. Certainly his abilities exceeded those of the average labour leader of his day, and long association with the Junta had reinforced his confidence that Londoners were shrewder in these matters than their provincial cousins, far more adept at playing the intricate parliamentary game.

On 11 May Howell sent the draft Bill to other members of the Parliamentary Committee and to trades councils around the country with no premonition of the trouble that lay ahead once the Bill received publicity. Reactions to the proposals were mixed. The Nottingham members of the Committee approved, as did several trades councils. Applegarth and J. D. Prior, his successor as Secretary of the Amalgamated Society of Carpenters and Joiners, both gave their qualified endorsement.[43] On the other hand, Daniel Guile protested that the Bill was 'little better than the Act and certainly not worth either the money or time it will cost to carry'.[44] Guile was an influential figure in the movement, and Howell sought to placate him, but to no avail. Although unable to refute the Secretary's premises, Guile's opposition continued despite Howell's warning that 'if they are not satisfied with our work, let them call on us to resign and let other and better men be elected to do the work'.[45]

Frederic Harrison was a more formidable antagonist, and in the weeks following the announcement of the Bill he tried, publicly and behind the scenes, to arouse labour circles against a measure he

G

regarded as inimical to their interest. He saw George Shipton, the new Secretary of the London Trades Council, whose jealousy of the Parliamentary Committee made him an immediate convert to the Harrison camp. The Council passed a resolution on 17 May demanding total repeal of the Criminal Law Amendment Act and repudiating the proposed Bill.[46] Howell's confidence was still unshaken, and he assured MacDonald that 'our Bill is unassailable as an amendment. As I have told all objectors, I should have preferred simple repeal, but what is the use of fighting windmills?'[47]

On 31 May the Positivists launched a full-scale attack in the *Bee-Hive*, with Beesly and Harrison denouncing the Bill as worthless. Amending only one part of the Act, it intended – with some rearrangement of clauses – to reimpose virtually all the objectionable provisions of the existing law. In most respects it was almost identical to Bruce's original measure, but it did add a sub-section prohibiting 'threats or acts calculated to intimidate'.[48] This was the clause which had been further simplified at Harcourt's prompting, by deleting the word 'threats', but Beesly and Harrison had evidently not seen the later version. Although Howell tried to dismiss the disagreement as a misunderstanding over the revisions, the disputed clause was not, in fact, the main focus of the Positivists' attack. They believed that Liberal concessions would not prevent continued convictions for peaceful picketing. Furthermore, the outcome of trade union collaboration in promoting the Bill might well be the subsequent refusal of the Liberals to undertake any more reforms on this issue. Howell saw the Bill as a partial and temporary solution, but the party leaders might feel that they had discharged their obligations to labour by granting this irrelevant concession.

As if the *Bee-Hive* castigation was not enough, Beesly wrote to the Shoemakers, apparently encouraging them to urge their representative on the Parliamentary Committee to disavow the Bill.[49] Beesly's appeal must have been effective, for on 6 June the Committee decided to ask George Thomas – absent from this meeting – to 'explain his conduct on the Bill question'.[50] Howell was told to inform the Shoemakers that Thomas 'had attended the meetings of the Committee and has concurred in all that has been done'. In other words, Howell, MacDonald, and Halliday wanted to impose collective responsibility for the measure on their colleagues. While Beesly approached Thomas through his union, Harrison tackled

Allan. According to Howell's report, Harrison told Potter that Allan denied all knowledge of and responsibility for the Bill.[51] While it was true that Allan had been ill in May, unable to give much attention to the Bill, he 'appeared to acquiesce' when Howell explained the provisions to him on 27 May.[52] At the 6 June meeting Allan denied Harrison's allegations, insisting that 'all he had said was that he unfortunately had been out of town during the drafting of the Bill and had not therefore seen its exact wording, but he held himself responsible for the work of the Committee'.[53]

Stung by the sudden onslaught of opposition, Howell set out at once to retrieve a situation which had seemed so promising only a few weeks earlier. During a long interview at the House of Commons on 3 June Harcourt and James conceded that the disputed clause might be misconstrued. They would not, however, agree to Howell's suggestion that guarantees for peaceful picketing be incorporated, and it was decided simply to omit the clause altogether.[54] Howell's next step was a bold, if somewhat inaccurate, reply to his critics in the 7 June Bee-Hive. In an article extending over almost the entire front page he denied that the promotion of this Bill would hinder efforts to secure total repeal, reiterating his conviction that only a limited measure was possible at present. The aim of the Parliamentary Committee was to relieve workmen from 'the terror of the existing law. It is an attempt to take the sting out of the Act of 1871, and it is neither opposed to the protest of last year, nor to the condemnation of the Nottingham Conference.' He further insisted that the proposal offered substantial benefits, preventing the recurrence of prosecutions like those which had recently taken place. He explained that the clause to which Harrison and Beesly objected had bothered him as well, and it had finally been removed. While his response to Harrison's remarks was reasonably temperate, Howell lashed out at Beesly for 'bespattering mud'. It was 'the Parliamentary Committee that the ill-tempered Professor tries to hit, rather than the Bill'. Howell was on shakier ground when he tried to associate Crompton with his actions, claiming that he had 'consulted him at every step taken up to the very day he left London for the Continent'.[55]

Unfortunately, there were several flaws in Howell's statement, although these were probably not wholly apparent to his readers. He failed to resolve the doubts as to whether similar prosecutions might occur under other clauses of the Bill. Nor did he mention that the alteration of the controversial words had been at Harcourt's suggestion, and that their ultimate omission was in part a response to the Positivist reproof. The constant consultation with Crompton at this stage was simply untrue: he rarely figures in Howell's painstaking 'Memorandum' after the March deputation to Bruce. Neither Harrison nor Crompton attended Parliamentary Committee meetings as they had those of the Conference of Amalgamated Trades. In a letter to Allan several days later Howell admitted that Crompton had departed for the Continent 'on the very day when the Bill was to have been drafted'.[56]

Harrison was not appeased by Howell's self-vindication, although he tried to reduce the level of personal recrimination which was entering the discussion. 'No one,' Harrison wrote in reply, 'accuses Mr Howell or anyone else. He and everyone concerned in the new Bill have acted with the best intentions. The only question is to see whether they have satisfied the wants of workmen as a body.' He denied that Crompton favoured the measure and repeated his own doubts about whether 'it is worthwhile to promote an Act of Parliament to make these infinitesimal changes in wording . . . If Mr Howell thinks there is any difference in law or in sense between "binding over to keep the peace the person threatening" and "binding over the person threatening to keep the peace", I am afraid he has been hoaxed.'[57]

At the Parliamentary Committee meeting on 6 June Howell made the allegations of the Positivist leaders an issue of confidence and rallied support around him. Allan, MacDonald, and Halliday – the other members present – agreed to issue a joint statement refuting the charges, and Howell was instructed to draft it.[58] The manifesto expressed their 'extreme regret' at the articles of Beesly and Harrison, and it went on to say that 'the Committee understood their duty to be to protest against the entire Act, and to do all in their power to promote its repeal; and meanwhile to seek such modification of the Act as would prevent the cruel prosecutions which have taken place, and are taking place under certain of its provisions'. The statement noted the lack of criticism of the Bill, except for that of Guile, and denounced Beesly and Harrison for 'rushing into print with their insinuations against our good faith', instead of taking up their grievances privately with the individuals concerned.[59] The full Parliamentary Committee endorsed the policy of its leaders on 13 June but, at the same time, called on trade unionists throughout the country to agitate for repeal, blaming the general apathy of working men for the Government's refusal to respond decisively.[60]

Once the loyalty of the Parliamentary Committee had been tested, Howell set about restoring harmony with the labour leaders who opposed his advocacy of the Bill, hoping in this way to prevent dissension at the forthcoming Congress. The most prominent of these was Guile, to whom the Secretary wrote in a deliberately conciliatory manner,

I give you full credit for the way in which you have objected to the Bill which we have got introduced. You are fully aware that my objections to the Act are quite as strong as yours, and I have never failed so to express myself. I am sorry to find you writing as though we had any desire to force you, or anyone, to swallow our dose, far from it. If we could only get the Act repealed, no one would work harder to achieve it. But are we, Sir, to prevent the passing of an Act which would at least render impossible the convictions of which we complain? I only ask you to recall the past in which I have sat by your side and I ask you if I ever faltered in my denunciation of this Act? Nay further, have you in any sense found me preferring modification to repeal? I only seek the one because *at present* I deem the other impossible. . . . If however my old friends think that I have in any way endangered repeal, I regret it very much, and only hope that their next appointed secretary will be as earnest a worker as I know myself to be in this work.[61]

Guile remained sceptical, but he was at least willing to show enough confidence in the Secretary and the Committee to contribute £20 towards expenses, one of the larger union donations of the year.[62]

The more troublesome Nottingham leaders were treated less gently. They had supported the Bill at first, belatedly expressing their dissatisfaction only when it proved abortive. At a Nottingham demonstration on 10 August Howell seized the opportunity to reprimand the dissenters. 'I had to give them a lesson on practical legislation,' he wrote MacDonald, 'for they talked as though it was only to speak and the job was done. I vindicated the Committee.' The Nottingham rebels had been incited by a man named Mathews, whom Howell believed to be an associate of Randal Cremer's. Mathews had advised the Nottingham trades to withhold their contribution to the Committee since it 'was a sham'. Howell challenged the Nottingham leaders to produce Mathews' statement, but they refused, charging Howell's informant with a 'want of confidence'. The Secretary replied that 'the want of confidence was on the other side as they were stabbing men in the dark without the chance of defence or reply'. He also suspected Odger's machinations in the background, probably a valid assumption in view of the scarcely concealed enmity between the Parliamentary Committee and London Trades Council.[63]

Despite the growing conflict in labour circles, the parliamentary dispute over Harcourt's Bill drew to a sudden close in the summer of 1872. Hinde Palmer introduced an amendment which confined the changes to the repeal of the 'watching and besetting' clause, in addition to a few minor alterations. Harcourt, who had incurred more blame than he had bargained for, disliked the mutilation of his Bill and contemplated withdrawing it, but Howell prevailed upon him to persist as far as the second reading.[64] Although it appeared on the Order Paper for several successive nights, during which time Howell and MacDonald canvassed for supporters, the second reading did not take place until late in the evening of 5 July. After a vigorous defence by Harcourt, James, Herbert, and Mundella, Lord Elcho succeeded in cutting off debate by an adjournment motion. The sponsors appealed to Bruce for the concession of government time before the summer recess, but he was hostile to the Bill and told Gladstone that he doubted the willingness of Parliament to go beyond its original measure.[65] The Bill was abandoned and gradually forgotten, a testimony to misguided intentions. It was Howell's last attempt to secure a partial concession through private negotiations. Thereafter he would adhere more strictly to the Congress insistence on repeal, realizing that the failure of his independent initiative could jeopardize his own security as Secretary. Looking ahead to the possibility of censure at Leeds, he felt both disappointed and betrayed by the parliamentary rebuff, lamenting the fact that 'the Bill was stabbed and thrust under the hedge in the darkness of night'.[66]

8

The Parliamentary Committee and the Labour Laws

Although the effort to change the Criminal Law Amendment Act overshadowed all other activities, the rest of the TUC legislative programme was attempted with far less controversy. The Parliamentary Committee supported the Government's Mines Regulation Bill, which passed into law in 1872, but it was MacDonald and the miners' delegates, rather than Howell, who assumed most of the responsibility for articulating the union position. Howell did help MacDonald to lobby MPs and offered sympathy when Beesly criticized him for agreeing to several of the employers' amendments that weakened the measure.[1] Somewhat relieved to find the attack shifting away from him, Howell agreed that Beesly had become 'nasty' and advised his colleague to 'just give him about three lines and finish him off.'[2]

After the TUC had passed several resolutions in favour of boards of arbitration to settle trade disputes, Rupert Kettle, the noted industrial arbitrator, had drafted a Bill which won the approval of the Nottingham Congress. Howell sent copies to friendly MPs who had agreed to promote such a measure. Mundella, however, regarded the Kettle draft as impracticable since it forced employers to open their books to arbitration boards.[3] He persuaded the Parliamentary Committee to submit it to a legislative draftsman and insisted on taking charge of its progress in the Commons, despite his obvious lack of enthusiasm for it.[4] At a Co-operative Congress in Bolton in early April Howell reported these developments to Kettle, who felt that Mundella neither desired nor really understood the principle of arbitration. He argued that Mundella's version contained nothing that was not included in earlier arbitration legislation 'except mischievousness'. Kettle's objections led to further negotiations between Howell and the MPs supporting the Bill, but despite additional changes in its wording Kettle remained dissatisfied. Howell was obliged to spend much of April and May trying to reconcile the differences between Kettle and Mundella, a more taxing job than he had imagined. 'With the egotism of both these men and the special predilection for their own handicraft,' he complained, 'I was put to considerable expense and trouble and work.'[5]

Finally, after a second reading on 12 June, Mundella's Bill, with certain modifications, was passed through the Commons by mid-July. Although Howell boasted that 'no more important Act has passed the legislature this session',[6] it had few admirers and proved an almost wholly ineffective measure. The cumbersome provisions for workshop rules and arbitration boards were rapidly consigned to oblivion. Proposals for legally-enforced arbitration appealed to the imagination of the TUC, but it was difficult to embody them in practicable legislation. In promoting this Bill Howell found himself in a predicament not unlike the crisis over the Criminal Law Amendment Act. The MPs who agreed to support it would only sponsor a more watered-down version than that envisaged by the TUC. In order to implement his mandate Howell felt compelled to accept the more modest Bill, but he had little more enthusiasm for it than its parliamentary proponents. While its passage was less thorny than its preparation, it was largely forgotten once placed on the statute books, and Howell earned little credit for his labours.

The Parliamentary Committee also supported a Government measure prohibiting payment of wages in 'truck'. After a first reading in February Crompton warned Howell that the Bill's opponents wanted to shelve it by referring it to a select committee. Howell sent out notices to trade societies urging them to petition in favour of the Bill, and he personally solicited support during frequent visits to the Commons. Howell and other Committee members addressed provincial meetings as part of an attempt to focus public attention on the issue.[7] But the Bill emerged from the committee in such a mutilated state that the TUC officers advised its withdrawal unless the original provisions were restored. On 6 June the London members decided to bring the matter before a full Parliamentary Committee meeting and instructed Howell to arrange a deputation to the Home Secretary.[8] In his memorial for the 13 June deputation Howell argued that the amended Bill was worse than the original. Trade unionists had sought weekly wages, but they feared that the new concessions permitted even greater laxity in payment than before, authorizing deductions by employers for food, fuel, and lodging.[9] In response to the resistance of labour opinion, Gladstone finally agreed to withdraw the Bill altogether. The Parliamentary Committee had thus succeeded not in securing an effective measure, but only in blocking a detrimental one.

As the Nottingham Congress had recognized, activity of this kind could not be carried out by voluntary labour. At its 13 January meeting the Parliamentary Committee proposed sending a circular to trade societies requesting donations for its expenses.[10] The response was encouraging, if not quite munificent. The Committee was obliged, just as the London Trades Council had been during the period of Junta control, to depend on the large amalgamated societies for support. In 1872 the Carpenters and Joiners contributed £20, the Engineers £25, and the two principal miners' unions £45. Coulson's Bricklayers was the notable exception, contributing nothing in 1872, probably because of its General Secretary's vendetta against Howell. Overall receipts in 1872 amounted to £295 16s 6d, while expenditure barely exceeded £200.

The largest single item in the Committee's budget was the salary of its Secretary, a total of £113 17s during the year between the Nottingham and Leeds Congresses.[11] This relatively modest sum covered not merely Howell's personal wages, but office rent and administrative expenses as well. The question of the Secretary's pay had come up first at a February meeting, at which time it was decided that Howell might draw £2 on account. The final determination of his salary was postponed, however, until a later meeting.[12] Within a few days George Thomas raised the issue again, urging that the salary be fixed immediately. The Secretary's work 'could only be done by constant application, and no one could do this unless paid for their [sic] services'.[13] Finally, in April the sum of two guineas per week was agreed upon, but Howell did not begin to draw a regular salary until some weeks later. The 13 June meeting, which was supposed to confirm this salary, indicated the degree of Howell's ascendancy over the Committee. Under

fierce attack from the outside for his conduct over the Criminal
Law Amendment Bill, he managed to persuade his colleagues not
only to approve his salary to date, but to raise it to £2 5s per week
until the next Congress.[14]

One of the penalties of Howell's rapid rise as an independent
figure in the labour movement – in contrast to leaders like Allan
and Applegarth – was that his enemies invariably sought to impugn
his trade union credentials. It was an almost unique phenomenon
to have attained a position of such prominence without having
controlled a major union. Men like Guile, MacDonald, and Kane
were always less vulnerable during their stints on the Parliamentary
Committee because of their secure positions as union leaders. On
the other hand, Howell, like Potter and to a lesser extent Odger,
was primarily a politician, for whom union affiliation had become
by this time only a prerequisite for his advance in labour politics.
He no longer considered himself a bricklayer by trade, but he
needed to maintain a union connection in order to give his position
legitimacy. His failure to displace Coulson in the Operative
Bricklayers' Society reinforced the political inclination of his
ambition, but, in fact, his tenure in the Reform League had
already made the direction of his career irreversible.

Howell's resignation from the London Order in 1871 followed
his appointment to the key office within the Parliamentary Committee. According to his own diary, Howell resigned in July. Since
he did not join the Sheffield branch of the Manchester Unity until
late January 1872, there was a gap of several months during which
he actually belonged to no union at all.[15] Indeed he remained
unaffiliated during the Nottingham Congress, at which he was
re-elected to office. In April – perhaps just at the time that the
Parliamentary Committee was seeking to confirm his salary –
rumours began to circulate denying that Howell was a union
member. Fearing that such reports might harm the reputation of
the TUC, the vigilant Kane brought them to the attention of the
Parliamentary Committee. Howell dismissed them, informing
Kane that he had retained membership in the Paddington Lodge
until March 1872, while joining the Manchester Unity in January.[16]
The claim to overlapping membership – which, in fact, seems
dubious – was calculated to dispel any doubts about his credentials.
At a May Committee meeting Howell offered to resign if his
colleagues were dissatisfied with his explanation. They certainly

had no desire to get rid of their diligent Secretary and rose to his defence, declaring that 'such calumnies and untruths are only intended and designed to injure the efforts of the Parliamentary Committee'. Since publicity 'would best suit the purpose of those circulating such slanders', they determined to make no public statement on the matter except for an explanatory letter to Kane.[17] The incident was soon forgotten, but similar rumours occasionally recurred to haunt Howell's later career. Imputations of peculation or dishonesty were the common currency of working-class politics, and the nature of Howell's functions made him particularly vulnerable to such attacks.

Once Parliament had adjourned for the summer recess, Howell could devote his attention to preparing standing orders, as the Nottingham Congress had instructed. Working with Allan and Kane, Howell drafted a comprehensive set of regulations which, with certain excisions and amendments, would be adopted at Leeds.[18] While most of the articles pertained to credentials and procedure, the standing orders finally defined the official duties of the Parliamentary Committee, consolidating previous resolutions with current practice: '(1.) To watch all legislative measures directly affecting the questions of labour, and (2.) to initiate, whenever necessary, such legislative action as Congress may direct, or as the exigencies of the time and circumstances may demand.'[19]

During the autumn of 1872 Howell busied himself with the report of the Parliamentary Committee, a detailed twelve-page narrative describing its activities since the previous Congress. Although unapologetic in tone, the report admitted its failure to secure the alteration of the Criminal Law Amendment Act.[20] Practical arrangements for the 1873 Congress were hardly less time-consuming than the preparation of the report. A stream of correspondence flowed out of Howell's office to the Leeds organizers and to various delegates. Societies which had been remiss in their contributions were urged to pay their share of the Committee's expenses. Sympathetic MPs and other friends had to be invited to attend the Congress.[21] Howell also chanced on a scheme for earning a bit of extra money by offering to represent societies that could not afford to send their own members, at a cost of only the ten shillings delegate's fee. At Leeds Howell was to represent the Glass Bottle Makers, the Dublin Trades Association, and the Miners' Provident Society.[22]

When the delegates assembled in Leeds on 13 January 1873 for the fifth annual Trades Union Congress, they were obliged to devote early sessions to procedural business. Determined to streamline the proceedings, a committee of TUC leaders advised the elimination of papers in defence of trade unionism, retaining only those relevant to their legislative objectives. In order to increase the revenue the suggestion was put forward that no candidate should be eligible for election to the Parliamentary Committee unless his society had contributed towards its expenses during the previous year. After Howell read the annual report and balance sheet, Crompton, once again restored as the main architect of Congress policy after his temporary eclipse in 1872, delivered an address on the operation of the Criminal Law Amendment Act. The time for compromise and concession, he warned, had passed: trade unionists should 'use all lawful means to stop these proceedings, by raising an excitement and agitation throughout the land. Parliament had trifled too long upon this matter, playing a game of deception.' Inciting the workers to action, Crompton outlined a six-point programme, headed by the demand for the repeal of the Criminal Law Amendment Act and the abolition of imprisonment for breach of contract.[23]

For the next two days the Congress discussed the report of the Parliamentary Committee. Its handling of the minor legislative measures provoked little comment, but once debate shifted to the CLAA, the officers were subjected to sharp criticism 'from all parts of the House'.[24] James Naylor of the Leeds Pattern Makers, who launched the attack, insisted that the Committee had exceeded its prerogatives by endorsing a compromise after the Nottingham Congress had specifically called for repeal. Delegate after delegate challenged the officers to justify their actions. Although the attack may have been instigated by the London Trades Council, seeking to supplant the Parliamentary Committee as the executive of the trade union movement, Odger, its longtime Secretary, took only a mildly reproving line. He argued that the delegates should not have accepted the report if they disapproved it, but having done so, no further justification was required. He believed that the Committee had done its best but conceded that its performance had been of a 'dilettante' quality. William Lishman of the Leeds Trades Council, the presiding officer, took a conciliatory approach: while agreeing that the Committee should explain its behaviour, he denied that this was tantamount to having to defend it. A Leeds delegate named Hustler, on the other hand, claimed that the leaders deserved the acclaim of the Congress for their efforts.

Facing a chorus of accusations, Howell rose to answer the dissident elements. His colleagues had tried to secure the total repeal of the Act, but finding that they could not do so, they looked for the next best thing. The Committee had not agreed to the compromise until all avenues had been explored. He expressed surprise that such opposition had not manifested itself before the Congress, since the Committee had kept affiliated societies informed about its activities. Some of the delegates, he continued, argued as though the passing of a parliamentary bill were the easiest thing in the world. In this they were mistaken, for it was a matter of the utmost difficulty. He did not for a moment concede that the Committee had exceeded its authority in sanctioning the compromise proposal.[25] This impassioned defence transformed Howell's vulnerability into a personal triumph. He realized that his policy had not succeeded, but he was certainly unwilling to offer himself as a scapegoat to appease the indignation of the delegates. The heated debate was terminated by Peter Shorrocks' (Tailors) resolution declaring 'that while the Congress acknowledged the valuable services of the Parliamentary Committee, the delegates desired to record their determination not to rest until they had obtained the total repeal of the Criminal Law Amendment Act'.[26] The officers not only survived the storm: Howell and MacDonald led the voting when the new Parliamentary Committee was elected. Rejecting a London Trades Council suggestion that the TUC scrap the Committee entirely, appointing instead provincial representatives to collaborate with the London body, the delegates elected a more impressive Committee than its predecessor. Howell headed the list with 86 votes to MacDonald's 73. Allan and John Kane remained, and the new members included Odger and Guile. J. D. Prior was nominated along with George Shipton and Henry Broadhurst – the London Trades Council contingent – but they fared badly in the voting.[27]

Howell emerged from the Leeds Congress with less room for personal manœuvre, but with his domination of the Parliamentary Committee guaranteed for the remainder of his term in office. Having survived the assault of the Positivists, the rivalry of the London Trades Council, and the recriminations of angry delegates, he settled down for his final two and a half years in the role of trade union statesman. The outlook for success improved in 1873 with the increase of working-class agitation and the conversion of more MPs to the cause of repeal, and the Parliamentary Committee began to encounter less resistance to its entreaties at Westminster. This meant less intense activity and virtually no controversy in the future for its Secretary.

Leeds represented much more than the test of a particular legislative policy for Howell. The position which he had built up in working-class politics over fifteen years had been endangered by the failure of his independent line in 1872. The 1873 Congress nearly undermined the basis of his strength – the trust of the trade union world – before he had made that ascent into bourgeois security to which he had long aspired. Had he not overcome the threat posed at Leeds, it might well have spelled the end of his political career. Unencumbered by the responsibility of running a union, he was a relatively free agent, the spokesman of the labour movement rather than the deputy of a single bloc. But this auton- omy deprived him of a secure power base, making him dependent on the confidence of the trade unions collectively. With the depart- ure of longtime associates like Applegarth from the labour scene and the waning influence of Potter and Allan, Howell faced a challenge from new men like Shipton and Broadhurst. With these men he lacked the fund of common experience dating back to the 1859 building trades dispute, although his relations with the newer leaders would in time become amicable. Without the support of loyal friends, Howell found himself in a precarious position, which might have brought defeat and ostracism. Thus Leeds – the most dangerous threat to his career in these years – marked an important milestone on the road to future success.

One reason for the virulence of the attack on the Parliamentary Committee at Leeds was the prior prosecution of London gas stokers on charges under the Criminal Law Amendment Act, the Master and Servant Act, and the conspiracy law. In 1872 they had formed a union to agitate for a raise in wages. When their leaders were victimized by the employers, the gas stokers decided to strike. Twenty-four of them were imprisoned for breach of contract, and another six were indicted for conspiring to intimidate the employ- ers' agent in order to secure the reinstatement of the locked-out workers. With Potter as Chairman, a committee was formed on 16

December to defend the gas stokers which included Howell, Applegarth, Guile, Shipton, Beesly, Crompton, Harrison, and Hughes.
Solicitors were engaged, and the trial took place at the Old Bailey
before Mr Justice Brett. A jury found the defendants guilty of
conspiracy, and Brett sentenced them to a year's imprisonment.

The verdict shocked the trade union world, revealing again that
legitimate labour agitation enjoyed no legal protection. Even if the
Criminal Law Amendment Act had been altered, workers would
still be liable to prosecution under the conspiracy law. Howell
himself commented, 'the gas stokers' prosecution, trial, conviction,
and sentence had given the deathblow to any compromise in the
matter of the Criminal Law Amendment Act'.[28] At a 21 December
meeting the committee decided to issue an appeal for funds to pay
for the trial and to support the prisoners' families. Howell was
selected to prepare a memorial on the case, which the committee
hoped to present at a deputation to the Home Secretary. On 7 January the committee met to discuss the memorial and a mass meeting
to be convened by the London Trades Council several days later.
Howell urged the members to concentrate on securing the release
of the victims. He felt that the legal issue could be left to the Leeds
Congress, insisting that the Government could not ignore the
opinion of such a body.[29] In his report, approved by the committee
and then endorsed by the TUC, Howell disputed the judge's
interpretation of the law, but noted that even if the conviction were
justifiable, 'the sentence [was] excessive and altogether disproportionate to the offence with which they were charged'.[30]
Protest meetings increased in number when Bruce declined to
receive a deputation. Although the Home Secretary refused to
acknowledge Howell's memorial when it was submitted to him,
he asked Hughes to arrange for the prisoners to send in their own
plea. As a gesture of mercy the Government agreed to commute the
sentence to four months. Remission in response to a direct appeal
allowed Bruce to extricate himself without yielding on the principles involved or disputing the validity of the sentence. Hughes
persuaded Howell to allow his own memorial to be dropped
quietly, and the Defence Committee decided to accept the Home
Office compromise.[31]

In the spring of 1873 Mundella consented to sponsor a Bill for
the repeal of the Criminal Law Amendment Act, a reversal of his

position of the previous year. The Bill received a first reading in May, but it proceeded no further during the remainder of the parliamentary session. Auberon Herbert's efforts to secure a select committee to consider changes in the law were also defeated, although Howell sent notices to sympathetic members to ensure a full House. The Home Secretary continued to obstruct reform, opposing alteration of either the CLAA or the Master and Servant Act at that time.[32] Harcourt brought in a Bill to amend the conspiracy law in June, which was passed by the Commons, but it was abandoned by the Government after the Lords imposed major alterations.

The burden of negotiation and correspondence, of arranging demonstrations and deputations fell largely on Howell. If the year brought no tangible benefits, it was not for want of effort. It was his own consciousness of unremitting work which made Howell resent letters from disgruntled trade unionists implying that the Parliamentary Committee was not getting its money's worth from its Secretary. An appeal for funds in February brought little response, although Howell's own salary rose slightly to £2 10s per week in 1874.[33] In the face of such meagre legislative returns, small societies were often reluctant to send in money to defray Parliamentary Committee expenses, and Howell had to reprimand them for lack of co-operation. As he wrote to one Maidstone official,

A Society that will not contribute to our funds is scarcely justified in criticizing our expenditure. I might say that the smallness of the sum contributed by Societies numbering 700,000 members is no reason why the Secretary should be starved. The sum you mention, £113, does not represent more than ⅛ a farthing per man to pay not only my salary but the office, rent and expenses included. Such stinginess and meanness is not compatible with the continual cry for increase of wages by the men. Are you aware that for two years I got nothing? Are you also aware that I have brought to this work 22 years of experience in active life? If you can find a better man at less pay, for God's sake have him.[34]

The replacement of Bruce by Robert Lowe as Home Secretary and Howell's restatement of trade union demands to Gladstone promised a fresh look at the labour laws by the Government.[35] On 29 October Hughes intimated to Howell that Lowe would be receptive to the idea of another trade union deputation. The Secretary immediately wrote to the Home Office, and a meeting was arranged for 5 November.[36] Hughes introduced the group, consisting of the Parliamentary Committee officers, Crompton, Mundella, and Hinde Palmer. Howell, the principal spokesman, assured Lowe that 'we do not, and never did, countenance or excuse acts of violence to persons, or injury of any kind to property by whomever committed. We ask no exceptions in legislation from that of any other citizen, but we do ask to be placed on an equality.'[37] The Committee felt that Lowe's sympathy had been enlisted, but it was to be of little use in the few months remaining to the ministry.

The Leeds Congress had resolved to support only those parliamentary candidates pledged to its programme, and, anticipating the coming election, the Committee issued a list of questions in early December to test the reliability of candidates. Unless they agreed to vote for the repeal of the Criminal Law Amendment Act, for the abolition of criminal prosecution for breach of contract, and for the amendment of the conspiracy law, working-class voters were urged to withhold support. Candidates were also to be held accountable for their endorsement of workmen's compensation, the nine hours factory Bill, a Bill to protect the lives of seamen by regulating shipping, and the prevention of truck payment of wages.[38]

When the sixth Trades Union Congress opened in Sheffield in January 1874, Howell read a brief, discouraging report to the assembled delegates. He stressed the Government's continued refusal to resolve the labour laws question. The failure, however, could no longer be blamed on the Secretary, whose report was accepted without discussion, in striking contrast to the imbroglio of the previous year. After debating the relation between repeal of the CLAA and support for parliamentary candidates, the delegates finally agreed on a resolution stating:

... that every delegate present pledges himself to assist in holding public meetings, arranging demonstrations, and making such other efforts as are in his power to remove this obnoxious piece of class legislation. If the Act is not repealed during the ensuing session of Parliament, it will be the duty of working men to oppose all candidates at the next General Election who uphold the Act.[39]

The Congress went on record again condemning the conspiracy law, the Master and Servant Act, the retention of unpaid magistrates, and the persistence of truck payment.

There was far less agreement when it came to the vital question of the direct representation of labour. Previous Congresses had always supported the principle, but they had been reluctant to implement it by concrete action. Broadhurst urged the Sheffield delegates to raise an electoral fund by a small levy on every trade union member, which would enable them to carry a dozen working men into the House of Commons. After several contradictory resolutions had been proposed, an attempt was made to formulate a compromise which recognized the duty of trade societies to 'exert themselves in the most strenuous manner' to assist labour candidates. The resolution called for society contributions of at least sixpence per member in order to raise a fund for these candidates, but most delegates still clung to the traditional trade unionist reluctance to bridge the gap between industrial activity and actual politics. It was one thing to agitate for parliamentary legislation; it was quite another to promote union-sponsored candidates. The split on this issue was not between those who favoured a militant, independent working-class party and the more moderate elements, as would occur in subsequent ideological splits within the TUC. Rather it was men like Broadhurst and Howell, identified with the Labour Representation League and committed to achieving a labour group within the Liberal Party, who urged the delegates to move into the political arena. Provincial leaders feared that the accumulation of such a fund would lead to the centralization of power in the hands of the Parliamentary Committee. Many of them preferred to leave political ventures, if they were to be undertaken at all, to local initiative. Ultimately only a mild resolution was carried, to the disappointment of those who hoped to mobilize the potential funds and organization of the unions. Repudiating any far-reaching ambitions, the Congress rejected any specific course of action in regard to labour representation, voting to leave each delegate to adopt whatever policy he believed appropriate for his locality.[40]

The efforts of the London Trades Council to transform the TUC into an industrial federation were as unsuccessful as its proposal to disband the Parliamentary Committee had been the year before. The delegates approved the idea of federation – it was always easy to endorse general principles – but felt that local trades councils should decide whether to implement such a policy. With the adoption of its standing orders and the growth of a Congress tradition, there was resistance to any effort to uproot the existing pattern. As with many such institutions, it developed its own internal stability and rejected designs for fundamental changes, especially when they came from groups of such equivocal loyalty as the London Trades Council.

The delegates decided to increase the size of the Parliamentary Committee, this time from nine to eleven. Just before the voting Coulson and Howell found themselves embroiled in another open quarrel. The Bricklayers' Secretary questioned Howell's eligibility for re-election since he was not attending the Congress as the representative of his new union, the Manchester Unity.[41] Howell retorted that he had been a member of the Manchester society ever since the Nottingham Congress and accused Coulson and his London Order of unwarranted harassment of the Manchester bricklayers.[42] Unlike their previous disputes, the two men were now fighting in safe Howell territory. As Secretary of the Parliamentary Committee, he had become a popular and respected T U C figure – especially after Leeds – and when Coulson rose to reply to Howell's charges, he was shouted down. Partly as a result of this ill-timed intervention, Coulson found himself at the bottom of the poll in the Committee elections. Howell tied for second place with 105 votes, behind A. W. Bailey of Preston, but ahead of Odger, MacDonald, Guile, Allan, Broadhurst, and Joseph Arch, the leader of the agricultural labourers, a newcomer to the T U C.[43]

Although Coulson's attack at Sheffield failed, Howell found these challenges to his position intolerable and vented his outrage in a letter to J. D. Prior: 'As to Coulson's slanders and lies, I don't know what I can do unless I put the matter into a lawyer's hand and go in for libel. You see, he mixes up member and delegate in an infamous manner. I never professed to be a *delegate* from the Bricklayers. He knows that. He is simply a scurrilous fellow – one of the Cremer type.'[44]

Howell was even more alarmed by the vindictive campaign which Coulson waged after the Sheffield Congress ended. The London Bricklayers decided to probe more deeply into Howell's affiliation with Manchester. Howell was alarmed lest their investigation uncover the brief lapse in membership after his resignation from the London Order, although such a revelation could hardly have jeopardized his position. Anticipating Coulson's inquiries, he warned the Sheffield branch that 'the Secretary [Coulson] intends asking you for information as to my entry into your lodge. Give him no information whatever for I am considering the propriety of prosecuting the malicious calumniator for libel.'[45] Unwilling to embarrass Howell or to abet the intrigues of his enemy, Houseley refused to furnish Coulson with any information. The London General Council admonished him for being unco-operative and accused Howell of making 'improper and totally untrue charges' against his former union.[46] When the truce between Houseley's and Coulson's men was broken once again in the North, the Manchester society suggested another round of arbitration, naming Howell as their agent. Coulson was willing to be conciliatory, but he would have nothing more to do with Howell. In October he informed the Manchester executive,

We are prepared to meet your members and agents at the earliest convenience and to go into the whole affair, except with Mr George Howell, who has made unfounded charges against our Society. Moreover we remind you that since then we have written to you twice for the date of Mr Howell's entrance into your Society, which you failed to furnish us with. Therefore, we decline to hold any intercourse with Mr G. Howell as your agent.[47]

Although no substantive progress in securing the reform of the labour laws could be reported at Sheffield, the Parliamentary Committee hoped that the Liberal administration was finally beginning to see the need for action. Within ten days of the Congress, however, Gladstone dissolved Parliament. During the ensuing campaign candidates of both parties promised to support measures to alleviate the workers' grievances, and, despite the fact that the few labour candidates, like Howell at Aylesbury, had run as Liberals, the union leaders expected Disraeli to move once he formed his ministry in February. The Parliamentary Committee planned to proceed through familiar channels: sympathetic members would be asked to bring forward motions in the Commons and to introduce private bills if the Government refused to act soon. Howell explained the arrangements to MacDonald, who had been elected for Stafford without Liberal opposition:

We met and decided to get our Bills and work ready. Mundella to take charge of the Criminal Law Amendment Act. You and [Thomas] Burt to back it. Conspiracy to be left to Harcourt, James and others. Masters

& Servants to be consulted on at interviews with Harcourt. You are to be asked to take charge of the Compensation Bill with one or two others.[48]

The new Prime Minister was obliged to make at least a gesture in recognition of the working-class support which had been partially responsible for his victory. He was determined at first to do no more than lay the foundations for future legislation and devised the strategy of yet another Royal Commission to re-examine the laws relating to trade unions. He wanted to pacify opinion by tacitly committing his Government to introduce measures in the future. Frustrated by this evasive approach, the Parliamentary Committee could not help but feel that 'all these preparations and the result of so much work has been dashed to pieces for this session by the appointment of this Commission'.[49] Many feared that Disraeli's diversionary tactics reflected his intention to avoid any legislation at all. The *Daily News* leaked the proposal for a Commission on 12 March, and on the same day Howell was summoned to a secret conference at the House. The Home Secretary, R. A. Cross, had appealed to 'one of our ablest and staunchest friends in the House' to join the Commission, but the unnamed member, who may have been Sir William Harcourt, refused to serve without the consent of Howell and Frederic Harrison.[50] Howell and Harrison, once again working in harmony, dissuaded him from serving on the grounds that all the information necessary for an immediate settlement of the question had already been gathered by the Home Office. The Parliamentary Committee saw the whole plan as a concession to the Federation of Employers, the pressure group agitating against repeal of the contested laws, and denounced it as 'an adroit movement on the part of the present Government for the purpose of closing the lips of our friends in the House and postponing legislative action'.[51]

Disraeli and Cross realized that the Commission would have been rendered innocuous without the inclusion of a recognized friend of labour and approached Crompton, who declined after consulting Howell.[52] Just as Cross was beginning to lose hope, he pulled off a political *coup* which astounded the trade union world. On 18 March Hughes and Burt were invited to join. Cross told them that since he had only a few hours in which to inform the Queen of the nominees, there was clearly not enough time to check with the Parliamentary Committee. None the less, after giving their hasty consent, the two men called on MacDonald. Discussions among the three led to Burt's replacement by MacDonald. At a dinner celebrating their elections to Parliament, neither they nor Hughes made any mention of their having agreed to serve.[53]

When the Commission was announced on 19 March, the Parliamentary Committee felt it had been betrayed by the two renegades. Hughes, indeed, had helped to prepare the resolution condemning the proposal only two days earlier. MacDonald's own position had now become untenable – the Chairman of the Committee which refused to acknowledge the Commission he had just joined. Howell summoned a full Parliamentary Committee meeting for the 20th, at which Hughes and MacDonald were called upon to justify their course of action. They explained that Cross had given them assurances that he would introduce legislation that year if they accepted. Moreover, they felt that if the Government were determined to stage another inquiry, it was in the interest of the movement for them to take part. Unmoved by these excuses, the Committee decided to 'repudiate' the two participants.[54] At this point MacDonald felt obliged to resign his chairmanship. A resolution deprecating the creation of the Commission was reaffirmed, and the Committee recommended that trade unions refuse to give evidence or to co-operate in any way. Hughes, whose ebbing sympathy for trade union demands had been apparent since 1872, was accorded greater hostility than MacDonald, whose lapse of judgement was gradually forgotten.

The Committee decided that its only reasonable course was one of defiance. Mundella agreed to introduce his Bill to repeal the Criminal Law Amendment Act, but the Government succeeded in stifling any legislative activity pending the report of the inquiry, and Mundella's Bill got no further than a preliminary printing. The London Trades Council seized the opportunity to contravene the Parliamentary Committee, and Shipton became one of the few trade unionists to testify. Early in June Francis Bacon, the Commission's Secretary, invited Howell to give evidence, but he declined. In a long letter listing grievances against the existing laws Howell explained his refusal: 'I am of the opinion that no such Commission should have been constituted by any Government without appealing to, and obtaining the consent of, Parliament. Especially in such a case as the present, where the inquiry has been so recent and so full, and where the points at issue are so well known and so fully understood.'[55]

The administration resorted to petty revenge in retaliation for Howell's refusal: they removed his name from the Speaker's List of those entitled to appear in the lobby of the Commons. The easy access, for which he had had to contend in the early years of the TUC, was withdrawn, and he confessed to Mundella,

I must own that I feel deeply hurt. Are publicans, Permissive Bill men, persons representing Church and State, pressmen, and some with their own personal claims to be admitted and the representative of a million unionists to be ordered to withdraw? . . . What am I to do? I can never put foot again in that Lobby without some explanation. I never go to the Lobby unless I have business for I dislike hanging about the House, but when I have business there I do feel that I ought not to be ordered to withdraw unless the Lobby is cleared of strangers.[56]

Mundella, Harcourt, and W. P. Adam, the new Liberal Chief Whip, took the matter up with the Sergeant-at-arms, and, with Gladstone's help, they were able to secure Howell's readmission.[57]

In order to avoid any recurrence of the embarrassing charges which Coulson had levied at Sheffield, Howell attended the Liverpool Congress in January as the official delegate of the Manchester Bricklayers.[58] For the last time he read a Parliamentary Committee report full of recriminations for the lack of official action. The Congress reiterated its regret that 'the obnoxious Criminal Law Amendment Act still remains unrepealed', but the debate rapidly deteriorated into an acrimonious dispute over the Royal Commission and trade union co-operation. Potter felt that 'they had been caught by the Conservative Government, and had been entrapped into a suspension of the decision of Parliament upon this question for an indefinite time'. Such remarks were typical of the leading delegates, more concerned with opposing the principle of another Commission than with condemning labour participation. Men like Howell, with their access to informed Westminster sources, were confident that repeal was imminent and preferred token reproof to a prolonged wrangle which might inflame potential disunity in the movement. The intervention of Cremer, whose penchant for abuse was familiar, prevented the Congress from quietly burying the divisive issue of participation. Once raised, the question awakened latent antagonism between London and provincial delegates – because of the London Trades Council's role – and between the Parliamentary Committee and the rank and file. Cremer claimed that it would be invalid to condemn the Commission because so many delegates were insincere in their opposition. He went on to accuse trade unionists of supporting non-working-class candidates 'who happened to have the needful'. Too many of them were unconcerned with a candidate's views on labour questions – despite the injunctions of the Congress – provided he had sufficient money. Cremer's indictment was exaggerated, but it contained a sufficient grain of truth to arouse the delegates to heights of self-vindication. His allegations were probably grounded in his electoral experience at Warwick, similar to Howell's at Aylesbury, but unsubstantiated charges of bribery and deceit were destined to offend self-righteous delegates.

The implications of his remarks were more complicated than is immediately apparent, since his target was not merely anonymous trade unionists in general, but MacDonald in particular. By rashly throwing out the charge of corruption when attention was focused on MacDonald's supposedly reprehensible behaviour, Cremer seemed to cast aspersions on the probity of the ex-Chairman. Broadhurst complained that Cremer had not only spoken harshly of members of the Congress, but had also attacked the Parliamentary Committee for betraying the trust vested in it by the rank and file. Lloyd Jones and others denied that the accusations could be sustained, and Broadhurst moved for the appointment of a committee to investigate them. Howell warned the delegates to nominate men of standing in order to avoid the appearance of London 'cliqueism' against which the Parliamentary Committee had to defend itself. Exonerating his colleagues and, by association, himself from the taint of Cremer's remarks, he continued,

If there were any man who would sell his interest and position, that man should be pointed out clearly to the delegates and the finger of scorn should rest on him for the future. But as far as [I have] had to deal with the Parliamentary Committee, [I can] only say that I always found the greatest nicety of honour, the greatest anxiety on their part to do their work and to carry out fully and faithfully the instructions of the Congress.

MacDonald defended his conduct with an impassioned plea that refusal to join the Commission would have constituted 'a crime against the action of his whole life', convinced as he was that the Government was bent on this course whether or not he or Burt decided to serve. Both men assured the gathering of their adherence to the principle of repeal.[59]

On the following day the committee of inquiry announced that Cremer had been unable to substantiate any of his allegations. He was then expelled from the meeting – on a motion by MacDonald – and proscribed from any future Congress 'until he has withdrawn the whole foul and unwarrantable charges'.[60] Before the Congress ended, Cremer recanted and was duly forgiven. After motions were carried favouring the extension of the factory acts, workers' compensation, and other legislative perennials, the 1875 Parliamentary Committee was chosen. Howell topped the poll with 117 votes, and most of the other prominent members were re-elected.[61]

The report of the Royal Commission, published in February 1875, disappointed both the trade unions and the Government. With only MacDonald dissenting, the majority had accepted the need for some modification of the existing laws, but they had rejected the broader proposal to repeal the Criminal Law Amendment Act and the Master and Servant Act. Disraeli and Cross recognized that it would be politically suicidal to adopt the limited programme of the commissioners. As in 1867, and once again spurred on by Liberal prodding, a Tory ministry seized the opportunity from which the Liberals had until now recoiled. But, as the Second Reform Bill had shown, the combined pressure of the working classes and Liberal politicians might produce in the end a more radical reform than the Government originally intended.

Howell obtained an advance copy of the report and helped Crompton to prepare an analysis of its conclusions which was issued at the same time that the report was made public. Immediately thereafter the Parliamentary Committee enlisted the support of friendly MPs to agitate for more comprehensive legislation than the Commission envisaged. The Committee prevailed upon Cross to receive a deputation, which reaffirmed the trade union insistence upon full repeal. The Home Secretary assured the delegation that the Government planned no further delay and would definitely legislate during that session.[62] On 10 June he introduced the Employers and Workmen Bill and the Conspiracy and Protection of Property Bill, which in their original form offered little more than the Commission report. Agitation was intensified to persuade Liberal supporters to undertake acceptable amendments. Lowe agreed to endorse the Parliamentary Committee's demands and was aided in his efforts by Harcourt, Mundella, and W. E. Forster. While the London Trades Council arranged public demonstrations, Howell kept provincial leaders informed of the Bills' progress.[63]

During the committee stage in July Howell sent out special instructions urging members to support Lowe's suggestions, but Liberal allies needed little prompting in their campaign to win Government concessions. Mundella rejoiced in their success:

It has been the best night for the Liberal party this Parliament. . . . The Tories were confounded and amazed, and we amended their Bills and we abandoned their clauses right and left. The workmen are delighted. . . . Last Friday night [Cross] declared to the workmen's Parliamentary Committee and myself in conference with them that nothing should induce him to *touch* this act. Tonight he has been compelled to re-open the whole question.[64]

Cross refused in the end to be outdone by Lowe or Mundella as the workers' benefactor and consulted Howell, who advised him to submit a new clause dealing with coercion and intimidation. Howell provided him with a draft amendment which had been drawn up by R. S. Wright, a leading parliamentary draftsman, and Cross adopted it as the basis of his revisions.[65] Howell reported these developments at once to Robert Knight, the new Chairman of the Parliamentary Committee:

We have a meeting on Mr Cross's clause today. We are, I assure you, working very hard at it and are consulting all our best friends on the question. Broadhurst and I were in the House for 10 hours and more on Monday watching, consulting, and promoting action. Cross's clause is even better than Lowe's clause. We want one or two words added which I hope will solve the whole difficulty. The whole debate in Committee was very satisfactory. Everyone vied with the other to do the best thing. Cross deserves our warmest gratitude for his conscientious work.[66]

On 16 July Cross moved his new clause repealing the Criminal Law Amendment Act and, with the addition of further alterations by Mundella and others, the new provisions were added to the Bill, which passed both Houses and was signed into law in August.

The years of struggle and frustration had been vindicated. Both the Criminal Law Amendment Act of 1871 and the Master and Servant Act of 1867 disappeared from the statutes. The new Conspiracy and Protection of Property Act established acceptable limits to the liability of workmen for the charge of conspiracy. Henceforth actions of two or more persons in the course of a trade dispute would be liable to criminal penalties only if the same actions would have been criminal when done by an individual. Moreover, the Act sanctioned peaceful picketing, eliminating the vague terms 'molest' and 'coerce' from the law. It continued to penalize violence and intimidation but interpreted these terms more judiciously. The Employers and Workmen Act finally provided legal equality between masters and workers in breach of contract disputes. The two measures, as Howell noted in his annual report, 'conceded all, and more than all, the demands made by successive Congresses'.[67] Indeed, as G. M. Young has written, 'it might fairly be questioned whether any measures ever placed on the Statute book have done more for the real contentment of the people'.[68]

With his most important task now successfully completed, Howell was eager to resign his position as Secretary of the Parliamentary Committee. The constant strain of long hours in the lobby of the House of Commons and of endless meetings and correspondence had undermined his health. Neuralgia and recurrent eye inflammations plagued him during 1875, and his anxiety was increased by the serious illness of his son in the winter of 1874-5. He was also discouraged by the personal enmities and frequent battles which disrupted the annual meetings. 'I feel unequal,' he told Wright, 'to the task of patching up eternally these dissensions. I have lost Allan, Guile will go, and I shall be very much alone.'[69] Crompton and MacDonald urged him to stay on, but Howell's decision was final. The rewards for his taxing labours had never been financial – at the end of his tenure he was receiving £3 10s per week – and he probably felt it an opportune moment to reap the dividends of his hard-won prestige in more profitable work, whether in journalism or politics. 'You are aware,' he informed MacDonald,

that I would have resigned at Leeds, only I was restrained by you, Allan, and Guile. There will no doubt be a scramble for the place, and it will be a sinecure in comparison to what it has been. I have to pay £60 a year out of my salary for the offices, and I have to work at night and day, Sundays included, to keep pace with my work. But then it has been a labour of love, my satisfaction is in its success.[70]

At the Glasgow Congress in October Broadhurst was elected as his successor, a choice which guaranteed the perpetuation of that policy of collaboration with Liberalism which Howell had engineered during the early years of the TUC. After the election of the new Secretary, Knight carried a unanimous vote of thanks to Howell for his six years of service to the Congress and proposed a testimonial fund as an expression of the gratitude of the entire movement.[71] Howell privately observed that the subscriptions were a means of compensating him for insufficient wages. 'The fact is,' he remarked, 'when they began to look at the remuneration given to me for over seven [sic] years' work as Secretary to the Parliamentary Committee, they found that I had not been receiving £50 [per year] for the long and anxious work given in their service.'[72] Broadhurst solicited contributions from affiliated unions and prominent friends of labour, and his personal efforts were aided by the editorial support of the *Bee-Hive*.[73] The Congress report carried an appeal which described the retiring Secretary in laudatory terms:

Few national organizations have possessed such able secretaries as the trades unionists of Great Britain have had in Mr George Howell. A man of cultured mind, he is a ready writer, a keen debater, a rare initiator and executor of business, and to him along with the various members of the Parliamentary Committee are owing the success of the legislative projects of the Congresses, more than to members of either house of Parliament.[74]

By the time the subscription list closed in September 1876, the committee had collected £250, a sum nearly equal to Howell's personal remuneration during his tenure in office. Heralded by an impressive contribution of £50 from Houseley's Manchester Bricklayers,[75] the fund included donations from Beales, Rathbone, Brassey, Forster, in addition to those from trade societies throughout the country.

Howell's departure amid tributes to 'the honest and able manner in which he performed the arduous and responsible duties of the office, and for his general conduct in public life during the last twenty years'[76] symbolized the end of an era. The pioneers who had created and shaped the Trades Union Congress – George Potter, William Allan, Daniel Guile, Alexander MacDonald and Howell himself – had now all retired from its activities. The resignation of Howell marked the passing of the generation of 1859, the young men from the provinces who had established a network of powerful, financially stable unions and then applied their moderate and conciliatory techniques to the association of trade societies. By 1876 the Congress which they had nurtured had earned a recognized place among the voluntary institutions of the nation. For five years Howell had personified the Parliamentary Committee and, in some ways, the Trades Union Congress itself. It was Howell as Secretary who shaped its policies and who embodied its virtues and failings.

Perhaps what contributed most to Howell's success in office was the nature of his own experience, a factor not to be discounted when considering the bureaucratic innocence of so many trade union leaders of the period. His apprenticeship in the early Radical movements and the intensive practical training of the Reform League secretaryship made Howell in some respects the ideal man to direct a large, but decentralized agitation for legislative reform. He had the time to devote to what became nearly a full-time task, in addition to familiarity with the organization of deputations, petitions, and meetings. What he lacked was the quality of selflessness, the ability to subordinate personal ambition to a cause. One can argue that his willingness to compromise over the repeal of the Criminal Law Amendment Act in 1872 reflected his duplicity or his overriding commitment to his Liberal friends. But in the absence of an actual financial arrangement at the time, it seems more likely that Howell was simply too susceptible to Liberal blandishments, too easily convinced by their estimation of political necessity. If his experience with politicians made him a more effective intermediary, it also made him an excessively pliant one. His confidence shaken by rebellion at the Leeds Congress in 1873, Howell learned to use his skill to better advantage. While the technique remained the same, the aspirations conformed more closely to the prescriptions of the TUC. Howell retained his autonomy in negotiation, but he could no longer try to set the dimensions of success.

Pragmatic, cautious, unresponsive to the more radical currents in the movement, he worked assiduously to promote the interests of trade unionism *as he conceived them*. Lacking any consistent ideological viewpoint on the relation of classes, he could not imagine the trade union movement as the vanguard of the proletariat. Compromise and concession were not the tools of class betrayal, but the means of securing the limited objectives which Howell and his associates envisioned. Identifying his own career with the progress of the working classes, Howell believed that success was only possible through the benevolent indulgence of bourgeois reformers. They had to be cajoled, implored, and, perhaps occasionally, threatened in order to win the legitimate rights of working men. But massive agitation was dangerous because it could not easily be controlled by trade union leaders and might unleash the submerged revolutionary potential of the labouring class.

Howell was admittedly remote from the rank and file union member. Furthermore, his own vanity made him yield more readily to the schemes of Westminster politicians whose dedication to trade union interests was less than wholehearted. Nor can it be denied that Howell's personal ambitions influenced his behaviour towards Liberal sympathizers. If his methods of parliamentary negotiation were overly accommodating, they reflected his conception of political expediency. Militant tactics helped to capture public attention, but the intricacies of legislative politics demanded more sophisticated techniques. Rightly or wrongly, Howell was firmly convinced that it was essential to press the workers' case in the 'corridors of power'. The almost daily pursuit of MPs and the diligence in administration suited his talents perfectly. He did not modify his approach to appease the politicians or intentionally compromise his constitutents in the hope of material reward for himself; rather his work on the Parliamentary Committee offered new scope within which to practise the skills developed during his term of office in the Reform League.

However narrow Howell's perspectives now appear, his tenure as Secretary was a personal and public success. Gradually but resolutely, he strove to convert men of influence to his cause, impressing them – and himself – with his astute advocacy of labour's demands. While the Reform League was ultimately a secondary factor in achieving franchise extension, the TUC deserves the major share of credit for securing legal protection for trade unionism. At the same time Howell established himself in the forefront of working-class politics. From the young collaborator of the Junta he had risen by 1876 to the role of statesman, secure from the petty intra-Congress squabbles. In his last years as Secretary he had won popularity, repeatedly securing re-election to the Parliamentary Committee near the top of the poll. Yet, his conduct during the TUC years reveal the same personal traits which marked Howell's earlier career: the desire to use his work as a means to social and political advancement, the defensiveness in personal relations, the predilection for the company of his social betters. He had still to learn that his enhanced reputation did not ensure greater success in the future. When he removed himself from the trade union world, he destroyed the basis of his strength. A decade was to pass before he finally won election to Parliament, seventeen years after his first attempt at Aylesbury and five years after his Parliamentary Committee successor, Henry Broadhurst. He continued fitfully to try to make a career for himself in working-class politics, but the most important chapter of his life was over, and he was never again to achieve the prominence he had earned in these years.

9

The Triumph of Respectability

When Howell resigned as Secretary of the Parliamentary Committee, he could look back on more than fifteen years of service to the labour movement. Still only forty-two, he might justifiably expect that his career had not yet reached its culmination. Although the achievement of his greatest ambition – to win election to Parliament – was still ahead of him, it is clear, at least in retrospect, that 1876 marked the summit of his career, not the threshold of greater success. He remained a useful, if not an essential, man, prominent on innumerable committees, active in organizing meetings, but he would not advance much further. His characteristically mid-Victorian Radicalism, changing little in his later years, became increasingly less relevant to the shifting mood of the labour movement. His values soon appeared archaic and even conservative to a new generation of working-class leaders, yet they were too much a product of his artisan background to facilitate his ascent into the middle class. Howell had neither the opportunities nor the abilities to transcend his relatively humble origins, to transform himself into a proper gentleman. He attained a level of respectability appropriate to his social and professional position: to the moderate trade union leaders and to bourgeois Radicals Howell had become an esteemed figure, but only in the context of working-class politics. He had achieved the status of a labour statesman whose advice on social problems and whose participation in movements was often sought. Men like Samuel Morley and Thomas – soon to become Lord – Brassey regarded him as their special emissary to the workers. But if he participated in the activities of middle-class reformers and relished their favour, he never became one of them, remaining in spite of himself firmly rooted in the world of labour.

As its second term drew to a close, the London School Board became a target for those who disliked its non-sectarian policy. Howell, like many of his former associates in the National Education League, would have preferred a compulsory, secular system to the one instituted under the 1870 Act, but he was 'prepared to give up something in order that the path to a higher, nobler, and better life should be thrown open to the children of the poor'.[1] Morley was equally convinced that Forster's compromise measure was having beneficial effects and launched a London School Board Policy Defence Committee in preparation for the 1876 election. Howell's administrative experience and the range of his London contacts made him the logical candidate for the secretaryship, and Morley, who put up £200 for the enterprise, left him in charge of all organizational details. The Committee did not attempt to select candidates, contenting itself with endorsing those who had pledged themselves to uphold the policy of the Board. Howell organized a working-men's Political Vigilance Committee and assisted local election groups in each of the ten London districts. These efforts resulted in the re-election of all thirty of the approved members, ensuring a favourable majority on the third School Board. Howell's own reward was not confined to the satisfaction he derived from the successful campaign: he received the major share of the £138 appropriated for salaries and office expenses.[2]

In view of his traditional sympathy for Continental nationalist movements, Howell's involvement in the Bulgarian atrocities agitation in 1876–7 was hardly surprising. The protest appealed to him on two counts. First, the moral issue resembled that of the Governor Eyre controversy, on which he had also taken the 'progressive' position, and, second, Radical friends, like Morley, Mundella, and Herbert, were active in the movement. Howell was invited to serve as one of the sixty sponsors of the meeting summoned by the League in Aid of the Christians of Turkey in Willis's Rooms on 27 July 1876.[3] Working-class participation was essential if the movement were to assume national proportions, and whatever prestige men like Freeman, Liddon, and Shaftesbury lent by their adherence, they had little influence over the workers. Once again, Howell's experience in labour politics made him an invaluable confederate.

From July until the Eastern Question Conference in December Howell was 'one of the pillars of the agitation'.[4] In September he

H

took part in a worker deputation to Lord Derby, at which he informed the Foreign Secretary that 'the time had come when the English Government should allay the anxiety that was being displayed as to their policy in the East, and that could only be done by a frank declaration . . . that everything had been done to put a stop to the atrocities'.[5] Howell was eager to rouse the working men, but at the same time he did not want to commit them to any specific policy. He had little faith in Russian intentions, and, in contrast to his attitude at the time of the Franco-Prussian War, did not regard military intervention as a practicable option.[6] Amid conflicting pressures on the working class either to avoid meddling in foreign affairs (a view that Potter adopted) or to rally to the defence of Turkey, Howell felt compelled to provide a cautious, if decidedly pro-agitation, lead. He presided over a working-men's meeting in early October which resolved to form a committee 'for the purpose of obtaining as far as possible a free government for the oppressed provinces of Eastern Europe'.[7]

Howell expounded his non-belligerent, Gladstonian position in a *Contemporary Review* article entitled 'Working Men and the Eastern Question'. In it he defended not only the right of the lower classes to interest themselves in foreign affairs, but also the standards they were likely to apply. 'The great mass of the people,' he maintained, 'look at the questions direct and straight from the moral point of view . . . Prudence, expediency, and diplomacy may have other methods to propose, but the people will judge of them by their sense of justice.' The sound instincts of the working men had been vindicated repeatedly in recent history – in regard to the American war, the Jamaican affair, the extension of the suffrage, and the disestablishment of the Irish Church. The impatience of the people with the equivocations of official policy reflected their outrage at the 'horrible cruelties and despotic rule' of the Turks. While he demanded that the Turks be expelled from Europe, Howell deliberately avoided any war-mongering. The working classes, he insisted, knew that in the event of war they would be 'the first and greatest sufferers'. The risk of rising taxes and scarcity of employment was enough to guarantee their pacific sentiments. The article underlined the persistently anti-imperialist cast of his own Radicalism – a moral 'Little Englandism', derived from the Bright-Cobden tradition, which failed to appreciate the latent chauvinism of the working classes that could be exploited during the Boer War. As an alternative to actual intervention, Howell argued that 'if the English Government were to put their foot down resolutely and firmly, other European Governments would act in concert with them' to impose a just solution. Deprecating the policy of Disraeli, Howell heaped praise on Gladstone, who 'understood and expressed the feeling and impulses of the people'.[8]

The climax of the 1876 agitation was the National Conference on the Eastern Question held in St James's Hall on 8 December. The meeting, which had been organized with expectations reminiscent of the Chartist Convention, proved to be little more than a successful protest rally. Howell, one of the eight hundred conveners and only working-class speaker besides Broadhurst, assured the audience that labour joined the educated classes in opposing war under any pretext on behalf of Turkey. 'What we have to do,' he continued,

is to stand by the other European Powers, and insist with our high prerogative amongst the nations. . . that justice shall be done to these provinces of Turkey, that something more shall be done by Turkey towards her own provinces and her own populations, and to tell her plainly and distinctly if this be not done, at whatever cost, she must pack up bag and baggage and leave Europe.[9]

Howell's credentials as a labour statesman entitled him to take a prominent part in movements like the Eastern Question agitation, but involvement with Radical organizations – as opposed to official duties within them – made inordinate demands on his time without offering remuneration. He was beginning to think that holding office in transitory groups, like the Reform League, was not worth his while whatever the personal and financial rewards. What he most desired was a secure, quasi-governmental job, one which would remove him from the hazards of pressure group politics. To his bitter regret, he was to find that his education and training were a disability and that his well-placed acquaintances did not always rush to intercede in his behalf. When he thought of applying for the post of Inspector of Schools in London, he took the precaution of writing to the Chairman of the London School Board to inquire 'whether it would be considered essential for the candidate to have had a university education, as I cannot boast of this and should not like to compete if this were one of the conditions'.[10] Sir Charles Reed's reply has not survived, but one can assume that Howell was not encouraged to apply. Yet, there were some official positions to which the Government was anxious to make working-class appointments. The offer of a factory inspectorship to Broadhurst must have rankled, since Howell clearly felt that his own claim took precedence over that of his TUC successor. He none the less decided to seek the job when Broadhurst declined it and urged Crompton to drop 'a kind word' in the right places for him:

I have determined to try for the appointment, as I think I have earned the right of such a position being offered to me. For over 20 years I have worked as hard as most men for the Liberal Party, without fee or reward, and often at great sacrifices and I think they might remember me now. . . . I have never made known how I was harassed while working night and day for the Unions, but my time was a hard time of it both for work and pay. I write thus privately to you, but not to make known my own privations, severe as these have often been while pleading for better terms and conditions for other people. As a matter of fact I am not so well off today as I was when I left my trade in 1864 [*sic*] to work for public questions.[11]

The appointment, however, went to J. D. Prior, and Crompton tried to console the disappointed office-seeker by writing, 'You know that in politics gratitude for past efforts finds no place'.[12]

Howell's resentment found expression in fulminations against the unappreciative politicians. 'The Liberals as a party,' he complained to John Holms, 'seem too poor to help their workers in the way of employment, or else some of us, at least I for one, have never been able to get into the stream, and the general movements which I have had in hand have barely sufficed for a mere existence'.[13] He resorted to a dignified form of begging, soliciting middle-class backing for various unpromising schemes. The letter to Holms mentioned the possibility of his subsidizing a parliamentary agency which Howell concocted, but nothing came of the project. At the same time he attempted to start a 'General Business Agency', which would collect rents, sell real estate, and handle property valuations. 'If I get ever so little here,' he told Beales, 'it will be my own and will I hope grow for the benefit of my son, who is now able to help me in my work.'[14] Although some business materialized, Howell never quite learned the lesson of his earlier experience with building societies: unless he could ensure reason-

able capital investment, such ventures were destined to fail. June
found him once again pleading for contributions:

I am just now in straitened circumstances, and a little help would
place me on my feet and enable me to establish a little business which in
the future would give me a living. No one can dislike begging more than
I do. It seems to me a very dreadful thing, but I have the satisfaction of
knowing that I am not placed in this position through any extravagance
or fault of my own. I am not a lazy man. In fact I like work and am
always at it, but most of it is gratuitous labour and that for which I have
been paid has not been either permanent or remunerative. . . . I feel sure
that there are many who would help me if they only knew, but I have
tried to keep things respectable and never allowed anyone to know how
severe the struggle has been.[15]

In November 1878 Potter's newspaper, which had changed its
name from the *Bee-Hive* to the *Industrial Review* at the beginning
of 1877, was on the verge of collapse. Howell had been a frequent
contributor since 1871, and Potter invited him to help salvage the
weekly. If he could manage to raise £150, Howell would become a
co-partner with full editorial control. He appealed to Frederick
Pennington, the wealthy merchant and MP for Stockport, to help
him purchase the half interest, assuring him,

I would not have troubled you if I did not believe that I can again
serve the cause to which for 25 years I have been devoted. Pray pardon
me for asking you. I have never before begged for myself, and even now
I hope to be able to return it in the shape of honest work for the Party,
to whose interest you are so devotedly attached.[16]

Pennington showed no inclination to swallow the bait: the Liberal
Party might have derived some advantage from the support of a
viable working-class journal, but the *Bee-Hive* had been a losing proposition for nearly a decade. Once this last appeal had been denied,
the newspaper was doomed and ceased publication at the end of
the year. Pennington did, however, commend Howell to his wife,
whose endorsement led to his appointment as Parliamentary Agent
for the National Society for Women's Suffrage.[17] His services
during the nine months before his dismissal were chiefly those of a
lobbyist, attempting without success to convert MPs and candidates
to the women's suffrage programme. His Liberal contacts were
useful in this work, but the results seemed to convince the women
that they could easily dispense with the services of an agent.[18]

Failing to find steady employment, Howell turned increasingly to writing as a source of income. In 1876 he had privately published *A Handy Book of the Labour Laws*, a popular guide to legislation of the 1870s, with which he had been so intimately involved. The work summarized each of the laws in terms comprehensible to unsophisticated readers and was well received by the Press.[19] Sold chiefly to trade union branches, it went through two editions of 2,000 each in the first year, but its low price and the considerable expense of publication left Howell with only £15 in profit.[20] The favourable reception accorded the *Handy Book* encouraged him to embark on a full-scale study of trade unionism. *The Conflicts of Capital and Labour Historically and Economically Considered* occupied much of 1877 and was finally published by Chatto & Windus early in 1878. The book, dedicated to Samuel Morley, traced the supposed evolution of trade unions from medieval craft gilds, a theory subsequently discredited by the Webbs.[21] Howell then proceeded to examine the constitutions of unions, their relevance to theories of political economy, their relationship to friendly societies, and the problems of apprenticeship, picketing, and strikes. Despite impressive research and interminable statistics, the book, written in an exceedingly turgid style, had little lasting merit except as an expression of trade unionist self-consciousness. It sold extremely poorly, but Howell received £105 from his publisher for it, as well as £40 for the two chapters published, on Morley's recommendation, in the *Contemporary Review*.[22]

Hoping to take advantage of the growing audience for popular literature, Howell tried his hand at fiction as well. The commercial market for scenes of rural life was large, and he drew upon the experiences of his Somerset childhood in a series of exemplary tales with titles like 'The Typical Farmer' and 'Radical of the Village'. Howell exhibited neither aptitude nor imagination in these cloyingly sentimental portraits of honest farmers and sturdy artisans. Although most of them appear to have been rejected by the better periodicals, such as *All the Year Round*, to which at least one was offered, some may have found their way into obscure temperance magazines.[23] Among the published pieces was 'Only a Workman! – A Life Sketch', a thinly disguised account of his friend Charles Bartlett's career. The hero, renamed Charley Bradley in the story, is portrayed as 'a man who quietly and without affectation plodded on and on, neither sighing for public recognition, nor seeking personal reward'. The author praised his devotion to 'books instead of beer', but he partly blamed Bradley's 'retiring disposition' for his failure to find a career in which he could take advantage of 'the fulness of his mind, and his solid acquirements in general literature, and in some branches of natural science'. In a particularly self-revealing observation Howell noted that Bradley may have lacked 'the necessary energy' to advertise his talents and 'thereby ensure recognition'. This deficiency notwithstanding, the moral of Bradley's life was clear: 'If the working classes only knew one half of the pleasure to be derived from [literature], they would discard smoking and drinking, avoid music-halls and haunts of vulgarity and vice, and instead thereof contrive to form a library at home for their own use and that of their families.'[24]

In February 1877 the German Consul in London informed Howell that his government was planning to introduce labour reforms and invited him to prepare a report on their effect in England. Howell agreed to do it if he were paid for his work, and for the next two months he pieced together material on trade unions, wages, apprenticeship, and hours of labour from the information he was using in *Conflicts of Capital and Labour*.[25] He hoped to demonstrate that 'so far from [labour legislation] being a dangerous experiment, it will be most advantageous in a political sense for it will produce a kind of reaction against what I consider the dangerous nostrums of the socialists'.[26] On 5 May he turned the report over to the Consul, receiving twenty guineas for his efforts.[27] Later in the same year he performed a similar service for Brassey, furnishing him with information about the rise of wages in the building trades since 1847.[28]

Howell found time during this interval of intense research to explore new areas of study. Crompton was pleased to discover that he was at last reading Comte. Offering to lend any books in the Positivist Library, he wrote, 'If you become practically one of us, no one would welcome you more than I should.'[29] Howell had always been closer to him than to either Beesly or Harrison, and Crompton reciprocated the esteem:

I was always sure that if you had only leisure, your mind would, if you read Comte, converge with our minds, on the great questions and leading features of Positivism. . . . I should value your adhesion – partly from personal motives – but chiefly because I think you would have the noblest career before you – and that you would be a most powerful help.[30]

Although Howell's exposure seems to have been brief, he embarked on his Positivist studies with great earnestness. He also regarded Crompton as a friend to whom he could turn in his bereavement over his son, George Washington Taviner, who died in August 1880:

I have lost my dear boy whom you have often seen when you have called on me. He was within a month or two of 21 years of age. We had become inseparable companions, so strong was the bond of sympathy between us, as well as of affection. We read together, conversed, discussed, planned. What I lacked in culture and scientific training, I hoped to have been able to make up by his help. How much I miss him no pen or words can tell. It has been his health – or rather want of it – that has kept me so much at home of late. We had been reading and discussing together on Comte often these last few months.[31]

Howell worshipped his only son, seeing in him the probable fulfilment of his grandiose plans. In an unpublished memoir of the boy, an extraordinary testament of grief, he extolled his flawless character and prodigious scholarship. From his earliest years books 'were part of the atmosphere he breathed and they filled his soul as with a perfume'.[32] This portrait of unremitting intellectual effort scarcely accords with the impression conveyed by the boy's own diaries, from which he emerges as a far more conventional, rather pompous and priggish young man. Moderately intelligent and eager for self-improvement, he seems to have been somewhat frivolous and lacking in purpose – a far cry from the ardent student of his father's wistful imagination. His death was the great tragedy of Howell's life. Not only did it deprive him of the focus of so much affection, an emotion perhaps all the stronger for its concentration on the boy; it also dispelled all hope of vicarious success through his son's career.

Although he was unlikely to shift his political allegiance, Howell continued to worry in the late 1870s about Liberal unresponsiveness to the challenge of the mass electorate. It was bad enough for its leaders to have disregarded his own claims on their gratitude; they seemed no more concerned to satisfy the grievances of the working classes.

I regret to say [he wrote Goldwin Smith] that the Liberals not only did not help us in our great labour battles but they positively threw every obstacle in our way. Of course there were many exceptions, noble and true, but the majority were as I have described.

There is much that is good in the great trade organization of this country; it can be utilized and made effective, but the Liberals discourage any effort to bring them into active work. . . . The Tories are doing their best to conciliate the artisan classes, and they will be repaid with the gratitude of those whom they help.[33]

He distrusted the Birmingham scheme for a National Liberal Federation, regarding it as a vote-manipulating device which aimed at strengthening one section of the community – the middle class – at the expense of the workers. 'Its main purpose,' he wrote, 'seems to be the substitution of local discipline for popular force.' Even if it did provide a necessary framework for Liberal Party organization in the country, it would impede working-class candidacies by concentrating local power in the hands of a few activists. Howell feared that the 'caucus' would 'lower the standard of parliamentary representation and reduce the measure of value of all public acts to a purely local gauge'.[34]

The inadequacy of its labour policy and the withdrawal of Gladstone from the party leadership forced Howell at last to question his belief that Liberalism would be the agency of further working-class progress. 'We are drifting into a sad state politically,' he wrote gloomily to Beales, 'and I can plainly see that Socialism will be the outcome unless we can stir up a healthy programme.'[35] Despite the failure of the Labour Representation League either to stimulate working-class insurgency or to revitalize the Liberal platform, Howell began to devise still another organization in 1878 based on Liberal-labour coalescence. In July he sent Samuel Morley a proposal for a National Political Union to 'attract the working classes and help turn back the tide of Conservatism'.[36] Morley was reassuring, but other Radicals, like Bright and John Morley, saw no purpose in proliferating leagues and federations.[37] The most stalwart advocate of the plan for an avowedly Liberal body in which the middle and working classes could collaborate in preparation for the next election was James Bryce, soon to be elected MP for the predominantly working-class constituency of the Tower Hamlets. Bryce was in contact with Howell and Broadhurst at least from January 1879, encouraging them to launch what would be called the National Liberal League. Bryce wanted the party to commit itself to a Radical, anti-imperialist line in foreign policy, and he felt that, coupled with pledges of domestic reform, it would greatly enhance electoral prospects.

Howell drafted a prospectus for the League, which he and Broad-hurst submitted for Bryce's approval.[38] While canvassing for supporters, Howell, who was to become Chairman of the new body, cautiously approached Samual Morley about a very different proposition:

Your reference today to the work done in the constituencies in 1868 emboldens me to revert to that work for a moment. You will recall that I had the management of that special fund, or rather the responsibility of it, for being under a committee of an association, it became very diffi-cult to manage. Now I would venture to suggest to you that a small committee of three or five who should be directly responsible to you for the money spent, and the way it was spent, would be better than any association for *that special work*. An association would have plenty to do in another way, such as by propagandism, lectures, meetings, publica-tions, etc. But the committee of whom I speak would be able to do good and useful work in a quiet way, the same as they did in 1868. . . . I shall be very happy to place myself in your hands to aid, direct, work or do whatever you assign me, and I hope that my past character, as well as experience, will serve to guarantee for the manner in which whatever duties I have to undertake will be discharged.[39]

It is not clear whether Howell foresaw the 'small committee' as a complement to the League or as a substitute for it, but, in any case, Morley, wary of another privately-financed undertaking, rejected the suggestion.

A series of public meetings in July and August 1879 launched the League with Broadhurst as Secretary, and William Morris, a recruit to Radical politics during the Bulgarian agitation, as Treasurer. The Provisional Committee included the Reverend Stewart Headlam, who had founded the Guild of St Matthew two years earlier in Howell's future constituency, Bethnal Green. The objects of the new body were the promotion of constitutional reform, the assertion of parliamentary control over the power to make treaties and declare war, 'a firm resistance to the spread of a degrading Imperialism, and a persistent opposition to the continu-ance of a mischievous foreign policy, at once demoralising and aggressive'. Such features were merely an expression of Liberal retrenchment, a reaction against the more extravagant aspects of Tory rule. The programme itself called for the extension of the suffrage to the counties on the same basis as in the boroughs, the revision of the land laws, local self-government, Church disestablishment, and tax reduction.[40] These were certainly principles on which the middle classes and the labour leaders could agree; what was missing was a programme of social reform geared to working-class needs.

The National Liberal League was, in fact, one more attempt to enlist working-class voters in the Liberal cause and to spread the Radical creed. It created even less of a stir than the Labour Representation League, and the few surviving reports of meetings indicate that its leaders were preoccupied with propaganda. By the following April Howell was complaining to Broadhurst that the organization would never get off the ground without an infusion of new money and the cultivation of a mass following.[41] Neither of these conditions for success materialized, and there is no evidence that the League played a significant role in the 1880 election. A committee appointed in April 1880 to assess its prospects decided that it would be to the advantage of the Liberal Party to continue operations, but the League disintegrated by 1882.[42]

In spite of his initial enthusiasm, Howell was too busy pursuing his own career to devote much attention to the League. In June 1878 the Greenwich Liberal Association had broached the subject of his standing for election in that constituency. His working-class background seemed to be an obstacle, and such misgivings as it aroused were not allayed by his refusal to answer questions about his religious beliefs. Reassuring the local leaders that his political views were inoffensive, he wrote, 'I cannot quite see in what sense I can be considered an extreme Liberal. The man who is more moderate than I am must be a weak-kneed Liberal indeed.'[43] In the end, the Greenwich Association refused to adopt him. The possibility of a candidacy in Kidderminster arose in 1880, but certain local interests were not well-disposed to him, and arrangements for his nomination were not made until it was too late to stand.[44]

In the meantime Howell had started working as London business agent for Ellis Lever, a Manchester coal merchant, a position he held until 1885. His duties were rather ill-defined, and there are intermittent complaints in his diary about not having enough work to do. He was obliged to make frequent trips to Manchester and went on a tour of Ireland with Lever in May 1882. Howell also helped him try to start a National Fatal Accidents Insurance Company in 1880, did research for him on accident statistics, and wrote several articles subsequently published under Lever's name. The position apparently paid at least £5 per week, leaving him with ample time for other activities.[45]

Howell's journalistic output increased in these years, with articles in *Social Notes*, the *Statist*, the *Citizen*, and the *Labour Standard*. In September 1880 the Reverend Henry Solly, whom Howell knew through the Working Men's Club and Institute Union, invited him to co-operate in launching a new labour weekly, *Common Good*.[46] The paper, a characteristically meliorist Solly project, stated as its aim 'the promotion of a better understanding and more mutually profitable relations between Capital and Labour'.[47] Once it had been constituted as a limited liability company, Howell was offered the job of Secretary, but he was reluctant to get involved:

I am afraid [he wrote Solly] that the post you offer me would not be of such a character as I could accept. In the first place I am not in a position to work and wait and depend on future results. I have to win my *daily bread* from week to week and cannot afford to await something in the future which may not come. Often and often I have done so, and have lost more than I care to say, and have learnt some terrible lessons.[48]

Solly made some arrangement as to stipend, and by December Howell was listed as Secretary, becoming co-editor in January.[49] His participation did not guarantee success, and by early February the newspaper's managers resolved to close it down. As usual, Howell hated to see any venture with which he was associated destroyed by financial pressures. Again and again during his career he had to watch promising – and often personally advantageous – projects disintegrate for lack of funds. As he remarked to Solly,

I think the Directors were most unwise in their determination to wind up the Company.... After all what is a deficit of £35 or £40 in a Journal account of this kind, especially with Ads coming in as they now are. If we could only find some enterprising man with a few hundreds to spare *as an investment* I believe that the Journal would pay in a comparatively short time.[50]

After its twentieth issue, on 19 February, *Common Good* was absorbed by the more successful businessman's paper, *Capital and Labour*. Howell ostensibly joined its staff to represent the working-class interest but, except for an occasional article, had virtually nothing to do with the publication.[51] He did take an active part, however, in the management of the *Labour Standard*, a working-class newspaper controlled by Shipton and Broadhurst. This weekly, the true successor to the *Bee-Hive*, lasted from 1881 to 1885.

The vacancy created by the death of Alexander MacDonald, MP for Stafford, on 31 October 1881 presented Howell with the chance for a contest in which there was a stong likelihood of victory. The veteran miners' leader had been one of three labour candidates to be elected in 1880, and it was therefore agreed that the local working men's committee should have the right to select the candidate to succeed him, as long as he was acceptable to the moderate Liberals in the borough.[52] At the instigation of the *Labour Standard* and with the encouragement of Liberal Party officials, Howell was invited to stand. In an election address issued on 9 November, he emphasized his dedicated service 'to the cause of Progress and to the interests of the Working Classes of this country'. At the same time his platform was moderate, focusing on land reform, the extension of local self-government, the reduction of taxation, and, more vaguely, 'equal and just laws for Ireland'. 'On all questions of general policy,' he added, 'I am a devoted follower of Mr Gladstone.'[53]

In his first public meeting in Stafford on the 10th Howell summed up the Liberal policy as 'order and progress', a phrase hardly likely to commend itself to dissident Irish and Radical elements. He refused to commit himself on the controversial Coercion Act, insisting simply that the Liberals only applied 'the strong arm of the Law' when the situation demanded it. A local alderman, seconding a resolution of support, declared that Howell 'brought with him a reputation which perhaps no other man who had sprung from the ranks of the people presented in the country today, because he had emancipated himself from the control [*sic*] which surrounded too many of them, particularly the class from which he sprang'.[54]

Howell's candidacy was immediately hailed by the *Labour Standard* and accorded sympathetic coverage by Liberal papers like the *Daily News*. For the first time he was fighting an election with the complete backing of the Liberal Party. But he was to find himself the target of a defamatory campaign exceeding anything he had experienced at Aylesbury. The Land League, smarting under the effects of the Coercion Act and the recent imprisonment of Parnell, used the by-election as an occasion to denounce the Liberal Government. Its local branch issued a manifesto full of invective:

[Howell] is a viper, and therefore take him not into your bosom. Despise him, scorn him, contemn him! Leave him at the poll with the odium and disgrace due to himself, his master, and his cause, and thus show Mr Gladstone, the chief slanderer of Ireland, and Mr Hypocrite Forster that tyranny and despotism can neither appal nor enslave a heroic and united people.[55]

To the candidate's misfortune, the attack was not confined to the scurrilous Irish. A testimonial had to be obtained from the Reverend John Oakley absolving Howell from the charge of atheism. In addition, two agents of the Fair Trade League, an association of landlords and capitalists favouring the reimposition of tariffs, conducted a campaign of vilification, alleging that he had misappropriated money from the Gas Stokers' Fund in 1872. They were referring to sums which had, in fact, been donated to the Parliamentary Committee and the Plimsoll Fund, but the money had not gone into Howell's own pocket. He refuted these charges and rebuked his Tory opponent for consorting with such disreputable characters.[56] The two agents, Thomas Kelly and a man named Peters, were probably behind a handbill distributed throughout the borough labelling Howell as 'the mere puppet of the Reform Club and the political wire pullers'.[57] More serious was a hostile editorial in the *Radical*, in which Francis W. Soutter denounced him as ill-equipped to succeed a true champion of the labour interest. Howell, he declared, was a man 'whose general demeanour was that of a respectable middle-class mediocrity' and whose principal motive was the desire for personal profit. He cited Howell's article on the International as proof of his 'Judas-like virtue – the love of the money-bag', since 'no representative of labour should have done the dirty work of the capitalists'.[58]

Howell's professions of his Gladstonian faith may have harmed his chances, although it is clear that the Irish, at least, were unalterably opposed to any candidate standing as a Liberal, whatever his political views. In the 19 November poll Howell received 1185 votes to 1482 for the Conservative, Thomas Salt. The *Labour Standard* attributed his defeat to several factors: the opposition of the Irish and the publicans, Liberal abstentions over Afghanistan and the Transvaal, the popularity of the local candidate, and the 'gross personal attacks by Tory hirelings'.[59] The local newspaper, on the other hand, blamed 'the lack of enthusiasm of working men for the candidate'.[60]

During the period from 1882 to 1885 Howell was less active politically than he had been at any time during the previous twenty years, devoting himself chiefly to journalism and his work for Ellis Lever. But after Hackney was divided into seven new constituencies in 1884, he was approached about the possibility of his standing in one of the two Bethnal Green divisions.[61] The procedure for selecting a candidate was complicated by the separate organization of local Liberal and Radical clubs, a phenomenon common to many London constituencies in the 1880s.[62] Preliminary negotiations lasted for five months, Howell first seeking the endorsement of the United Radical Club and subsequently that of the Bethnal Green Liberal Association. On 17 June he was adopted for the North-East division. In contrast to his earlier ventures at Aylesbury and Stafford, Howell had ample time in which to 'nurse' his constituency: between February and the 25 November poll he addressed several dozen meetings and canvassed voters.[63] Hamilton Hoare, a Liberal banker, started a subscription fund to pay his election expenses, to which Samuel Morley donated £200 and Brassey £50.[64] Howell's election address, somewhat more advanced than prevailing Liberal policy, was singularly lacking in social content. Although Bethnal Green was one of the poorest boroughs in England, its prospective member offered no solutions for the problems of housing and unemployment. To the traditional Radical nostrums of land tenure reform, non-intervention, reduction of taxation, and triennial Parliaments, he added only proposals for the equalization of poor rates, a system of elective government for London, Church disestablishment, and the abolition of a hereditary House of Lords.[65] With Liberal domination of London still secure and partisan sentiment in the borough running high, his tepid programme proved no obstacle to victory with a comfortable majority of 1251.[66] Finally, after three unsuccessful election contests and numerous abortive attempts Howell had achieved his lifelong ambition, but the event was not as dramatic as victory in 1868 would have been. Ten other working men, most of them miners, were elected in 1885, the beginning of a substantial 'Lib-Lab' contingent in the House of Commons.

The only disturbing incident in an otherwise uneventful contest was the circulation of a placard reiterating the Gas Stokers' Fund allegations. Mixing half-truths and invective, Patrick Kenny, its author, insinuated that Howell had personally misappropriated some of the funds intended for the gas stokers' families, citing particularly the money paid to the Parliamentary Committee and the Plimsoll Fund. Kenny did his research quite thoroughly, uncovering, for example, the lapse in Howell's union membership in 1871. On the other hand, he accused Howell of misrepresentation for stating in Stafford that he had worked as a shoemaker during his early life. Denouncing him as an 'intriguer' and a 'renegade', Kenny urged the electors to reject the Liberal candidate.[67] Immediately after the election Howell took criminal action against Kenny for libel. During the Old Bailey trial in January Howell denied having received any money himself from the fund, insisting that the sums voted to the Parliamentary Committee and the Plimsoll movement were appropriated after payments had been made to the gas stokers and their families.[68] Kenny's defence counsel admitted that there were mis-statements in the alleged libel, but he maintained that the charges were substantially true. 'It was that system of terrorism,' he asserted, 'which prevented discussion at all Mr Howell's meetings during the Bethnal Green election that forced Kenny to do what was his undoubted right – to inform the electors as to certain matters of public interest.'[69] To Howell's shock and dismay, the jury found Kenny not guilty.

His first term in Parliament was exceptionally brief, coinciding with the introduction and defeat of Gladstone's Home Rule Bill. In June 1886 the Prime Minister dissolved Parliament, and less than eight months after his first contest Howell once again faced his constituents. His election address hardly differed from his previous one, although he now endorsed 'the proposal to give Ireland a Domestic Legislature, with the right to manage her own Local affairs'.[70] None the less, his contribution to a brief collection of essays entitled *The New Liberal Programme* indicated his belief that other questions should be pressed more energetically. The settlement of the Irish issue, he argued, 'must of necessity await events', and the appropriate policy for the present would be 'masterly inactivity'.[71]

One of these questions which Howell took in hand after his re-election was the simplification and amendment of the laws relating to parliamentary elections. The Bill which he introduced unsuccessfully in every session from 1886 to 1895 called for the substitution of simple residential manhood suffrage for all existing franchises, with the necessary term of residence reduced to three months. He also proposed that the duration of Parliaments not exceed three years and that election expenses be charged to the Consolidated Fund.[72] The cry of 'one man – one vote', long a Radical tenet, would soon be included in the Newcastle Programme, but most of Howell's suggestions were treated with disdain by the party leaders. On the other hand, his appeal to the Government to sponsor publication of a working-man's edition of the Statutes bore immediate fruit. The Statute Law Committee, under Lord Thring's leadership, took up the idea, and in 1887 the plan for a cheap edition was approved, prompting the passage of several consolidation Bills to discard obsolete regulations and to bring the Statutes into conformity with contemporary practice.[73]

Howell made his early parliamentary reputation largely as a 'muckraker'. When rumours of fraud in the Cardiff Trustee Savings Bank began to circulate in 1887, he prodded the Government to set up an inquiry which led to legal proceedings against the defaulting trustees and the recovery of much of the depositors' money.[74] Howell was also one of the instigators of the Select Committee's investigation into charges of malversation by the City Corporation. The Committee's findings disclosed that the Corporation had spent nearly £20,000 in organizing opposition to the proposals for elective government in London.[75] In 1889 Howell carried a Merchant Shipping Bill regulating the load-line on ships and in 1892 a measure to secure the inspection of provisions on all vessels undertaking foreign voyages. Samuel Plimsoll, who had resigned from the House in 1880, employed him as his principal spokesman on Bills for the improvement of seamen's conditions.[76]

Despite these accomplishments, it would be wrong to depict the Member for NE Bethnal Green as either influential or inordinately diligent. For the most part he was content to follow the dictates of the London group in the Commons, refraining from an independent role as a labour champion. He was hampered in the performance of his duties by the need to make a living, having no income except that derived from journalism, although he did accept a position with the National Home Reading Union in 1889–90.[77] At the suggestion of H. O. Arnold-Forster, Howell was engaged by Cassells to edit the *Imperial White Books*. Intended as a long-term project, these volumes were a compilation of summaries of official papers and parliamentary speeches. It was the ideal job for Howell, involving laborious examination and abridgement of a vast quantity of documentary material. After four volumes had been published between the end of 1886 and the beginning of 1888, for which Howell had been paid £160, Cassells decided to abandon the unprofitable enterprise.[78]

With the spread of militant, class-conscious 'new unionism' in the late 1880s, Howell's writings assumed a more polemical character. His animosity was aroused less by the aggressive trade policies of these bodies or by their inclusion of unskilled labourers than by their advocacy of socialist measures. It was their demand for a statutory eight-hour day which, in Howell's view, epitomized the dangerous tendencies in the movement. Decrying its endorsement by the Liverpool TUC in 1890, he warned that

we shall be plunged into a whirlpool of turmoil, until the workmen of England have awakened from the fascinating dream that the State can do everything for the individual, and do it better than he can for himself. But it will pass away, like many another dream. Self-reliance and self-restraint are characteristics of our race; these qualities, supported and sustained by associative effort, will triumph in the future as they have in the past, to the discomfiture of social innovators who know not whither they are tending or wending their way.[79]

Earlier that year Thomas MacKay invited him to contribute to a collection of essays 'of an anti-socialistic nature'. MacKay denied that the project emanated from the Liberty and Property Defence League, although he admitted that its sponsors were 'more or less disciples of Mr Herbert Spencer'.[80] In his essay entitled 'Liberty for Labour' Howell tried to distinguish between appropriate areas for state intervention – protection of workers in hazardous occupations, compensation for injury, public health – and those in which legislative action was unwarranted. He condemned a statutory eight-hour day as impracticable: it would be inelastic in application; it would require an army of inspectors to enforce it; it would abolish the possibility of profitable overtime work. Inherent in such regulation was the danger that it might subvert individual liberty. 'The demand for more law,' he concluded in a peroration worthy of Spencer himself, 'indicates a decadence of manhood, an absence of self-reliant, self-sustaining power. It marks an epoch of dependence, the sure precursor of decay in men and in nations.'[81]

Howell continued the indictment in his second major literary work, *Trade Unionism New and Old*, first published in 1892. Its descriptive passages recapitulated material included in *Conflicts of Capital and Labour*, but most of the book was devoted to a comparison of the objectives of amalgamated craft unions and those of new unionism. He conceded that recent developments had infused a new vitality into the movement, but at the same time he castigated the new leaders for 'their persistent, cowardly and calumnious attacks upon the old leaders, upon men who have borne the brunt of labour's battles'.[82] Their reckless and violent strike policy was a throwback to a more primitive form of trade unionism, appropriate only to an era when freedom of association was denied to the workers. The new unions were willing, Howell argued, to turn themselves into 'party political machines', a trend which would assuredly 'destroy their significance and usefulness as industrial associations'.[83] He condemned their demand for state intervention, their propensity towards ill-conceived, costly demonstrations, and their promotion of 'a bastard socialist propaganda'[84] as a sign of complete irresponsibility.

In the evolution of society [he concluded] the Unions will have much to do; they must look after the welfare of their members in the changes that may have to take place. They may also greatly assist in promoting such changes as may lead to beneficial results. But to organize a crusade to promote vast social and industrial changes would involve an abnegation of their present functions, possibly to the detriment of useful reforms, and certainly to the disadvantage of labour.[85]

Similar allegations might well have been levelled against Howell and his associates a quarter of a century earlier, as they sought to enlist organized labour in the movement for political and social reform. What had happened in the intervening years was a steady widening of labour's horizons, a growing disposition to seek collectivist solutions to economic grievances. The assumptions of at least the more advanced elements in late-Victorian working-class politics were diametrically opposed to Howell's Radical creed. It was not that he had grown more conservative, but rather that younger leaders had discarded the ideal of accommodation within a liberal, capitalist society. The aggressive forces in the movement were no longer content with the minimal concessions of a benevolently paternalistic regime. For the new generation, the deferential attitude of their forbears, the sense that working-class progress depended on the indulgence of their social betters, implied a servility incompatible with both the enhanced self-awareness of the workers and the heightened class tensions of the last decades of the century. With his political ideas rooted in the context of the 1860s, Howell found the new militancy completely uncongenial. 'I cannot forgo the convictions of a lifetime,' he wrote in 1892, 'to win temporary applause.'[86] Thus he found himself in the anomalous position of being outside the middle-class Liberal world to which he aspired while becoming increasingly unrepresentative of the new currents in labour politics. His attacks on new unionism provoked the particularly abusive form of retaliation reserved for class traitors. The *Trade Unionist* remarked that 'the spirit [Howell] displays suggests not the seeker after truth or the social reformer, but the petulant manner of a professional advocate who knows that his brief cannot stand daylight'.[87]

Howell toyed with the idea of retiring from Parliament after his second term, but the Bethnal Green Liberal Association prevailed upon him to reconsider.[88] The Liberal central office, responsive to the waning enthusiasm for its programme in working-class constituencies, poured money in to bolster registration, and Arnold Morley urged Howell to take precautions against possible inroads by his rivals.[89] When the contest began in June 1892, three candidates challenged Howell for his seat: Harry H. Marks, the Conservative editor of the *Financial News* and a member of the London County Council, Richard Ballard, an independent running on a Radical-imperialist platform, and Hugh Robert Taylor, the Social Democratic Federation nominee.[90] The *North Eastern Leader* endorsed Howell even though he did not 'entirely meet the views of the Labour leaders'.

He is opposed to an eight hours day by legislation, and in one or two other instances holds independent views; but a great part of his service in the House, it must be remembered, has been for the amelioration of the condition of the working classes. He is a good, sound Radical, and though differing with many because he opines it is impossible for legislation to restrict the hours of labour, he is no doubt far and away the best candidate before the constituency, and in reality a sound friend of the working man.[91]

Defending himself against Taylor's charge that he was a traitor who had fulfilled none of his promises, Howell stressed his record in carrying measures for the benefit of the workers and his commitment to the programme of the London Liberal and Radical Union. 'I have always been present and voted in accord with the promises I made you,' he announced. 'I have never been content with doing the political drudgery of the Party.'[92] The Liberals, anxious to regain the ground that had been lost in London in 1886, offered the Newcastle Programme, a Radical platform calculated to strengthen its appeal among working-class voters. In the July election Howell, assisted by an improved local organization, received 2918 votes for a majority of 597 over his Tory opponent. Taylor secured only 106 votes, but his candidacy, however fruitless, testified to the discontent of the more extreme labour elements with their MP.[93] Moreover, while Howell increased his margin of victory over the 1886 election, the Conservatives too had made progress. In view of the unwillingness of the Social Democratic Federation to work for an independent labour party in the 1890s, it was the ability of the Conservatives to capture a consistently larger share of the working-class vote which posed the greatest threat to Liberal control and to Howell's political survival.

Between 1892 and 1895 he managed to carry a Bill exempting trade union provident funds from the income tax and to work for the further revision of statute law. These were small gains compared to the failure of the Liberal Government to implement the Newcastle promises or to find a solution for the growing unemployment of the 1890s. As Howell later recorded,

The fact is we, as a Party, had got into a helpless and hopeless muddle. We have been raising hopes and expectations which we could never satisfy; we had raised a storm by the variety of interest attacked, or marked out for attack; we were carrying our political trade by show-card and dummies, and there was consequently something like disgust both in Parliament and the country.[94]

In the 1895 election Howell's Tory opponent was an Indian barrister and journalist, Mancherjee Merwanjee Bhownaggree. Despite the ineffectiveness of his local organization – Howell had to act as his own election agent – and the obvious unpopularity of the Liberals, he did expect a fourth victory. When Bhownaggree defeated him by a vote of 2591 to 1431 in a straight fight, he felt hurt and resentful. 'After ten years' hard labour in Parliament,' he wrote Charles Bartlett, 'I was kicked out by a black man, a stranger from India, one not known in the constituency or in public life.'[95] Howell blamed the outcome on the over-confidence of his supporters, his own lack of money, and the opposition of the new unionists, who refused to work on his behalf.[96] In fact, he was suffering the consequences of the Liberal refusal to alter its middle-class, Nonconformist image in response to working-class demands.[97]

In poor health and short of money, Howell had fifteen years of retirement, and obscurity, before him. He withdrew almost entirely from public life, preserving his diminishing strength for his writing. Three years earlier he had been commissioned to prepare a biography of Ernest Jones for £250, but the committee which engaged him abandoned the project without paying him for the effort. Macmillans refused to publish the manuscript, completed in 1896, and Howell was obliged to sell it for serialization in the *Newcastle Weekly Chronicle*.[98] While *Reynolds* and trade journals continued to publish his articles in the years after his election defeat, he was afflicted with failing eyesight and the worsening alcoholism of his wife, who died in 1897. His appeal for a Civil List pension earlier that year had been denied, but Applegarth, now his closest friend, came to the rescue with a testimonial fund in his honour. The subscribers included men with whom Howell had been associated in activities ranging over thirty years – Harrison, Harcourt, James, Plimsoll, Thring, and even Rothschild, and the £1650 which was raised for an annuity served as a welcome tribute to his years of service.[99]

Howell's health and fortunes improved in 1898, and he was able to return to several literary projects, including his memoirs, never completed, a history of the Chartist London Working Men's Association, and his major work, *Labour Legislation, Labour Movements and Labour Leaders*, published by T. Fisher Unwin in 1902. Dedicated to Applegarth, this book was Howell's only significant literary contribution – a comprehensive and partially autobiographical study of the progress of the working classes in the nineteenth century. He found time for several trips to the Continent, usually with the companion of his last years, Mrs Emily Price, and devoted himself to the affairs of the National Liberal Club, to which he had been elected in 1887. Political developments troubled him, but he tended increasingly to restrict his comments to the pages of his diary. Shocked by the jingoism of the Boer War, he was appalled to find that 'the Press, the Pulpit, and the Platform reek with blood'.[100] He could only view the party situation at the time of the 1900 General Election with despair:

My interest is gone so far as party conflicts are concerned for we have no leader, no policy, no cohesion. All are atoms, floating about, often in collision, the impact in some cases being like explosions. There are not 20 who can be said to agree upon leader and policy. This is the Great Liberal Party broken into fragments. . . . The Socialists are nowhere. Their boasted capture of the labour unions and of the Liberal Party is a doleful farce. They also are without a policy – except of brag, and in this respect they are like sick ducks in a farmyard.[101]

He found the campaign pronouncements 'a hash and jumble – worse than an Irish stew' and felt 'really sick of the inanities on all sides'.[102]

In 1900 he was temporarily lured out of retirement to take part in the fiftieth anniversary banquet of *Reynolds*, a curious 'popular front' assemblage, including H. M. Hyndman, Tom Mann, Ben Tillett, George Jacob Holyoake, Applegarth, and Howell.[103] W. M. Thompson, the newspaper's editor, persuaded him to join the provisional committee of his ephemeral National Democratic League, a short-lived attempt to resuscitate the old Radical political platform.[104] In 1904 Howell was stricken with partial blindness, and Applegarth assumed the responsibility for raising money to buy his library, a proposal Howell had first mentioned to Professor H. S. Foxwell in 1899. This second subscription brought in £1100, and the books and papers were deposited in the new Bishopsgate Institute at the invitation of its librarian, Charles W. F. Goss.[105]

In July 1906, at the suggestion of Professor Foxwell, Campbell-Bannerman awarded Howell a Civil List pension of £50 a year 'in recognition of [his] merits as a writer upon labour questions'.[106] With his health deteriorating rapidly, he was soon compelled to give up all of his writing except his weekly 'Industrial Notes,' published in the trade journal *Engineering* since 1889. On 16 September 1910, three weeks before his seventy-seventh birthday, he died at his home in Shepherd's Bush. *The Times* acknowledged his death with the laconic note: 'Mr Howell, who was in his 78th year, was a familiar figure in Labour politics 20 years ago.'[107]

Conclusion

In the search for authentic British working-class heroes, George Howell has, perhaps justifiably, been neglected. There was nothing of the stuff of greatness about him and little enough to warrant the admiration of posterity. From the perspective of our own time the harsh judgement of many of his contemporaries seems more deserved than the encomium of Aaron Watson, a poem which began,

> To have lived for the welfare of others –
> That is the praise that is yours,
> That is what men will remember
> Long after your life has its end.
> To have laboured for men as a man –
> That is the work which endures,
> And the gates will be opened at last
> To the cry of George Howell, a friend.
> And the world will go on, growing better,
> The world which you helped us to mend.[1]

Howell was doubtless a vain, self-important man, lacking either the humility or the noble virtues that might excuse his sometimes less-than-exemplary conduct. Still, he figures in the history of the nineteenth century as one of the principal architects of the English labour movement, a role worthy of rehabilitation whatever his personal failings.

Those who judge working-class history in terms of the progress of revolutionary consciousness tend to dismiss the middle years of the century as a period of regression. After the incipient revolts that followed Waterloo and the Chartist threat of social upheaval, the labour movement seemed to retreat into quiescence before the revival of political and industrial militancy at the end of the century. Yet the loss of heroic vision which marked Howell's generation, the attempt to reach accord with the existing powers rather than to displace them, was not an historical aberration. The tradition was passed on to the modern Labour Party, based on an alliance of middle-class reformers and trade unionists and oriented towards a welfare state. This pattern of social accommodation has, in fact, been characteristic of periods in which economic benefits have been widely diffused, no less of the post-World War II decades than of the era of mid-Victorian prosperity. While the 'New Jerusalem' has survived as a Socialist dream, working men in practice have settled for tangible gains, even if it meant accepting only the half-loaf, and their leaders have sought them through the traditional channels of voluntary associations and Parliament.

Howell belongs to the mainstream of English labour history not merely because of his limited horizons, his striving for the practicable rather than the ideal. He also shared a common tendency among working men to emulate the middle class, to adopt the prevailing social values. If Victorian liberalism, with its stress on individual progress through self-help and the removal of privilege, derived from middle-class experience, it seemed at the same time to offer a valid ideology for upwardly-mobile artisans. Their political attitudes were reinforced by religious sanctions, especially within the Nonconformist *milieu*. Howell identified with men like John Bright and Samuel Morley not only because they represented the kind of success to which he aspired, but equally because, despite the class barrier, he shared a common set of values with them, a common concern with progress through individual effort. No statement better illustrates his social attitudes than a remark in his autobiography: 'I have always found that working men will go long distances for the sake of pleasure; I preferred long distances for self-improvement.' Although characteristically self-satisfied, it provides a good deal of insight into his behaviour. Self-improvement was not merely a moral and intellectual concept to Howell, although his early religiosity, his disdain for frivolous pursuits, and his appetite for knowledge testified to that aspect of it. There was also an economic side, manifested in his social pretensions. His desire to rise above his circumstances stemmed from the same preoccupation with individual progress. Frightened by the perils of working-class life, by the economic reversals that drove working men to lethargy and to drink, he identified progress with respectability, and respectability with a materially-secure position in life. His snobbery towards many of his fellow workers was reserved for those less dedicated to the ideals of advancement through self-help.

That he was insecure and defensive in personal relations, eager to please those who might help his career, reflected not a lack of principle, but rather the tension between his goals and his opportunities. He knew what he was looking for, but he was never quite sure of how it was to be attained.

It was as an organizer and administrator that Howell achieved prominence. From the time he abandoned his trade at the age of thirty-two, he found an avenue for his talents in working-class politics. The extension of democracy and the growth of labour institutions afforded him the opportunity to make a career out of service to his fellow workers. Less an agitator than a professional bureaucrat, he belongs to the tradition of Thomas Hardy and Francis Place, of William Lovett and Robert Applegarth, of Arthur Henderson and Walter Citrine, the men who devoted themselves to the administrative chores of labour politics. In their concern with details, with the endless paper work involved in correspondence and propaganda, they served an essential function without which these institutions could not have survived. The Feargus O'Connors, the Keir Hardies, and the James Maxtons inspired the English workers, arousing within them the indignation from which a political movement could be forged. But it was men like Howell who built the organizations, ensuring that the energies awakened would not be dissipated in futile outbursts of protest. By their industry and dedication they showed that working-class institutions could be managed as efficiently as industrial and commercial concerns. It was not enough for the individual worker to prove himself worthy; the organizations to which he belonged also had to establish their credibility.

His success as an administrator turned Howell into something of an organizational entrepreneur. No longer a craftsman, he was largely dependent on groups like the Reform League and the Trades Union Congress for his livelihood. Once he had mastered the formula, he was continually trying to set up new organizations or to find a position in existing ones. In this way he was able to keep himself at the centre of labour politics for over twenty years, each new association opening up additional possibilities to be exploited. To each he brought the same combination of self-interest and diligence, discovering in the achievements of pressure group politics the means to his own advancement. He found the work congenial, relishing the thousands of letters he had to write, the hundreds of meetings he had to arrange, attend, and address, but, most of all, his contacts with eminent people. Although he was deferential, and at times even fawning, in his relations with them, Howell performed the crucial task of interpreting working-class opinion to men of influence. While he never fully appreciated the power that organized labour might exert, he was an effective exponent of its interests and was instrumental in persuading well-disposed politicians that concessions were necessary.

He discovered in the principles of Gladstonian Liberalism the embodiment of his own personal values, and he looked to middle-class Radicals for political leadership. He accepted as an article of faith that these men were as sincerely devoted to the improvement of the working classes as he was himself. Since he shared their professed goals, he could conceive of no alternative to their methods of bringing about political and social changes. If this meant gradual, piecemeal reforms, then the workers should respond by organizing to promote these reforms and by educating public opinion to recognize their importance. Workers should prove their worthiness by putting forward realistic demands and behaving peaceably, not by mobilizing the discontented elements for an assault on the bastions of power. It was necessary to build bridges to the middle class, not only so that some workers could cross into it, but also to foster greater understanding between classes. Conciliation would lead to concessions, and concessions were a necessary concomitant to self-help. In Howell's view, the ideal of self-improvement never implied that the working class should seek to better its position unaided, but rather in partnership with the more enlightened leaders of the country. In the progress of the nation the role of the workers was as an auxiliary to the champions of reform, not as the vanguard of the revolution.

Howell took pride in his contribution to the progress of the English workers during his lifetime, but he regarded his own career as something of a failure. His expectations of wealth, honour, and position were never realized. He was too greedy for success, too eager to climb out of the working class into bourgeois security. In his last years he came to be discredited as an apologist for Liberalism, and his reputation never revived. In the more militant, class-conscious phase of the labour movement at the end of the century he seemed old-fashioned, his ideas irrelevant to the aspirations of a new generation. However his ambitions coloured his personal conduct, his adherence to Liberalism was genuine. Although he hoped that collaboration with Radical politicians would prove personally advantageous, he believed that it was in the best interest of the working class. Lacking in foresight and imagination, he never moved beyond the values inculcated in childhood. His cautious Radicalism was, in some ways, profoundly conservative, but it reflected the dominant mood of the labour movement before the late 1880s. The faith of men like Howell in the possibility of accommodation within the system acted as a brake on social conflict. As long as the working men trusted to their trade unions and to the traditional leadership to ameliorate their condition, they avoided political disruption, while at the same time imposing restraints on the forces of change.

Notes

1 : *The Making of an Artisan*

1 The only detailed source of information on Howell's early life is his own fragmentary autobiography in manuscript at the Bishopsgate Institute in London. There is a brief article by Aaron Watson, published in *The Millgate Monthly* in August 1908, presumably based either on an interview with Howell or an examination of his papers. In addition, a brief summary of his life was published in the *Weekly Dispatch* on 7 June 1885 as a result of Howell's parliamentary candidacy and was reprinted as a campaign pamphlet. Another sketch appeared in the 'Men of Mark' series, *Reynolds's Newspaper,* 3 February 1895. The article in the *Dictionary of National Biography,* written by J. Ramsay MacDonald, is inaccurate and largely disregards the early years. Although he attempted to re-write it several times, Howell was unable to complete very much of his autobiography. Seven overlapping fragments survive, providing reasonably complete details about the first thirty years of his life. This chapter and the beginning of the next depend chiefly on the narrative which Howell himself provides in order to reconstruct the events of this period. Textual contradictions have been reconciled as much as possible, but, for the most part, I have accepted Howell's own account. Since the fragments follow no practical or consistent order of pagination, citation is virtually impossible, and I have merely noted direct quotations.

2 G. D. H. Cole, *Chartist Portraits*, 2nd ed. (London, 1965), p. 149.

3 Howell, 'Autobiography' (Howell Collection, Bishopsgate Institute. Hereafter cited as HC).

4 Early interruption of schooling was by no means uncommon. Webb notes that a working-class child was rarely expected to attend school after the age of ten or eleven. Robert K. Webb, *The British Working Class Reader, 1790-1848 : Literacy and Social Tension* (London, 1955), p. 19.

5 E. P. Thompson, *The Making of the English Working Class* (New York, 1964), p. 401; Richard D. Altick, *The English Common Reader : A Social History of the Mass Reading Public, 1800-1900* (Chicago and London, 1963), pp. 67-8, 148.

6 Howell, 'Autobiography' (HC).

7 Hobsbawm comments that 'the Bible, the *Pilgrim's Progress*, and Foxe's *Book of Martyrs* were the texts from which English labouring men learned the ABC of politics, if not the ABC of reading.' E. J. Hobsbawm, *Primitive Rebels: Studies in Archaic Forms of Social Movements in the 19th and 20th Centuries*, 2nd ed. (New York, 1963), p. 145.

8 Thompson, *Making of the English Working Class*, p. 193.

9 Howell, 'Autobiography' (HC).

10 Howell, 'Labour Politics, Policies, and Parties', *Reynolds's Newspaper*, 4 June 1905.

11 About 1850 Howell obtained a membership card, signed by Kossuth and Mazzini, for a society known as the Friends of European Freedom. Howell, 'Labour Politics, Policies, and Parties', *Reynolds's Newspaper*, 4 June 1905.

12 J. F. C. Harrison, *Learning and Living 1790-1960: A Study in the History of the English Adult Education Movement* (London, 1961), p. 48.

13 Howell to the Editor of the *British Controversialist*, 4 May 1867 (HC). (Copies of nearly 10,000 of Howell's letters are preserved in thirteen copy books. It is these copies – all in his own hand – rather than the originals which are cited below. The copy books follow a somewhat irregular chronological order, and I have simply cited the recipient and the date, instead of noting the respective volume and page.)

14 Howell, 'Autobiography' (HC); see Mark Rutherford, *The Revolution in Tanner's Lane*, ed. Reuben Shapcott (London, 1936), p. 6; Samuel Bamford, *Early Days*, ed. Henry Dunckley) London, 1893), p. 166.

15 Altick, *The English Common Reader*, p. 256.

16 Howell, 'Autobiography' (HC).

17 Howell, 'Autobiography' (HC).

18 Altick, *The English Common Reader*, p. 205; also see Webb, *The British Working Class Reader*, p. 20. J. F. C. Harrison calls the mutual improvement society 'the most truly indigenous of all attempts at working class adult education'. Harrison, *Learning and Living*, p. 53.

19 Howell, 'Working Class Movements of the Century', XIII, *Reynolds's Newspaper*, 15 November 1896.

20 Howell, 'Autobiography' (HC).

21 Howell, 'Autobiography' (HC).

22 The *Christian Observer* insisted that by reading Shakespeare 'the mind is enervated and deranged at a time when it ought to be braced and organized'. Quoted in Altick, *The English Common Reader*, p. 112.

23 Howell, 'Autobiography' (HC).

24 Howell, 'Autobiography' (HC).

25 Royden Harrison, *Before the Socialists : Studies in Labour and Politics 1861 to 1881* (London, 1965), p. 207.

2: *A Political Apprenticeship in London*

1 Howell, 'Autobiography' (HC).

2 Ms. of 'Notes of a Workman's Life' written by Howell in December 1871 at the request of Hodgson Pratt for a series of biographical sketches on English labour leaders to be published in the French newspaper, *Le Cloche*. (HC).

3 Jonathan R. T. Hughes, *Fluctuations in Trade, Industry and Finance : A Study of British Economic Development, 1850–1860* (Oxford, 1960), pp. 225–6.

4 Arthur L. Bowley, *Wages in the United Kingdom in the Nineteenth Century* (Cambridge, 1900), p. 90. Howell claimed that the average bricklayer in London in the 1850s earned 5s 6d per day. Howell to Thomas Brassey, 26 June 1869 (HC).

5 Howell, 'Autobiography' (HC).

6 James Winstanley, one of the first English Positivists, found in Howell 'a kind of intellectual, moral and even physical beauty'. James Winstanley to Pierre Lafitte, 30 August 1861, quoted in Harrison, *Before the Socialists*, p. 261 n. His fellow Positivists were distinctly less impressed.

7 Howell, 'Working Class Movements of the Century', XV, *Reynolds's Newspaper*, 29 November 1896.

8 John Bedford Leno, *The Aftermath with the Autobiography of the Author* (London, 1892), p. 55.

9 Howell, 'Autobiography' (HC).

10 Aaron Watson, 'George Howell', *The Millgate Monthly*, Vol. III, Part II (August 1908), p. 668.

11 Howell, 'Autobiography' (HC).

12 Howell, 'Autobiography' (HC).

13 Howell, 'Autobiography' (HC).

14 Howell to T. H. Huxley, 1 September 1880. Huxley Papers, Vol. 18, f. 244 (Imperial College).

15 Henry Collins and Chimen Abramsky, *Karl Marx and the British Labour Movement : Years of the First International* (London, 1965), p. 14.

16 Howell, 'Working Class Movements of the Century', XIII, *Reynolds's Newspaper*, 15 November 1896.

17 Sidney and Beatrice Webb, *The History of Trade Unionism*, Rev. ed. (New York, 1920), p. 233.

1

18 Webb, *The History of Trade Unionism*, p. 239.

19 See, for example, G. D. H. Cole, 'Some Notes on British Trade Unionism in the Third Quarter of the Nineteenth Century', *International Review of Social History*, Vol. II (1937), pp. 1–22; Harrison, *Before the Socialists*, pp. 6–19; Stephen Coltham, 'George Potter, the Junta, and the *Bee-Hive*', *International Review of Social History*, Vol. IX (1964), Part 3, pp. 4–6.

20 John Malcolm Ludlow, Ms. Autobiography (1893). Ludlow Papers, Add. 7348, Box 1 (Cambridge University Library).

21 *The Nine Hours' Movement in the Building Trades: A Report of the Proceedings of a Conference of Delegates from the Building Trades held in Temperance Hall, Curzon Street, Derby on the 1–4 January 1861, to consider the best means to be adopted for obtaining the proposed Reduction in the Hours of Labour* (London, 1861), p. 8.

   This report, probably written by Howell and Cremer, and the *Balance Sheet of the Late Strike and Lockout in the London Building Trades* (May 1860), probably written by Potter, provide the fullest account of the dispute. Both pamphlets are in the Howell Collection. Howell also offers a detailed summary in his *Labour Legislation, Labour Movements and Labour Leaders* (London, 1902), pp. 128–34. The best modern histories are Raymond Postgate, *The Builders' History* (London, 1923) and Stephen Coltham, 'George Potter and the "Bee-Hive" Newspaper', Unpublished Oxford D. Phil. thesis (1956).

22 Howell, *Labour Legislation*, p. 131.

23 *Balance Sheet of the Late Strike and Lockout*.

24 London Operative Bricklayers' Society, *Report and Balance Sheet of the Dispute relating to the Attempt to Introduce the System of Hiring and Paying by the Hour* (London, 1861), p. 2. (HC).

25 Report of the Derby Conference, p. 6.

26 Howell, 'Notes of a Workman's Life' (HC).

27 2 April session, *Minutes of Evidence of the Royal Commission on Trade Unions* (London, 1867).

28 Howell, 'Working Class Movements of the Century', XIII, *Reynolds's Newspaper*, 15 November 1896.

29 *Balance Sheet of the Late Strike and Lockout*, p. 14.

30 Bricklayers' *Report and Balance Sheet*, pp. 3–4.

31 Bricklayers' *Report* . . . p. 16.

32 Bricklayers' *Report* . . . pp. 4–6, 14–16.

33 *Operative Bricklayers' Society Circular* [n.d.] (HC).

34 Preamble to 1867 edition of the Operative Bricklayers' Society Rules (HC).

35 Operative Bricklayers' Society Rules [1861]; Revised Rules and Circular (HC).

36 Howell, Preface to Operative Bricklayers' Society Revised Rules (HC).
37 Howell, 'Why I am a Trades Unionist', *Operative Bricklayers' Society Trade Circular,* 1 December 1861.
38 Howell, article appended to Circular [n.d.] (HC).
39 Howell, 'Why I am a Trades Unionist', *Operative Bricklayers' Society Trade Circular,* 1 December 1861.
40 Howell, Preface to Revised Rules (HC).
41 *Operative Bricklayers' Society Trade Circular,* 1 September 1861.
42 *Operative Bricklayers' Society Trade Circular,* 1 December 1861.
43 See Chapter 7, p. 148.
44 Annual Report of the Operative Bricklayers' Society (December 1862). (HC).
45 See Chapter 7, p. 148–9
46 *Operative Bricklayers' Society Trade Circular,* 1 August 1870.
47 The report was presented to the executive at a meeting on 28 September 1863 and published in the October issue of the *Trade Circular.*
48 Minutes of the General Council, 21 and 28 February, 21 March 1865, *Documents of the First International : The General Council of the First International,* Vol. I: 1864–1866 (Moscow, 1963), pp. 73–6, 82–4.
49 Second Annual Report of the London Trades Council (1862). (HC).
50 Minutes of the London Trades Council, 14 May 1861 (Microfilm).
51 Rules of the London Trades Council (HC).
52 Minutes of the London Trades Council, 4 June 1861.
53 Minutes of the London Trades Council, 18 March 1862.
54 Account Book of the London Trades Council (Microfilm).
55 Howell, 'Working Class Movements of the Century', XIV, *Reynolds's Newspaper,* 22 November 1896.
56 Minutes of the London Trades Council, 17 December 1861, 9 January, 17 February 1862.
57 Second Annual Report of the London Trades Council.
58 Minutes of the London Trades Council, 4 and 18 March, 1 April 1862; Howell to Walter Morrison, 23 April 1872 (HC).
59 Address to the General Neapolitan Society of Working Men, 10 March 1862 (HC).
60 Second Annual Report of the London Trades Council.
61 Minutes of the London Trades Council, 17 February, 18 March, 1 April 1862.
62 Minutes of the London Trades Council, 6 May 1862.
63 Minutes of the London Trades Council, 17 June 1862.
64 Coltham, 'George Potter and the "Bee-Hive" Newspaper', and, more succinctly, in his article, 'George Potter, the Junta, and the

Bee-Hive'. Also see *Mr. Potter and the London Trades Council* and the Fifth Annual Report of the London Trades Council. Potter's side of the case is presented in the *Bee-Hive*.

65 *Bee-Hive*, 18 March 1865; Howell's Diary, 15 March 1865 (HC).

66 *Bee-Hive*, 2 September 1865; *Miner and Workman's Advocate*, 2 September 1865.

3: *The Revival of Reform Agitation*

1 Richard Cobden to William Hargreaves, 1 March 1861, Cobden Papers, Add. MSS. 43655, f. 205 (British Museum).

2 Address to the General Neapolitan Society of Working Men, 10 March 1862 (HC).

3 Frederic Harrison to Richard Cobden, 26 February 1864, quoted in John Vincent, *The Formation of the Liberal Party, 1857–1868* (London, 1966), p. 191.

4 Frances Elma Gillespie, *Labor and Politics in England 1850–1867* (Durham, North Carolina, 1927), pp. 162–6, 238.

5 *Bee-Hive*, 25 October, 22 November 1862.

6 *Bee-Hive*, 28 May 1864.

7 *Bee-Hive*, 17 September 1864.

8 Howell's Diary, 21 September 1864 (HC); *Bee-Hive*, 24 September 1864.

9 Howell, 'Working Class Movements of the Century', XV, *Reynolds's Newspaper*, 29 November 1896.

10 *Operative Bricklayers' Society Trade Circular*, 1 October 1861.

11 Howell to the London Trades Council, published in the *Bee-Hive*, 8 November 1862.

12 Henry Adams had been sent by his father, the American Ambassador, as an observer at the suggestion of Beesly. See Charles Francis Adams to Edward Spencer Beesly, 28 March 1863, Beesly Papers (University College, London). Cobden was impressed by the performance of the 'Cockney Trades Unionists'. He found them to be 'very able logical talkers' and remarked that 'it was refreshing to read such straightforward utterances after the namby-pamby middle class oratory we have been so long used to'. Richard Cobden to John Bright, 30 March 1863, Cobden Papers, Add. MSS. 43652, f. 86 (BM).

13 *Bee-Hive*, 28 March 1863.

14 Howell to John Bright, 7 October 1867 (HC).

15 Howell to unnamed correspondent, 24 September 1867 (HC); *Bee-Hive*, 30 April 1864.

16 *Bee-Hive*, 2 May 1863.

17 *Bee-Hive*, 23 May, 5 September, 31 October 1863.

18 John Malcolm Ludlow and Lloyd Jones, *Progress of the Working Class 1832–1867* (London, 1867), p. 288.

19 *Bee-Hive*, 19 and 26 December 1863, 16 and 23 January 1864.

20 *Bee-Hive*, 21 May 1864.

21 *Bee-Hive*, 28 May 1864; Howell's Diary, 20 June 1864 (HC).

22 *Bee-Hive*, 25 June 1864.

23 Howell's Diary, 12 July 1864 (HC).

24 *Bee-Hive*, 30 July 1864.

25 Howell's Diary, 7 September 1864.

26 Report of the St Martin's Hall meeting in *Founding of the First International (September–November 1864) : A Documentary Record*, ed. L. E. Mins (Moscow, 1935), pp. 1–17.

27 Howell's Diary, 28 September 1864 (HC).

28 Minutes of the General Council, 5 October 1864, *Documents of the First International*, I, p. 35.

29 Minutes of the General Council, 12 October 1864, *Documents of the First International*, I, p. 40; Collins and Abramsky, *Karl Marx and the British Labour Movement*, p. 42.

30 *Documents of the First International*, I, p. 289.

31 Collins and Abramsky, *Karl Marx and the British Labour Movement*, p. 17.

32 Howell to Walter Morrison, 23 April 1872 (HC).

33 Howell, 'The History of the International Association', *Nineteenth Century*, Vol. IV, No. XVII (July 1878), pp. 26–7.

34 In October 1867 Howell promised to attend meetings more faithfully, but did not in fact do so. Howell to George Eccarius, 29 October 1867 (HC).

35 Minutes of the General Council, 22 November 1864, *Documents of the First International*, I, p. 50.

36 Minutes of the General Council, 21 February 1865, *Documents of the First International*, I, p. 73.

37 Karl Marx, 'A Reply on the First International: Mr George Howell's History of the International Working Men's Association', *Labour Monthly* (September 1954), p. 419. Marx's reply to Howell was originally published in *The Secular Chronicle* in August 1878.

In 1865 Leno became the proprietor of the failing *Miner and Workman's Advocate*, formerly the organ of the miners hostile to Alexander MacDonald of the NAM. He offered to put the paper at the disposal of the International after the *Bee-Hive* refused to give its activities regular coverage. Sponsorship by the International – itself in financial straits – did little to recoup the journal's fortunes, and by the end of 1865 it was necessary to seek a subsidy from middle-class patrons. Arthur Miall, son of the editor of the *Nonconformist*, became the proprietor of the paper, renamed the *Commonwealth* in February

1866. Marx was temporarily able to impose Eccarius as editor, much to the consternation of Howell and Odger, who disliked him and coveted the position themselves. Within two months the English trade union faction engineered Eccarius' removal and his replacement by Odger, who, with Howell as accomplice, turned the *Commonwealth* into the unofficial mouthpiece of the Reform League. George Odger and Arthur Miall to Howell, 23 April 1866 (HC).

38 Minutes of the General Council, 17 July 1866, *Documents of the First International*, I, p. 210.

39 Minutes of the General Council, 31 January 1865, *Documents of the First International*, I, p. 70.

40 Ernest Jones to Karl Marx, 7 February 1865, *Bulletin of the Society for the Study of Labour History*, No. 4 (Spring, 1962), p. 12.

41 *Bee-Hive*, 25 February, 5 August 1865, 3 and 10 November 1866.

42 *Bee-Hive*, 18 March 1865; Howell's Diary, 16 March 1865 (HC).

43 Rules of the Reform League [1865] (HC). The Reform League papers constitute the largest manuscript holding in the Howell Collection. Copies of about 5,000 letters from Howell fill four copy books, and there are several hundred manuscript letters relating to League affairs received during his years as Secretary. In addition, there are seven volumes of Executive and General Council and other committee minutes, five volumes of account books and ledgers, a volume of reports of deputations to boroughs before the 1868 election, and a large body of miscellaneous manuscript and printed materials, including pamphlets, newspaper clippings, memoranda, handbills, annual reports, and balance sheets. See my 'Notes on Sources: The George Howell Collection', *Bulletin of the Society for the Study of Labour History*, No. 10 (Spring, 1965), pp. 38–40.

4: *The Workers Demand the Vote*

1 Minutes of the Reform League Executive Committee [hereafter cited as EC Minutes], 15 April 1865 (HC); *Bee-Hive*, 15 and 22 April 1865; letter from F. Milne Edge, *Bee-Hive*, 15 December 1866.

2 EC Minutes, 24 May 1865.

3 Howell, 'Autobiography' (HC).

4 Letter from Edmond Beales, *Bee-Hive*, 5 January 1867.

5 *Bee-Hive*, 2 September 1865.

6 Letter from Edmond Beales, *Bee-Hive*, 12 August 1865.

7 *Bee-Hive*, 8 December 1866.

8 Letter from F. Milne Edge, *Bee-Hive*, 15 December 1866.

9 Letter from Edmond Beales, *Bee-Hive*, 22 December 1866. The

exchange of letters and mutual recriminations continued in the *Bee-Hive* through January 1867.

10 Aldon D. Bell, 'Administration and Finance of the Reform League, 1865–1867', *International Review of Social History*, Vol. X, Part 3 (1965), p. 388. Professor Bell's unpublished Oxford thesis, 'The Reform League from its Origins to the Reform Act of 1867' is the first comprehensive study of the League's organization and activities.

11 Howell to David Chinery, 2 November 1865 (HC); Goldwin Smith to Howell, 14 January 1866 (HC).

12 E. S. Beesly to Howell, 18 October 1865 (HC).

13 John Malcolm Ludlow to Howell, 26 June 1865 (HC).

14 Howell, 'Autobiography' (HC).

15 *Report of Proceedings at the National Reform Conference held in Free Trade Hall, Manchester, May 15 and 16, 1865* (HC); *Bee-Hive*, 20 May 1865.

16 Ernest Jones to Karl Marx, 17 May 1865, *Bulletin of the Society for the Study of Labour History*, No. 4 (Spring, 1962), p. 19.

17 Ernest Jones to Karl Marx, 22 May 1865, *Bulletin of the Society for the Study of Labour History*, No. 4 (Spring, 1962), p. 20.

18 Minutes of the Reform League Permanent Committee, 22 May 1865 (HC).

19 Bell, 'The Reform League from its Origins to the Reform Act of 1867', p. 322; *Bee-Hive*, 23 February 1867.

20 Howell, 'To the Trades' Unionists of the United Kingdom' (HC). This printed letter was issued just before the General Election and again in a slightly revised version shortly thereafter. A similar injunction to the members of the Operative Bricklayers' Society (29 May 1865) appeared in the *Operative Bricklayers' Society Trade Circular*, June 1865.

21 Reform League Cash Book (HC).

22 Letter from F. Milne Edge, *Bee-Hive*, 15 December 1865.

23 EC Minutes, 24 May 1865 (HC).

24 Minutes of the Reform League Permanent Committee, 21 July 1865 (HC).

25 George Odger to Howell, 28 June 1865 (HC).

Although the League helped to solicit funds to defray Hughes's expenses, his biographers' assertion that Howell paid the £635 of election costs is without foundation. Neither Howell nor the League had such funds at their disposal, nor as yet such willing donors to tap. Hughes was grateful for the aid he did receive, reciprocating with a one guinea donation and acceptance of a vice presidency. EC Minutes, 4 August 1865 (HC); Edward C. Mack and W. H. G. Armytage, *Thomas Hughes: The Life of the Author of Tom Brown's*

School Days (London, 1952), p. 146; Thomas Hughes to Howell, 23 July 1865 (HC).

26 Minutes of the Reform League Permanent Committee, 14 July 1865 (HC).

27 Howell to John Bright, 19 October 1865 (HC).

28 Howell to John Bright, 16 November 1865 (HC).

29 EC Minutes, 11 August 1865 (HC).

30 EC Minutes, 25 August 1865 (HC).

31 EC Minutes, 10 November 1865 (HC).

32 Howell obtained clerical assistance in June 1866, but he continued to write all his own letters – often several dozen a day.

33 Howell to Mr Wynne, 6 December 1865 (HC); Howell to A. Wilson, 20 February 1866 (HC); EC Minutes, 16 and 23 February, 23 March 1866 (HC).

34 Howell to E. Dresser Rogers, 27 November 1865 (HC).

35 Howell to D. Low, 21 October 1865 (HC). The obligation to hand over one-third of receipts was a theoretical one. Howell admitted that the branches generally 'were not able to remit anything, for their own expenses more than swallowed up all that they could obtain'. Howell, 'Autobiography' (HC).

36 Howell to R. Griffiths, 11 December 1866 (HC).

37 Howell to C. Heen, 11 October 1865 (HC).

38 Bell, 'The Reform League from its Orgins to the Reform Act of 1867', pp. 207, 211.

39 First Annual Report and Balance Sheet of the Reform League [April 1866] (HC).

40 Howell's Diary, 3 January 1866 (HC).

41 Howell to Edwin Charles Howell, 8 March 1866 (HC).

42 Howell to Edward Owen Greening, 6 November 1865 (HC).

43 EC Minutes, 24 November 1865 (HC); Howell to J. D. Morton, 11 December 1865 (HC); *Bee-Hive*, 16 December 1865, 20 January 1866.

44 Howell's Diary, 24 January 1866 (HC); *Commonwealth*, 17 February 1866.

45 EC Minutes, 10, 16, and 20 March 1866 (HC).

46 Howell to J. D. Morton, 4 May 1866 (HC).

47 Ernest Jones to Howell, 4 May 1866 (HC).

48 Howell to Ernest Jones, 7 May 1866 (HC).

49 Ernest Jones to Howell, 17 May 1866 (HC).

50 Reform League Cash Book, (HC).

51 EC Minutes, 10 April 1866 (HC).

52 *Commonwealth*, 5 May 1866; *Bee-Hive*, 5 May 1866.

53 George Macaulay Trevelyan, *The Life of John Bright*, 2nd ed. (London, 1925), pp. 361–3.

54 *Bee-Hive*, 30 June 1866.

55 EC Minutes, 29 June 1866 (HC).

56 EC Minutes, 4 July 1866 (HC); Howell to J. D. Morton, 9 July 1866 (HC).

57 John Bright to Howell, 19 July 1866 (HC).

58 Telegram from John Bright to Howell, 20 July 1866 (HC). Trevelyan calls it a 'public letter', but Bright seems to have had second thoughts about its inflammatory implications. Trevelyan, *John Bright*, p. 60.

59 Letter from Mason Jones, *The Times*, 23 July 1866.

60 The incident was documented extensively in contemporary newspapers and recounted in subsequent biographies and memoirs. See, for example, Hypatia Bradlaugh Bonner, *Charles Bradlaugh: A Record of His Life and Work*, 3rd ed. (London, 1895), I, pp. 223–6; Henry Broadhurst, *The Story of His Life from a Stonemason's Bench to the Treasury Bench* (London, 1901), pp. 33–40; Howard Evans, *Sir Randal Cremer: His Life and Work* (London, 1909), pp. 44–5; A. W. Humphrey, *Robert Applegarth: Trade Unionist, Educationist, Reformer* (Manchester, 1913), pp. 60–61; Howell, 'People I Have Met: The Fall of the Park Railings', *Reynolds's Newspaper*, 10 June 1906. Also see The Hyde Park Cases, 1866: Report of the [Reform League] Sub-Committee. (HC).

61 *Bee-Hive*, 28 July 1866; Report of the Reform League deputation to the Home Secretary, 25 July 1866 (HC).

62 John Bright to Howell, 26 July 1866 (HC).

63 *Bee-Hive*, 4 August 1866.

64 Vincent, *Formation of the Liberal Party*, p. 192.

65 *Bee-Hive*, 24 February, 2 June 1866.

66 *Bee-Hive*, 18 August, 1 September 1866; EC Minutes, 24 August 1866 (HC).

67 Howell to John Jeffrey, 24 October 1866 (HC).

68 Howell to Robert Cooper, 10 December 1866 (HC).

69 Howell to F. Milne Edge, 26 November 1866 (HC).

70 *Commonwealth*, 1 December 1866.

71 Robert Applegarth, 'Some People I Have Known', Typescript of speech to the Hotspur Club, 12 March 1898 (HC).

72 Howell to George Jackson, 31 October 1866 (HC).

73 Howell to S. Bennett, 24 December 1866 (HC).

74 Howell to Edmond Beales, 26 December 1866 (HC).

75 Howell to Edmond Beales, 12 January 1867 (HC).

76 EC Minutes, 27 October, 9 and 16 November 1866 (HC).

77 EC Minutes, 14 November 1866 (HC); Howell to J. J. Colman, 8 November 1866 (HC).

78 Howell to George Mantle, 11 November 1866 (HC).

79 Minutes of the Reform League General Council [hereafter cited as GC Minutes], 18 December 1866 (HC).
80 Howell to W. Smith, 15 September 1866 (HC).
81 Howell to W. Chester, 19 March 1867 (HC). Bell calculates a maximum figure of at least 619 branches, including 354 provincial ones. Bell, 'Administration and Finance of the Reform League', p. 404.
82 Howell to R. E. Oliver (Lower Clapton), 2 February 1867 (HC).
83 Howell to Sam Dodd, 6 October 1866 (HC).
84 GC Minutes, 2 January 1867 (HC).
85 Howell's Diary, 7 January 1867 (HC).
86 GC Minutes, 9 January 1867 (HC).
87 Howell to Edmond Beales, 10 January 1867 (HC).
88 Howell to E. Dresser Rogers, 26 January 1867 (HC).
89 Reform League Cash Book (HC); Bell provides a more general breakdown of income, listing several sources together, which brings the total of donations during the second year to £1,960. Bell, 'Administration and Finance of the Reform League', p. 401.
90 Howell to Robert Kell, 17 October 1866 (HC).
91 EC Minutes, 2 November 1866 (HC).
92 Howell to Samuel Morley, 5 November 1866 (HC).
93 Reform League Cash Book (HC).
94 Howell to P. A. Taylor, 15 November 1866 (HC).
95 Minutes of the London Trades Council, 19 December 1866.
96 EC Minutes, 21 December 1866, 11 January 1867 (HC).
97 Howell to J. G. West, 1 January 1867 (HC).
98 EC Minutes, 21 December 1866, 11 January 1867 (HC).
99 EC Minutes, 14 January 1867 (HC).
100 Howell to John Bright, 24 January 1867 (HC).
101 EC Minutes, 18 January 1867 (HC).
102 Printed letter from Howell to Reform League Branch Secretaries, 4 February 1867 (HC).
103 Reform League Cash Book (HC).
104 Reform League: General and District Organization for a Demonstration, 11 February 1867 (HC).
105 Howell to George Mantle, 17 February 1867 (HC).
106 Robert Blake, *Disraeli* (London, 1966), p. 456.
107 Howell to William Osborne, 23 March 1867 (HC).
108 Reform League Cash Book (HC).
109 *Bee-Hive*, 20 April 1867.
110 EC Minutes, 18 April 1867 (HC).
111 *Bee-Hive*, 27 April 1867.
112 Minutes of the Delegate Meeting, 1 May 1867 (HC).
113 EC Minutes, 3 May 1867 (HC).
114 Howell to Thomas Hughes, 5 May 1867 (HC).

115 Howell to Dorcas Howell, 6 May 1867 (HC). Another letter two days earlier declared, 'I write today as a great difficulty might occur on Monday next. One false step on either side might be *fatal.*' Howell to the Editor of the *British Controversialist*, 4 May 1867 (HC).

116 GC Minutes, 8 May 1867 (HC).

117 Goldwin Smith to Howell, 11 June 1867, quoted in *The Times*, 17 June 1867.

5: *The Reform League and the Liberal Party*

1 Howell to William Dell, 2 September 1867 (HC).

2 Harrison, *Before the Socialists*, p. 208. Harrison offers a critical analysis of the Special Fund and its implications in his chapter on The Reform League and the General Election of 1868, in *Before the Socialists*, pp. 137–209. Also see H. J. Hanham, *Elections and Party Management : Politics in the Time of Disraeli and Gladstone* (London, 1959), pp. 333–43.

3 Howell to Samuel Morley, 5 June 1867 (HC).

4 EC Minutes, 21 June, 5, 8, and 12 July 1867 (HC); Printed letters from Howell to Members, Branch Secretaries, and Subscribers, 12 and 15 July 1867 (HC).

5 John Bright to Edmond Beales, 26 July 1867 (Courtesy of Professor Herman Ausubel). Printed Subscriber List for Registration Fund [1867] (HC).

6 EC Minutes, 7 August, 13 September 1867 (HC); Printed letter from Howell to Branch Secretaries and other Officers, 18 September 1867 (HC).

7 Howell to J. J. Merriman, 16 September 1867 (HC).

8 EC Minutes, 6 September 1867 (HC); Howell to W. S. Grayson, 7 September 1867 (HC).

9 EC Minutes, 13 and 20 September 1867 (HC).

10 Howell to George Jackson, 14 September 1867 (HC).

11 Howell to E. Dresser Rogers, 22 September 1867 (HC).

12 Howell to William Malthouse, 23 September 1867 (HC).

13 Howell to J. J. Merriman, 23 September 1867 (HC).

14 Howell to E. Dresser Rogers, 22 September 1867 (HC). Mantle resigned from the Executive Committee in May 1868 after default-ing on his racing debts. See Howell to W. Morris, 6 May 1868 (HC).

15 Howell to Dorcas Howell, 28 September 1867 (HC). Mrs Howell was in Brighton at the time.

16 Howell to E. Dresser Rogers, 19 October 1867 (HC).

17 Edmond Beales to Howell, 19 October 1867, quoted in GC Minutes, 23 October 1867 (HC).

18 GC Minutes, 23 October 1867 (HC).

19 Howell to J. M. Gee, 10 January 1868 (HC).

20 GC Minutes, 1 November 1867 (HC).

21 Reflections on 1867, Howell's Diary, 1 January 1868 (HC).

22 Personal Financial Review of 1867, Howell's Diary, 1868 (HC).

23 Howell's Diary, 3 January 1868 (HC).

24 EC Minutes, 15 March 1867 (HC).

25 Howell to Ernest Jones, 23 February 1868 (HC).

26 Howell's Diary, 17, 28, and 31 January 1868 (HC).

27 Howell's Diary, 3 February 1868 (HC).

28 Reform League Cash Book (HC).

29 Howell's Diary, 6 February 1868 (HC). Beales condemned the 'dictation of the middle classes' in pressing for a fusion of the reform groups. EC Minutes, 12 February 1868 (HC).

30 Howell to Robert Kell, 11 February 1868 (HC).

31 Howell to Dr [James Robert] Black, 22 February 1868 (HC).

32 Howell to James Stansfeld, 10 November 1867 (HC).

33 Howell to James Stansfeld, 15 February 1868 (HC).

34 Howell's Diary, 8 February 1868 (HC).

35 Prospectus for the Adelphi Club (HC); John Stuart Mill to Howell, 26 April 1868 (HC); Howell to W. T. Malleson, 15 June 1868 (HC).

36 Howell to Robert Applegarth, 15 June 1868 (HC).

37 GC Minutes, 4 December 1867 (HC).

38 EC Minutes, 16 January 1868 (HC).

39 Howell to F. Clayton, 28 February 1868 (HC).

40 Howell to George Jackson, 28 October 1867 (HC).

41 Howell to Titus Salt, 3 April 1868 (HC).

42 Draft of lecture to the Pimlico branch of the Reform League on 'Work for the Future', 28 March 1868. Ms. in 1868 Letter Book (HC).

43 Howell to George Jackson, 11 May 1868 (HC).

44 EC Minutes, 24 June 1868 (HC).

45 Howell to William Thomas, 4 May 1868 (HC). Morley's defeat was not unexpected. See George G. Glyn to W. E. Gladstone, 10 February 1868, Gladstone Papers, Add. MSS. 44347, f. 100 (BM). Bristol was torn by local rivalries, and Morley's opposition to the Permissive Bill angered many of the temperance men. Howell to Sir Wilfrid Lawson, 15 July 1868 (HC).

46 Howell to William Hargreaves, 9 July 1868 (HC).

47 Howell to Samuel Morley, 12 August 1868 (HC).

48 Charles Bradlaugh to Howell, 4 July 1868 (HC); Howell to S. Clarke, [Secretary of the Northampton branch], 11 July 1868 (HC).

49 Howell to the Editor of the *Daily Telegraph*, 6 August 1868 (HC).

50 Charles Gilpin to Howell, 25 July 1868 (HC).

51 Howell to James Wells, 10 August 1868 (HC).

52 Howell to Mr Yorke, 14 August 1868 (HC).

53 George G. Glyn to W. E. Gladstone, 10 September 1868, Gladstone Papers, Add. MSS. 44347, f. 157 (BM).

54 GC Minutes, 4 September 1868 (HC).

55 George G. Glyn to W. E. Gladstone, 8 October 1868, Gladstone Papers, Add. MSS. 44347, f. 190 (BM).

56 EC Minutes, 15 and 31 July, 6 August 1868 (HC); The Reform League Report and Balance Sheet from May 1st to November 30th, 1868 (HC); A. F. Thompson, 'Gladstone's Whips and the General Election of 1868', *English Historical Review*, Vol. LXIII, No. CCXLVII (April 1948), pp. 193, 199.

57 Reform League Cash Ledger (HC). The money was given to Howell in ten instalments between 8 August and 20 November. Howell noted in a letter to Stansfeld that Morley's personal share of the first £1,000 was £630, but there is no indication that Morley did not pay all of the remaining £900 himself. Howell to James Stansfeld, 6 January 1869 (HC). See Edwin Hodder, *The Life of Samuel Morley*, 2nd ed. (London, 1887), p. 268.

58 Howell to John Hales and Samuel Brighty, 13 August 1868 (HC).

59 Howell to W. Brumfitt, 13 August 1868 (HC).

60 Howell to James Stansfeld, 26 August 1868 (HC).

61 George G. Glyn to W. E. Gladstone, 9 September 1868, Gladstone Papers, Add. MSS. 44347, f. 154 (BM).

62 Howell to James Stansfeld, 18 September 1868 (HC).

63 Howell to James Stansfeld, 26 September, 2 October 1868 (HC).

64 Howell to Samuel Morley, 26 October 1868 (HC).

65 Howell to James Stansfeld, 6 January 1869 (HC).

66 Howell to George G. Glyn, 30 September 1868 (HC). Glyn's father was the Chairman of the London and North-Western Railway. The Chief Whip was interested in ousting Sir Daniel Gooch, the incumbent. While Glyn himself tried to secure the neutrality of unfriendly railway directors, Howell was delegated to apply pressure to the railway workers. Hanham, *Elections and Party Management*, p. 86 n.

67 Howell to J. Butcher, 22 September 1868 (HC). Samuelson saw no need to accommodate the workers by modifying his position, and it was Howell who took a conciliatory line, writing him that 'Trades Unionists, like Employers, are not over wise. They want everything their own way. But some of us must step between them and folly and try and test all questions by reason and common sense. We cannot satisfy all.' Howell to Bernhard Samuelson, 7 October 1868 (HC).

68 Howell to William Dronfield, 27 June 1868 (HC).

69 A. J. Mundella to Howell, 25 September 1868 (HC).

70 Howell to William Dronfield, 26 September 1868 (HC).

71 Howell to Leigh Ellis, 12 October 1868 (HC); Howell to John Hales and Samuel Brighty, 2 and 7 October 1868 (HC).

72 Howell to William Rathbone, 27 October 1868 (HC).

73 Howell to James Thompson, 28 October 1868 (HC).

74 Howell to William Conningham, 21 November 1868 (HC); Harrison, *Before the Socialists*, pp. 173–4.

75 Howell to W. H. White, 24 September 1868 (HC). See Howell to James Stansfeld, 15 and 22 September 1868 (HC); Harrison, *Before the Socialists*, p. 177.

76 Henry Pelling, *The Origins of the Labour Party, 1880–1900*, 2nd ed. (Oxford, 1965), pp. 40, 68.

77 Minutes of the Finance Committee, 25 September 1868 [Agenda Book] (HC); Special Fund Account, Reform League Ledger (HC); EC Minutes, 20 January 1869 (HC).

78 Howell to Samuel Morley, 1 December 1868 (HC); The Reform League Report and Balance Sheet from May 1st to November 30th 1868 (HC).

79 Report of the Finance Committee, 9 December 1868 (HC).

80 EC Minutes, 18 November 1868 (HC).

81 EC Minutes, 25 November 1868 (HC); GC Minutes, 25 November 1868 (HC).

82 Howell to G. J. Goschen, 27 November 1868 (HC).

83 Howell to George G. Glyn, 30 November 1868 (HC).

84 EC Minutes, 2 December 1868 (HC). Odger had in fact decided not to contest Stafford.

85 Howell to Edmond Beales, 2 December 1868 (HC). Also see Howell to Samuel Morley, 1 December 1868 (HC) which explains more fully the points in the letter to Beales. The letter to Morley is extensively quoted in Harrison, *Before the Socialists*, pp. 186–7.

86 EC Minutes, 9 December 1868 (HC).

87 Howell to Edmond Beales, 10 December 1868 (HC).

88 Howell to George G. Glyn, 11 December 1868 (HC); EC Minutes, 16 December 1868 (HC). Howell's first letter to Glyn was sent on 3 December, but Glyn did not reply until the 15th.

89 Howell to George G. Glyn, 11 December 1868 (HC).

90 Howell to George G. Glyn, 17 December 1868 (HC).

91 GC Minutes, 16 December 1868 (HC); Samuel Morley to Edmond Beales, 22 December 1868 (HC).

92 EC Minutes, 23 December 1868 (HC).

93 EC Minutes, 8, 13, and 20 January 1869 (HC).

94 EC Minutes, 20 January 1869 (HC).

95 EC Minutes, 26 February, 3 March 1869 (HC).
96 Howell to Edmond Beales, 10 March 1869 (HC).
97 EC Minutes, 12 March 1869 (HC).
98 Howell to John Bright, 22 June, 2 July 1869 (HC); Howell to Sir James Watts, 20 December 1869 (HC).
99 Howell to Edmond Beales, 10 March 1869 (HC).
100 Howell to Charles Bartlett, 25 March 1870 (HC).

6: The Business of Politics

1 *Bucks Chronicle*, 10 October 1868.
2 George G. Glyn to W. E. Gladstone, 13 November 1868, Gladstone Papers, Add. MSS. 44347, f. 107 (BM).
3 *Bucks Advertiser*, 24 October 1868.
4 *Bucks Advertiser*, 7 November 1868.
5 Howell's 1868 Election Address, published in *Bucks Chronicle*, 24 October 1868.
6 *Bucks Herald*, 10 October 1868.
7 *Bucks Chronicle*, 24 October 1868.
8 Howell's experience was not unusual. Bright remarked to Gladstone, 'The corruption, bribery, compulsion & tumult of this general election have probably never been exceeded.' John Bright to W. E. Gladstone, 27 November 1868, Gladstone Papers, Add. MSS. 44112, f. 67 (BM).
9 *Bucks Advertiser*, 7 November 1868.
10 *Bucks Chronicle*, 21 November 1868.
11 *Bee-Hive*, 7 November 1868.
12 Nathaniel Mayer de Rothschild to William Morris [a local Baptist minister], 1 November 1868, *Bucks Advertiser*, 7 November 1868.
13 *Bucks Chronicle*, 14 November 1868; Leno, *Autobiography*, p. 70.
14 John Stuart Mill to Charles Stuart Walther [Secretary of Howell's London committee], 25 October 1868, *Bee-Hive*, 31 October 1868. Mill contributed £10.
15 Walter Morrison to Charles Stuart Walther, n. d., *Bucks Advertiser*, 7 November 1868.
16 Morrison tried to work through Rothschild's uncle, the MP for Hythe. Walter Morrison to Howell, 12 and 14 November 1868 (HC); George G. Glyn to W. E. Gladstone, 22 September 1868, Gladstone Papers, Add. MSS. 44347, f. 174 (BM).
17 George G. Glyn to W. E. Gladstone, 13 November 1868, Gladstone Papers, Add. MSS. 44347, f. 107 (BM).
18 *Bucks Advertiser*, 31 October 1868.
19 *Bucks Advertiser*, 24 October 1868.

20 *Bucks Advertiser*, 21 November 1868. (My italics).

21 *Bucks Herald*, 21 November 1868.

22 Howell to John Porter, 2 December 1868 (HC). Howell's election expenses came to £417, of which more than half was spent on agents, canvassers, and on transporting voters to the polls. Ms. Statement of Election Expenses, 1868 Letter Book (HC). Howell's campaign was financed by £50 donations from Walter Morrison and Samuel Morley, and smaller sums from M. T. Bass, William Hargreaves, James Stansfeld, E. Lyulph Stanley, J. Baxter Langley, S. C. Kell, W. E. Forster, W. Leaf, John Stuart Mill, Edmund Potter, and Auberon Herbert. In January 1869 the Reform League agreed to absorb his remaining debts of £136 16s.

23 Hanham, *Elections and Party Management*, p. xi n; Howell to Walter Morrison, 13 September 1877 (HC).

24 Howell to Walter Morrison, 19 November 1868 (HC).

25 *Bucks Advertiser*, 21 November 1868.

26 *Bucks Chronicle*, 21 November 1868.

27 Walter Morrison to Howell, 27 November 1868 (HC).

28 Howell to Samuel Morley, 21 January 1869 (HC).

29 Howell to W. Thomas, 3 February 1869 (HC).

30 Howell's Diary, 3 February 1869 (HC).

31 W. R. Cremer and Howell to an unnamed correspondent, 13 February 1869 (HC). The letter was undoubtedly to Glyn. Howell's diary entry for that day notes, 'Sent letter to Glyn about fee on account of work done. Cremer supplied copy of letter which I moderated . . . both signed and sent it off.' Moreover, Howell refers to it in a subsequent letter: Howell to George G. Glyn, 16 February 1869 (HC).

32 Howell's Diary, 17 and 20 February 1869 (HC).

33 Howell to James Stansfeld, 18 February 1869 (HC).

34 Draft copy of Howell to James Stansfeld, 15 April 1869 [included in 1869 file of letters received by Howell] (HC). The proposals were formulated more concretely in a printed prospectus for the Liberal Registration and Election Agency, 27 April 1869 [Volume on Representation] (HC). A pamphlet spelling out the provisions for registration was issued on 28 June [Miscellaneous Pamphlets] (HC).

35 Ms. report entitled Registration and Election Agency, 1869. The document in Howell's handwriting provides an account of his activities and expenditure during the Agency's brief existence.

36 Howell to Samuel Morley, 11 June 1869 (HC).

37 Registration and Election Agency, 1869 (HC).

38 Howell to James Stansfeld, 8 November 1869 (HC).

39 Howell's Diary, 12–14 June 1869 (HC); Howell to George G. Glyn, 16 June 1869 (HC).

40 Howell's Diary, 11–18 November 1869 (HC); Howell to James Stansfeld, 15 December 1869 (HC).
41 Howell to James Stansfeld, 2 November 1869 (HC).
42 Howell's Diary, 15 December 1869 (HC).
43 Registration and Election Agency, 1869 (HC); Howell to William Shaen, 24 May 1870 (HC).
44 Thomas Brassey to Howell, 7 November 1871 (HC); Registration and Election Agency, 1869 (HC).
45 Howell to James Stansfeld, 5 April 1870 (HC). He explained to Langley his reason for giving up the agency, noting that 'that path, as a means of living, must be one of political apostasy and dishonour'. Howell to J. Baxter Langley, 4 May 1870 (HC).
46 Howell provided a detailed account of the origins of the League in the Ms. Notes and Memoranda as to the History of this League [Labour Representation League Volume] (HC). Also see Howell's Diary, 22 January, 3 and 11 August 1869 (HC); G. D. H. Cole, *British Working Class Politics* (London, 1941), pp. 49–53.
47 Prospectus of the Labour Representation League (HC).
48 Rules of the Labour Representation League (HC).
49 *Bee-Hive*, 27 November 1869; Francis William Soutter, *Recollections of a Labour Pioneer* (London, 1923), pp. 29–53.
50 Howell's Diary, 28 March 1870 (HC); Howell to Robert Applegarth, 28 March 1870 (HC); Humphrey, *Applegarth*, pp. 71–3.
51 Howell's Diary, 7 April, 30 May 1870 (HC).
52 William Rathbone to Lucretia Rathbone, 13 March 1870, quoted in Eleanor F. Rathbone, *William Rathbone: A Memoir* (London, 1905), p. 270.
53 Howell to Charles Bartlett, 25 March 1870 (HC).
54 Howell to Charles Bartlett, 27 June 1870 (HC). Of course Howell was exaggerating here: he constantly appealed to Liberal friends in his quest for a secure position.
55 'The Labour Representation League and the War', *Bee-Hive*, 30 July 1870.
56 The Labour Representation League and the War, 7 September 1870 [Labour Representation League Volume] (HC). This manifesto was published in the *Bee-Hive*, 10 September 1870. Howell expressed similar sentiments in a letter to the Editor of the *Daily News*, 29 September 1870 (HC).
57 Howell to Charles Bartlett, 11 September 1870 (HC).
58 *Bee-Hive*, 7 January 1871.
59 *Bee-Hive*, 18 February 1871; Harrison, *Before the Socialists,* pp. 231–3; Collins and Abramsky, *Karl Marx and the British Labour Movement*, p. 212. Odger resigned from the General Council of the International in June.

60 Howell's Diary, 4 April, 10 May 1871 (HC).
61 Ms. of article by Howell on 'Working Men in Parliament', [December 1872], 1872 Letter Book (HC); *Bee-Hive,* 14 December 1872.
62 Printed Labour Representation League circular, 17 March 1873, Mill-Taylor Collection, Vol. II (LSE).
63 T. Grant Facey, for example, was appointed as League agent in Aylesbury, where Howell was standing again. Minute Book of the Labour Representation League, 27 January 1874, Broadhurst Collection (LSE).
64 Minute Book of the Labour Representation League, 13 February 1874, Broadhurst Collection (LSE).
65 Howell to Henry Broadhurst, 6 May 1876 (HC); Minute Book of the Labour Representation League, 31 March, 13 April, 5 May 1876, Broadhurst Collection (LSE).
66 In contrast to its quasi-independent stance in 1873-4, the League declared in November 1875 that 'we have ever sought to be allied to the great Liberal party, to which we, by conviction, belong'. An Address to the People of Great Britain, November 1875 [Labour Representation League Volume] (HC).
67 Howell to Charles Bartlett, 29 May 1870 (HC).
68 Prospectus of the Adelphi Permanent Building Society (HC); Howell's Diary, August 1870 (HC).
69 Howell to Charles Bartlett, 11 September 1870 (HC).
70 Howell to Robert Applegarth, 29 November 1870 (HC).
71 Howell to Charles Bartlett, 9 January 1871 (HC).
72 Howell to Charles Bartlett, 1 October 1871 (HC).
73 Howell to Edmond Beales, 19 December 1871 (HC); Cash Account, June 1872, Howell's Diary, 1872 (HC).
74 Prospectus of the People's Garden Company, 10 December 1870 (HC).
75 Howell to Charles Bartlett, 14 August 1870 (HC); Howell's Diary, 12 August 1870 (HC).
76 Howell to Charles Bartlett, 9 January 1871 (HC).
77 Howell to W. R. Warner, 29 January 1871 (HC); Howell to Charles Bartlett, 1 October 1871 (HC).
78 Prospectus of the Metropolitan Dwelling House Improvement Company (HC).
79 Howell's Diary, June 1871 (HC).
80 Howell to Edmond Beales, 29 July 1871 (HC).
81 Howell to Thomas Brassey, 4 August 1871 (HC). There is no indication in Howell's papers of how long the financial arrangement with Brassey lasted.
82 Howell to Edmond Beales, 19 August 1871 (HC).
83 Howell to Edmond Beales, 23 August 1871 (HC).

84 Howell to Hodgson Pratt, 28 February 1872 (HC). He also turned down the secretaryship of the Metropolitan Poor Rate League and of the *Cooperative Bazaar*. See Howell to Capt. W. Warner Dennis, 12 July 1871 (HC); Howell to E. O. Greening, 20 January 1872 (HC).

85 Howell to Goldwin Smith, 30 September 1871 (HC); Howell to Charles Bartlett, 1 October 1871, 17 March 1872 (HC).

86 Howell to John Malcolm Ludlow, 22 June 1868 (HC).

87 Howell to Arthur A. Burbridge, 16 September 1869 (HC).

88 Walter Morrison to Howell, 5 November 1874 (HC).

89 Howell to Walter Morrison, 6 November 1874 (HC).

90 Howell's Ms. notes on the 3 August 1869 Land Tenure Reform Association meeting [LTRA Papers] (HC); Howell to Charles Bartlett, 26 September 1869 (HC).

91 Howell to James Stansfeld, 8 November 1869 (HC).

92 Programme of the Land Tenure Reform Association, 8 July 1870 [LTRA Papers] (HC); Howell's Diary, 12 and 18 April 1870 (HC).

93 Howell's Diary, 10 August, 12 and 13 October 1869 (HC); Howell to George Dixon, 11 August 1869 (HC).

94 *Report of First General Meeting of Members of the National Education League* (Birmingham, 1869).

95 Howell to Francis Adams, 8 November 1869 (HC).

96 Howell's Diary, February and March 1870 (HC); Howell to Francis Adams, 19 March 1870 (HC).

97 Howell to J. Oxley, 21 March 1870 (HC).

98 Cash Account, Howell's Diary, 1870 (HC).

99 Treasurer's Account, Liberation Society Papers (London County Record Office).

100 Ms. Minute Book of the Executive Committee of the Liberation Society, 3 July 1871 (LCRO) [Hereafter cited as LS Minutes].

101 LS Minutes, 17 July 1871 (LCRO).

102 LS Minutes, 31 July, 18 September, 2 October 1871 (LCRO).

103 Howell to George Potter, 28 October 1871 (HC). J. Carvell Williams was the Secretary of the Liberation Society.

104 Address of the Working Men's Committee for Promoting the Separation of Church and State, published in the *Bee-Hive*, 21 October 1871.

105 Howell, for example, spoke in London on 3 November, Brighton on 15 November, and Wolverhampton on 5 December. LS Minutes, 13 November, 18 December 1871, 29 January 1872 (LCRO); Howell to Charles Bartlett, 17 March 1872 (HC).

106 LS Minutes, 3 June 1872 (LCRO).

107 LS Minutes, 9 December 1872 (LCRO).

108 Report and Balance Sheet of the Plimsoll & Seamen's Fund

Committee, 15 May 1875 (HC); Howell, *Labour Legislation,* pp. 263–82.

109 Howell's Ms. draft of 1871 Norwich Election Address, 16 January 1871, 1871 Letter Book (HC).

110 Howell to Charles Bartlett, 19 January 1871 (HC).

111 Howell's Diary, 25 January, 4 and 6 February 1871 (HC). Glyn paid Howell £44 2s. to cover the expenses he had incurred in Norwich.

112 Howell to R. A. Cooper, 28 January 1871 (HC).

113 Howell to Samuel Morley, 28 January 1871 (HC).

114 Howell to Joseph Arch, 24 January 1874 (HC); Howell to Goldwin Smith, 28 January 1874 (HC); Howell to W. E. Gladstone, 28 January 1874 (HC); Howell to William Rathbone, 28 January 1874 (HC). Rathbone contributed £50. Harcourt was willing to donate £25 once Howell assured him that he was not endangering Rothschild's seat. Sir William Harcourt to Howell, 28 January, 7 and 16 February 1874 (HC). Lord Russell refused to use his influence with Rothschild on the grounds that any interference on his part in an election would be 'contrary to the Constitution'. Lady Fanny Russell to Henry Crompton, 27 January 1874 (HC).

115 Howell to Sir William Harcourt, 28 January 1874 (HC).

116 Printed letter from W. E. Gladstone to Edmond Beales, 27 January 1874. Issued as an election handbill (HC).

117 *Bucks Advertiser,* 31 January 1874.

118 *Bucks Herald,* 31 January 1874.

119 *Bucks Advertiser,* 7 February 1874; Howell to Edmond Beales, 31 January 1874 (HC).

120 Howell to W. Thomas, 18 March 1874 (HC).

121 Howell to Samuel Morley, 24 January 1874 (HC); Samuel Morley to Howell, 28 January 1874 (HC).

122 Howell to J. J. Colman, 8 May 1875 (HC); Howell to R. A. Cooper, 8 May 1875 (HC); Address to the Electors of the City of Norwich, 20 May 1875 (HC); *Bee-Hive,* 19 June 1875.

123 *Bee-Hive,* 15 May, 19 June 1875. Howell's expenses were paid by the Labour Representation League. Ms. Account of Howell's Norwich election costs, 8 May–15 June 1875, Letter Book (HC).

124 Howell to Peter Shorrocks, 4 June 1875 (HC).

7 : The Rise of the Trades Union Congress

1 *Minutes of Evidence of the Royal Commission on Trade Unions* (London, 1867); Frederic Harrison to Howell, [March 1867] (HC). See Webb, *History of Trade Unionism,* pp. 264–9; Howell, *Labour Legislation,* pp. 161–5.

2 See B. C. Roberts, *The Trades Union Congress, 1868–1921* (London, 1958), pp. 44–9. A. E. Musson, *The Congress of 1868: The Origins and Establishment of the Trades Union Congress* (London, 1955).

3 Howell to the General Secretary and Members of the Executive Council, Operative Bricklayers' Society, 20 July 1869 (HC).

4 *Operative Bricklayers' Society Trade Circular*, August 1869.

5 Howell to William Fordham, 26 July 1869 (HC).

6 Howell to Robert McRae, 9 August 1869 (HC).

7 *Operative Bricklayers' Society Trade Circular*, September 1869.

8 William Fordham to Edwin Coulson, 26 August 1869, published in *Operative Bricklayers' Society Trade Circular*, October 1869.

9 Edwin Coulson to William Fordham, 28 August 1869, published in *Operative Bricklayers' Society Trade Circular*, October 1869.

10 W. S. Hilton, *Foes to Tyranny: A History of the Amalgamated Union of Building Trade Workers* (London, 1963), p. 148.

11 Henry Markley to the Members of the Operative Bricklayers' Society, 20 October 1869. Printed letter (HC).

12 Hilton, *Foes to Tyranny*, pp. 149–151; *Operative Bricklayers' Society Trade Circular*, October 1869.

13 To the London and Manchester Bricklayers' Societies, 9 July 1869. (Printed report of the arbitration proceedings) (HC).

14 Markley to Members of the Operative Bricklayers' Society, 20 October 1869 (HC).

15 Edwin Coulson to Members of the Operative Bricklayers' Society, 22 July 1869. Printed Letter (HC); Notes in Howell's handwriting on printed letter announcing of 29 September meeting (HC); *Operative Bricklayers' Society Trade Circular*, October 1869.

16 Howell to Brothers of the No. 6 Lodge of the Operative Bricklayers' Society, 2 July 1870 (HC).

17 Howell to William Fordham, 1 July 1871 (HC).

18 Ms. minutes of 7 March session, Third Annual Trades Union Congress, London, 6–11 March 1871 (HC).

19 Minutes of 8 March session, report of London TUC (HC).

20 Howell, *Labour Legislation*, p. 183; [Howell,] 'The New Labour Laws and the Parliamentary Committee', *Bee-Hive*, 4 September 1875.

21 Minutes of 10 and 11 March sessions, Report of London TUC (HC).

22 Ms. minutes of the Parliamentary Committee, 1871 (HC); Howell's Diary, 25 March 1871 (HC).

23 Howell to William Rathbone, 29 March 1871 (HC).

24 Minutes of the Parliamentary Committee, 5 July 1871 (HC).

25 Harrison, *Before the Socialists*, pp. 282–91.

26 Howell, *Labour Legislation*, p. 191.

27 Howell to William Hicking, 6 September 1871 (HC).

28 E. S. Beesly, 'The Division on the Trades Union Bill', *Bee-Hive*, 29 July 1871.
29 Howell, 'Professor Beesly and the *Pall Mall Gazette*', *Bee-Hive*, 4 November 1871.
30 Report of the Parliamentary Committee for 1871 (HC).
31 Minutes of the 9 and 10 January sessions, Report of the Fourth Annual Trades Union Congress, Nottingham, 8–13 January 1872 (HC).
32 Minutes of 13 January session, Report of Nottingham TUC (HC).
33 Ms. minutes of the Parliamentary Committee, January to June 1872 (HC); Howell's Diary, 13 January 1872 (HC).
34 Minutes of 13 January session, Report of Nottingham TUC (HC).
35 Minutes of the Parliamentary Committee, 13 January 1872 (HC).
36 Howell to John Kane, 6 April 1872 (HC).
37 Ms. memorandum on the activities of the Parliamentary Committee from January to August 1872, kept by Howell. [Hereafter cited as 'Howell Memorandum'] (HC).
38 Howell to Henry Crompton, 16 March 1872 (HC); Henry Crompton to Howell, 19 March 1872 (HC).
39 Published report of the Parliamentary Committee deputation to the Home Secretary, H. A. Bruce, 19 March 1872 (HC).
40 Henry Crompton to Howell, 30 March 1872 (HC).
41 Minutes of the Parliamentary Committee, 3 May 1872 (HC); 'Howell Memorandum' (HC).
42 Howell to Charles Bartlett, 18 May 1872 (HC).
43 'Howell Memorandum' (HC).
44 'Howell Memorandum' (18 May 1872) (HC).
45 Howell to Alexander MacDonald, 25 May 1872 (HC).
46 Howell to William Allan, 17 June 1872 (HC); *Bee-Hive*, 14 June 1872.
47 Howell to Alexander MacDonald, 25 May 1872 (HC).
48 Frederic Harrison, 'The New Criminal Law Amendment Act'; E. S. Beesly, 'The Criminal Law Amendment Act', *Bee-Hive*, 31 May 1872.
49 Howell to William Allan, 17 June 1872 (HC); Minutes of the Parliamentary Committee, 6 June 1872 (HC).
50 'Howell Memorandum' (HC).
51 Minutes of the Parliamentary Committee, 6 June 1872 (HC).
52 'Howell Memorandum' (HC).
53 Minutes of the Parliamentary Committee, 6 June 1872 (HC).
54 'Howell Memorandum' (HC).
55 Howell, 'The Criminal Law Amendment Act (1871) Amendment Bill', *Bee-Hive*, 7 June 1872.

56 Howell to William Allan, 17 June 1872 (HC).
57 Frederic Harrison, 'The Criminal Law Amendment Bill', *Bee-Hive*, 14 June 1872.
58 Minutes of the Parliamentary Committee, 6 June 1872 (HC).
59 'The Criminal Law Amendment Act, 1871, Amendment Bill' *Bee-Hive*, 14 June 1872.
60 Minutes of the Parliamentary Committee, 13 and 14 June 1872 (HC).
61 Howell to Daniel Guile, 16 July 1872 (HC).
62 Howell to Daniel Guile, 26 July 1872 (HC).
63 Howell to Alexander MacDonald, 14 August 1872 (HC).
64 Howell to W. V. Harcourt, 26 June 1872 (HC).
65 H. A. Bruce to W. E. Gladstone, 14 July 1872, Gladstone Papers, Add. MSS. 44087, f. 52 (B.M).
66 Howell to Charles Bartlett, 15 August 1872 (HC).

8: *The Parliamentary Committee and the Labour Laws*

1 E. S. Beesly, 'The Mines Regulation Bill', *Bee-Hive*, 6 July 1872.
2 Howell to Alexander MacDonald, 24 August 1872 (HC).
3 A. J. Mundella to Howell, 7 April 1872 (HC).
4 Minutes of the Parliamentary Committee, 9 April 1872 (HC); W. H. G. Armytage, *A. J. Mundella, 1825–1897: The Liberal Background to the Labour Movement* (London, 1951), pp. 120–21.
5 'Howell Memorandum' (HC).
6 Report of the Parliamentary Committee for 1872 (HC).
7 'Howell Memorandum' (HC).
8 Minutes of the Parliamentary Committee, 6 June 1872 (IIC).
9 Memorial on Payment of Wages (Truck) Bill, presented to the Home Secretary at a deputation of the Parliamentary Committee, 13 June 1872 (HC).
10 'Howell Memorandum' (HC); Printed letter soliciting contributions, February 1872 (HC).
11 Report of the Parliamentary Committee for 1872 (HC).
12 Minutes of the Parliamentary Committee, 17 February 1872 (HC).
13 Minutes of the Parliamentary Committee, 26 February 1872 (HC).
14 Minutes of the Parliamentary Committee, 9 April, 13 and 14 June 1872 (HC).
15 Howell's Diary, 1 July 1871 (HC); Howell to Robert Byron, 26 January 1872 (HC).
16 Howell to John Kane, 4 May 1872 (HC).
17 Minutes of the Parliamentary Committee, 3 May 1872 (HC).
18 Howell to Alexander MacDonald, 24 August 1872 (HC).
19 Article 26 of the Proposed Standing Orders for the Trades Union

Congress, appended to the Report of the Parliamentary Committee for 1872 (HC).

20 Report of the Parliamentary Committee for 1872 (HC).

21 Howell invited Frederic Harrison to Leeds after the latter had solicited an invitation through Henry Crompton. Crompton assured the Secretary that Harrison desired to attend 'in a friendly spirit'. Howell replied that 'we had no wish to control him. We did what we conceived to be our duty. He differed from us, that is all.' Howell to Alexander MacDonald, 28 December 1872 (HC). See Harrison, *Before the Socialists,* p. 261 n.

22 Report of the Fifth Annual Trades Union Congress, Leeds, 13–18 January 1873 (HC).

23 Henry Crompton's Report on the Criminal Law Amendment Act, appended to the Report of the Parliamentary Committee for 1872 (HC).

24 Howell's Diary, 15 January 1873 (HC).

25 *Bee-Hive,* 18 January 1873.

26 Minutes of 15 January session, Report of Leeds TUC (HC).

27 Minutes of 17 January session, Report of Leeds TUC (HC).

28 Howell, *Labour Legislation,* pp. 284–5.

29 *Bee-Hive,* 11 January 1873.

30 [Howell,] *The London Gas Stokers: A Report by the Committee of their Trial for Conspiracy, of their Defence, and of the Proceedings for their Liberation* (London, 1873) (Goldsmiths' Library).

31 Howell, *Labour Legislation,* pp. 245–9; Howell to Alexander MacDonald, 28 December 1872 (HC).

32 H. A. Bruce to W. E. Gladstone, 6 July 1873, Gladstone Papers, Add. MSS. 44087, f. 92 (BM).

33 Howell to William Allan, 9 February 1874 (HC).

34 Howell to Robert Peters, 29 July 1873 (HC). Peters' critical remarks, to which Howell alludes, seem to have been sent in lieu of a contribution.

35 Howell to W. E. Gladstone, 12 and 14 July 1873, Gladstone Papers, Add. MSS. 44439, ff. 152, 163 (BM).

36 Howell's Diary, 29 October, 1 November 1873 (HC); Howell to Lord Edmond Fitzmaurice, 1 November 1873 (HC).

37 Report of Deputation to the Home Secretary, 6 November 1873, published by the Parliamentary Committee (1873) (HC).

38 'Questions for Candidates' published by the Parliamentary Committee [1873] (HC).

39 Minutes of 14 January session, Report of the Sixth Annual Trades Union Congress, Sheffield, 12–17 January 1874 (HC).

40 Minutes of 16 and 17 January sessions, Report of Sheffield TUC (HC).

41 As he had done at Leeds, Howell was representing several small societies which could not afford to send their own men.
42 Discussion of Sheffield TUC in Report of General Council Meeting, Operative Bricklayers' Society Business Paper No. 10, July-August 1874 (HC).
43 Minutes of 16 January session, Report of Sheffield TUC (HC).
44 Howell to J. D. Prior, 16 February 1874 (HC).
45 Howell to John Callah, 25 February 1874 (HC).
46 Operative Bricklayers' Society Business Paper No. 10, July-August 1874 (HC).
47 *Operative Bricklayers' Society Trade Circular*, November 1874.
48 Howell to Alexander MacDonald, 16 February 1874 (HC).
49 *The Royal Commission on the Labour Laws and the Trades Union Congress Parliamentary Committee,* published by the Parliamentary Committee (1874) (HC).
50 Howell, *Labour Legislation*, p. 341.
51 *The Royal Commission and the Parliamentary Committee* (HC).
52 Henry Crompton to Howell, 20 March 1874 (HC); Howell to Henry Crompton, 21 March 1874 (HC).
53 *The Royal Commission and the Parliamentary Committee* (HC); A. J. Mundella to Robert Leader, 21 March 1874, quoted in Armytage, *Mundella*, pp. 148-9.
54 Howell to Thomas Halliday, 21 March 1874 (HC).
55 Howell to Francis Bacon, 10 June 1874 (HC).
56 Howell to A. J. Mundella, 18 June 1874 (HC).
57 W. P. Adam to Howell, 19 June 1874 (HC); A. J. Mundella to Howell, 22 June 1874, quoted in Armytage, *Mundella*, p. 149; Sir William Harcourt to Howell, 23 June 1874 (HC).
58 Howell to George Houseley, 26 January 1875 (HC).
59 Minutes of 19 January session, Report of the Seventh Annual Trades Union Congress, Liverpool, 18-23 January 1875 (IIC).
60 Minutes of 20 January session, Report of Liverpool TUC (HC).
61 Minutes of 22 January session, Report of Liverpool TUC (HC).
62 Report of the Parliamentary Committee for 1872 (HC); Howell to the Editor of the *Birmingham Morning News*, 9 March 1875 (HC).
63 Howell to J. D. Prior, 21 and 23 June 1875 (HC).
64 A. J. Mundella to Robert Leader, 15 July 1875, quoted in Armytage, *Mundella*, p. 151.
65 Howell, *Labour Legislation*, pp. 374-5.
66 Howell to Robert Knight, 14 July 1875 (HC).
67 Report of the Parliamentary Committee for 1875 (HC).
68 G. M. Young, *Victorian England: Portrait of an Age,* 2nd ed. (London, 1953), p. 123.

69 Howell to R. S. Wright, 21 July 1875 (HC). William Allan had died in October 1874 after a long illness.
70 Howell to Alexander MacDonald, 4 October 1875 (HC).
71 Minutes of 15 October session, Report of the Eighth Annual Trades Union Congress, Glasgow, 11–16 October 1875 (HC).
72 Howell to Auberon Herbert, 13 May 1876 (HC).
73 Auberon Herbert to Howell, 12 May 1876 (HC); *Bee-Hive*, 26 February 1876.
74 The Suggested Testimonial to Mr George Howell, Report of the Glasgow Trades Union Congress (1875) (HC).
75 Howell to George Houseley, 14 June 1876 (HC).
76 *Bee-Hive*, 30 September 1876.

9: *The Triumph of Respectability*

1 Howell's 'Autobiography' (HC).
2 Printed Report of the London School Board Policy Defence Committee, December 1876 (HC). The success of this first venture led to the reconstitution of the committee, again controlled by Howell and Morley, in 1879 and in 1882. Howell was paid £5 5s per week for four months during 1879 and nearly £50 *in toto* in 1882. Howell to Samuel Morley, 2 August 1879 (HC); Minute Book of the London School Board Election Committee, 1879 (HC); Report and Balance Sheet of the London School Board Election Committee, 1882 (HC).
3 R. T. Shannon, *Gladstone and the Bulgarian Agitation, 1876* (London, 1963), p. 48; Announcement of the League in Aid of the Christians of Turkey meeting, 27 July 1876 (HC).
4 Shannon, *Gladstone and the Bulgarian Agitation*, p. 233.
5 *Reynolds's Newspaper*, 17 September 1876.
6 Howell to Walter Morrison, 13 September 1877 (HC).
7 *Daily News*, 9 October 1876.
8 Howell, 'Working Men and the Eastern Question', *Contemporary Review*, Vol. XXVIII (October 1876), pp. 866-72.
9 The Eastern Question Association, *Report of Proceedings of the National Conference at St James's Hall, London* (1876). Howell was, of course, echoing the celebrated phrase from Gladstone's *Bulgarian Horrors*. Gladstone, however, had called for the extinction of Turkish administrative action in the Balkan provinces, not Turkish expulsion from Europe.
10 Howell to Sir Charles Reed, 7 April 1877 (HC).
11 Howell to Henry Crompton, 15 January 1881 (HC).
12 Henry Crompton to Howell, 9 March 1881 (HC).
13 Howell to John Holms, 7 April 1877 (HC).

14 Howell to Edmond Beales, 6 April 1877 (HC).
15 Howell to Dr W. C. Burnett, 13 June 1877 (HC).
16 Howell to Frederick Pennington, 9 November 1878 (HC).
17 Howell to Mrs Frederick Pennington, 7 November 1878 (HC); Howell to Miss Kate Thornbury, 15 November 1878 (HC).
18 Howell to Mis Kate Thornbury, 8 June 1879 (HC).
19 *Daily Telegraph*, 4 July 1876; *Pall Mall Gazette*, 1 September 1876.
20 Howell's 'Autobiography' (HC); Howell to Edmond Beales, 1 March 1878 (HC).
21 Webb, *History of Trade Unionism*, p. 13. The Webbs claimed that Howell's historical chapters are a 'close paraphrase' of Luigi Brentano's *History and Development of Gilds and the Origin of Trades Unions* (1870).

    Beatrice Webb records that when she and Sidney visited the Bodleian Library in search of material for their *History*, they were curtly received by the librarian who 'repelled our inquiries with the remark that we should find all we required in Howell's *Conflicts of Capital and Labour*'. Beatrice Webb, *Our Partnership* (London, 1948), p. 87.
22 Howell to Andrew Chatto, 8 October 1877 (HC); Howell to Samuel Morley, 6 April 1877 (HC). See 'Intimidation and Picketing: Two Phases of Trade Unionism', *Contemporary Review*, Vol. XXX (September 1877), pp. 598–624 and 'Trade Unions, Apprentices, and Technical Education', *Ibid.* (October 1877), pp. 833–57.
23 Howell's Diary, January 1879 (HC). Potter helped to place some of these pieces. One called 'Ellen Ashbury's Choice' appeared in *Temperance World*.
24 A copy of the story is included in a bound volume of Howell's journalistic publications. [Miscellaneous Articles] (HC). There is no indication of the magazine in which it appeared.
25 Howell's Diary, 21 February 1877 (HC); Howell to A. J. Mundella, 7 April 1877 (HC). Howell discussed the report with Mundella.
26 Howell to the Reverend Alfred Steinthal, 26 April [1877] (HC).
27 Howell to the Consul-General of the German Empire, 14 April, 4 May [1877] (HC). The report itself has not survived, although Howell's notes for it are in his collection.

    Collins and Abramsky misconstrued Howell's activities when they wrote, 'It seems likely that in 1878 the secrets of the International were sold to the German consulate in London, not by Eccarius, but by George Howell.' (*Karl Marx and the British Labour Movement*, p. 307) In January 1878 Howell wrote James Knowles, the editor of the *Nineteenth Century*, to ask whether the magazine might be interested in an article he had begun on the history of the International. Knowles accepted it, and the article

appeared in the July issue. Collins and Abramsky refer to Howell's
4 May letter to the German Consul, in which he promises to deliver
'the Report' and notes that 'much of the information given is not to
be found elsewhere'. They assign this letter to 1878 and imply that
the report was on the 'secrets of the International'.

To Howell's credit, this allegation cannot be substantiated. The
letter in question was written in 1877, not in 1878, and it appears in
a section of his letter book containing only letters written that
spring. The 1877 date correlates with Howell's rough notes on the
report, stating that it was written between 28 March and 28 April.
Collins and Abramsky disregard a more significant letter to the
Consul, dated 14 April 1877, in which Howell notes that he had
been working on 'the report on Trade Unions in England' ever
since he had been invited to prepare it and had submitted his notes
to Mundella. Nor is there any mystery about the information which
was 'not to be found elsewhere'. Howell explains this when he
writes that 'the information brought together in this report cannot
be obtained through any printed books, parliamentary or otherwise,
but it is the result of more than 20 years of close study of these questions and an intimate knowledge of the operations of these unions
throughout Great Britain'.

28 Howell was paid £10 for his research. Thomas Brassey to Howell,
    17 December 1877 (HC); Howell to Thomas Brassey, 1 and 12
    January 1878 (HC).
29 Henry Crompton to Howell, 2 December 1879 (HC).
30 Henry Crompton to Howell, 30 December 1879 (HC).
31 Howell to Henry Crompton, 6 September 1880 (HC). Howell's son
    had been a partial invalid since an attack of rheumatic fever in 1871.
32 'In Memorium GWTH 1880, Being the Memoirs of a Young Stu-
    dent Showing what books he read; what studies he pursued; what
    difficulties he encountered; how manfully battled with them; and
    what he achieved. And the End of it all.' (HC).
33 Howell to Goldwin Smith, 6 July 1877 (HC).
34 Howell, 'The Caucus System and the Liberal Party', *New Quarterly
    Magazine*, X (October 1878), pp. 583, 585. Also see Howell's article
    on the caucus in *Industrial Review*, 9 November 1878.
35 Howell to Edmond Beales, 21 March 1878 (HC).
36 Howell to Samuel Morley, 29 July 1878 (HC); Draft proposal for
    National Political Union [1878] (HC).
37 John Bright to Henry Broadhurst, 14 June 1879, Broadhurst Col-
    lection, Vol. I (LSE); John Morley to James Bryce, 14 December
    1878, Bryce Papers (Bodleian Library).
38 Ms. draft prospectus for National Liberal League, August 1879,
    1879 Letter Book (HC); Henry Broadhurst to James Bryce, 7

August 1879 and printed draft prospectus of National Liberal League (with ms. corrections), Bryce Papers (Bodleian Library).

39 Howell to Samuel Morley, 28 July 1879 (HC).

40 Draft prospectus for National Liberal League, Bryce Papers (Bodleian Library).

41 Howell to Henry Broadhurst, 26 April 1880 (HC).

42 Report of the Special Committee appointed to consider and report on the future work of the [National Liberal] League, [April 1881] (HC).

43 Howell to the Secretary of the Greenwich Liberal Association, 18 June 1878 (HC). See *Industrial Review*, 29 June 1878.

44 Howell to B. E. Morris, 11 March and 13 May 1880 (HC); Howell's Diary, 16 March 1880 (HC).

45 Howell's Diary, 1879–1885 *passim* (HC); Howell to Ellis Lever, 17 June, 14 October 1880 (HC); Ms. prospectus for National Fatal Accident Insurance Fund Ltd. [July 1880] (HC).

46 Benjamin T. Hall, *Our Fifty Years : The Story of the Working Men's Club and Institute Union* (London, 1912), p. 29 ff; Henry Solly to Howell, 16 September 1880 (HC). See Henry Solly, *These Eighty Years* (London, 1893), II, pp. 519–22.

47 *Common Good*, 9 October 1880.

48 Howell to Henry Solly, 22 November 1880 (HC).

49 *Common Good*, 4 December 1880, 15 January 1881; Howell's Diary, 8 January 1881 (HC); Howell's Cash Accounts for 1881 (HC).

50 Howell to Henry Solly, 9 February 1881, Solly Collection, Vol. V (LSE).

51 *Common Good*, 19 February 1881; Printed letter on the future of the paper by Henry Solly, 2 March 1881, Solly Collection, Vol. V (LSE).

52 *Stafford Chronicle*, 12 November 1881.

53 Address to the Freemen and Electors of the Borough of Stafford, 9 November 1881 (HC).

54 *Stafford Chronicle*, 12 November 1881; *Daily News*, 11 November 1881.

55 *Stafford Chronicle*, 19 November 1881.

56 *Daily News*, 18 November 1881; *Stafford Chronicle*, 19 November 1881; Webb, *History of Trade Unionism*, pp. 394–5 n.

The TUC cleared the administrators of the Gas Stokers' Fund of the charge of malversation. See *Mr H. Broadhurst, M.P. and the Gas Stokers' Fund* (Manchester, 1882), Webb Trade Union Collection, Section B, Vol. XXIV (LSE). Also see Daniel Guile to the Chairman of Howell's Election Committee, 29 November 1881, published in the *Labour Standard*, 3 December 1881.

57 Handbill: 'To the Electors of the Borough of Stafford', signed 'A Radical Elector' (HC).

58 *Radical*, 19 November 1881; Soutter, *Recollections*, pp. 118–21.

59 *Labour Standard*, 26 November 1881.

60 *Stafford Chronicle*, 26 November 1881.

61 Howell's Diary, 27 January 1885 (HC).

62 See Paul Thompson, *Socialists, Liberals and Labour: The Struggle for London, 1885-1914* (London, 1967), p. 92.

63 Howell's Diary, 1885 (HC); *Hackney Standard*, 11 July 1885; *Eastern Argus*, 18 July, 26 September, 10 and 31 October, 7 November 1885.

64 Howell's Diary, 24 June 1885 (HC); Samuel Morley to Howell, 2 July 1885 (HC); Thomas Brassey to Howell, 21 October 1885 (HC).

65 Address to the Electors and Non-Electors of the North-East Division of the Borough of Bethnal Green, August 1885 (HC).

66 In a straight fight with a Conservative, Howell received 3095 votes and his opponent, John Dawson Mayne, 1844 votes. *Eastern Argus*, 28 November 1885.

67 Handbill: 'To the Working Men Electors', signed 'Old Gas Stokers' [1885] (HC); George Shipton to Howell, 26 November 1885 (HC). Kenny was a disreputable agitator who founded the General Amalgamated Labourers Union in the 1870s. He subsequently became a Conservative *agent provocateur* and was in the pay of the Fair Trade League. In 1888 he was arrested for stealing silverware from a restaurant and sentenced to fifteen months in prison.

68 *Daily Telegraph*, 19 January 1886; *Hackney Standard*, 23 January 1886.

69 *Daily Telegraph*, 20 January 1886.

70 Address to the Electors of the North-East Division of Bethnal Green, June 1886 (HC).

71 See the essay by Howell in Andrew Reid, ed., *The New Liberal Programme* (London, 1886); *The Liberal Home Ruler*, 27 November, 4 December 1886.

72 Howell, 'The New Political Charter', *The Liberal Home Ruler*, 25 September 1886; Ernest Davies, 'Mr George Howell's New Political Charter', *The Liberal Home Ruler*, 16 October 1886; Howell, 'One Man, One Vote and Registration Reform', *North Eastern Leader*, 30 July 1892.

73 Howell, 'Statute Law Revision', *North Eastern Leader*, 4 June 1892; Lord Thring to Howell, 16 August 1887 (HC). See Preface to *The Statutes*, 2nd rev. ed. (London, 1888), I, p. iv.

74 C. G. Mander to Howell, 8 February 1887 (HC); Alfred Milner to Howell, 21 May, 29 June 1887 (HC).

75 Howell's Diary, March 1887 (HC); *Eastern Argus*, 1 October 1887.

76 Howell, *Labour Legislation*, pp. 282, 471; Joseph Havelock Wilson, *My Stormy Voyage Through Life* (London, 1925), I, p. 251.

77 Owen Roberts to Howell, 8 October, 4 November 1889 (HC); Howell's Diary, August, November, December 1889 (HC).

78 Howell's Diary, September, October 1886, January 1887 (HC); H. O. Arnold-Forster to Howell, 25 January 1888 (HC).

79 Howell, 'Social Democracy and the Trades Congress', *New Review*, Vol. III, No. 17 (October 1890).

80 Thomas MacKay to Howell, 30 May 1890, 12 January 1891 (HC).

81 Howell, 'Liberty for Labour', *A Plea for Liberty: An Argument against Socialism and Socialistic Legislation*, ed. Thomas MacKay (London, 1891), pp. 109–41.

82 Howell, *Trade Unionism New and Old*, 4th ed. (London, 1907), pp. 133–4.

83 Howell, *Trade Unionism* . . . p. 68.

84 Howell, *Trade Unionism* . . . p. 162.

85 Howell, *Trade Unionism* . . . p. 231.

86 Howell, 'The Eight Hours' Agitation', *North Eastern Leader*, 14 May 1892.

87 *The Trade Unionist*, 23 January 1892.

88 *Eastern Argus*, 14 March 1891.

89 Arnold Morley to Howell, 1 July 1889, 28 July 1891, 25 June 1892 (HC).

90 Ballard called for abolition of the House of Lords and the party system, payment of members of Parliament, abolition of Sabbatarian legislation, opposition to local option, a compulsory eight-hour day, and the annexation of Egypt. Ballard election handbill (HC).

   Eleanor Marx and Edward Aveling came to the aid of Taylor against that 'horrible beast Howell'. Quoted in Chushichi Tsuzuki, *The Life of Eleanor Marx, 1855-1898 : A Socialist Tragedy* (Oxford, 1967), p. 225. The money for Taylor's campaign came in part from H. H. Champion. See Pelling, *Origins of the Labour Party*, p. 106.

91 *North Eastern Leader*, 18 June 1892.

92 *North Eastern Leader*, 25 June 1892; *Eastern Argus*, 25 June 1892.

93 *North Eastern Leader*, 7 July 1892.

94 Howell's 'Autobiography' (HC).

95 Howell to Charles Bartlett, 26 December 1905 (HC). Bhownaggree was the second Indian to win a seat in Parliament. Dadabhai Naoroji had been elected as a Liberal for Central Finsbury in 1892. Bhownaggree held Bethnal Green in 1900 but lost his seat in the Liberal landslide of 1906.

96 Howell to William Rathbone, 13 June 1900, Rathbone Papers

(Courtesy of the University of Liverpool Library); Howell's 'Auto-biography' (HC).

97 The Liberals, who managed to win 24 London seats in 1892, after securing 10 in 1886, held only 8 seats in 1895. See Paul Thompson, *Socialists, Liberals and Labour : The Struggle For London, 1885–1914*, pp. 107–11.

98 Howell to Haworth Barnes, 4 March 1892 (HC); Ms. Preface to 'Ernest Jones' [1896] (HC); Frederick Macmillan to Howell, 11 June 1896 (HC); Howell to W. E. Adams, 9 July 1896 (HC). The work was published in 41 instalments from January to October 1898, and Howell received £60 from the *Newcastle Weekly Chronicle* for it. An abridged version appeared in the *Dewsbury Reporter* in February and March 1899.

99 Circular for George Howell Testimonial Fund and List of Contributors (HC); Howell to Robert Applegarth, 3 November 1897 (HC).
    Former associates occasionally sent him small contributions in later years. See Arnold Morley to Howell, 4 June 1903 (HC); R. K. Causton to Howell, 26 June, 18 October, 18 November 1903, 21 November 1904 (HC).

100 Howell's Diary, March 1900 (HC).

101 Howell's Diary, 24 September 1900 (HC).

102 Howell's Diary, 26 September 1900 (HC).

103 *Reynolds's Newspaper*, 17 June 1900.

104 *Reynolds's Newspaper*, 28 October 1900; Cole, *British Working Class Politics*, pp. 165–6.

105 Foxwell, a Professor of Political Economy at University College, London, accumulated two collections of books on politics and economics. The first forms the basis of the Goldsmiths' Library in the University of London. The second was purchased by Harvard University for the Kress Library in 1929.
    H. S. Foxwell to Howell, 7 August 1899 (HC); Robert Applegarth to Professor [H.S.] Foxwell, n.d. (HC); Howell's Diary, 31 December 1905 (HC). Andrew Carnegie contributed £105 towards the purchase of Howell's library. Robert Applegarth to Frederic Harrison, 12 July 1906, Harrison Papers, Section C, Vol. 4 (LSE).

106 Henry Campbell-Bannerman to Howell, 31 July 1906 (HC); H. S. Foxwell to Howell, 8 August 1906 (HC).

107 *The Times*, 19 September 1910. See Howard Evans, *Radical Fights of Forty Years* (London, 1913), p. 20.

Conclusion

1   *Westminster Gazette,* 13 November 1906.

Select Bibliography

A. PRIMARY SOURCES
    I. Howell Collection
        1. Manuscripts
        2. Published Reports and Journals
        3. Election Data
        4. Miscellaneous Printed Material
    II. Additional Manuscript Collections
   III. Howell's Published Writings
   IV. Newspapers and Periodicals

B. SECONDARY WORKS
    I. Unpublished Material
   II. Books and Pamphlets
  III. Articles

A. PRIMARY SOURCES

I. *George Howell Collection, Bishopsgate Institute, London*

  1 Manuscripts
    a Howell's Autobiography
      Seven autobiographical fragments written between 1896 and
      1907 and chiefly concerned with Howell's early years. Includes
      brief memoirs of many political associates and organizations.
    b Howell's Letters
      Copies of nearly 10,000 letters are preserved in thirteen copy
      books covering the years from 1865 to 1884. Four of these
      volumes comprise Howell's correspondence as Secretary of
      the Reform League. Also include drafts of speeches, reports,
      articles, and election addresses.
    c Howell's Diaries
      Fragmentary entries between 1864 and 1909, plus some finan-
      cial accounts.

K

d Letters to Howell

Approximately 1,600 original letters written to Howell between 1865 and 1910.

e Diaries of George Washington Taviner Howell, 1873–80

f Reform League Papers

Executive Committee Agenda Book

Executive Committee Minute Books (4 volumes)

General Council Minute Book

Finance Committee Minute Book

Ledgers and Account Books (5 volumes)

Election Reports (1868 deputations to constituencies)

Miscellaneous Papers

g International Working Men's Association

Minute Book of the General Council, 1866–9

Howell's notes and summary of minutes

h Liberal Registration and Election Agency

Howell's notes on its origins and finances

i Labour Representation League

Howell's notes on the founding of the organization

j Trades Union Congress

Reports of the 1868, 1871, and 1872 Congresses

Minutes of the Parliamentary Committee, 1872

Memorandum on Parliamentary Committee activity, 1872

Secretary's notes on 1872 and 1873 Congresses

Howell's review of TUC history, 1868–83

k Beales Testimonial Fund Minute Book

l Account Book, 1873–4

m Plimsoll and Seamen's Fund Committee

Papers and accounts

n London School Board Election Committee, 1879

Minute Book

o Parliamentary Motions and Questions

p Memoir of George Washington Taviner Howell

q Ms. copy of 'A History of the Working Men's Association, 1836–1850'

r Ms. copy of biography of Ernest Jones

s 'Industrial Notes'

Articles for *Engineering*, 1909–10

t Robert Applegarth, 'People I Have Known'

Typescript of a speech to the Hotspur Club, 12 March 1898

2 Reports and Journals

a London Trades Council

Rules

Reports, 1861–92

b Operative Bricklayers' Society
  Rules
  Strike Reports
  Trade Circular, 1861–81
  Annual Reports, 1862–70
  Report and Balance Sheet of the Dispute relating to the Attempt to Introduce the System of Hiring and Paying by the Hour (1861)
c *Balance Sheet of the Late Strike and Lock-out in the London Building Trades* (1860)
d *The Nine Hours' Movement in the Building Trades : A Report of the Proceedings of a Conference of Delegates from the Building Trades held in the Temperance Hall, Curzon Street, Derby on the 1–4 January 1861, to consider the best means to be adopted for obtaining the proposed Reduction in the Hours of Labour.* (London, 1861)
e *Mr Potter and the London Trades Council* (1865)
f *Report of Proceedings at the National Reform Conference held in Free Trade Hall, Manchester, 15 and 16 May 1865*
g R. S. Kirk, *The Second Annual Congress of Trades Unions* (Birmingham, 1869)
h Reports of the Parliamentary Committee of the Trades Union Congress, 1872–5
i Reports of the Trades Union Congress, 1873–80
j *The Royal Commission on the Labour Laws and the Trades Union Congress* (1874)
k Eastern Question Association: *Report of Proceedings of the National Conference at St James's Hall, London* (1876)
3 Election Data
  Election addresses, posters, handbills, newspaper clippings and other material relating to Howell's parliamentary election campaigns, 1868, 1871, 1874, 1875, 1881, 1885, 1886, 1892, 1895
4 Miscellaneous Printed Material
  Reports, pamphlets, handbills, form letters, and other documentary material on the following organizations:
  Committee for Mr Trevelyan's Motion for Parliamentary Reform
  Eastern Question Association
  1884 Demonstration Committee
  Gas Stokers' Defence Committee
  Labour Representation League
  Land Tenure Reform Association
  Leasehold Enfranchisement Association
  Liberal Registration and Election Agency
  Liberation Society
  London Liberal and Radical Union

London Municipal Reform League
London School Board Election Committees, 1876, 1879, 1882
London Working Men's Association
National Democratic League
National Education League
National League for the Independence of Poland
National Liberal League
National Reform Union
National Women's Suffrage Society
Parliamentary Committee of the Trades Union Congress
Plimsoll and Seamen's Fund Committee
Reform League
Representative Reform Association
Universal League for the Material Elevation of the Industrious Classes
Working Men's Club and Institute Union
Working Men's Committee for Promoting the Separation of Church and State

II. *Additional Manuscript Collections*
1 Bodleian Library, Oxford
James Bryce Papers
2 British Library of Political and Economic Science, London
a Henry Broadhurst Collection
Broadhurst Letters, 1873–86
Minute Book of the Labour Representation League, 1873–8
b Frederic Harrison Papers
Letters from Harrison to E. S. Beesly and John Morley
Letters to Harrison from Applegarth, Beesly, Beales, Bright, Dilke, Herbert, and Odger
c Mill-Taylor Collection
Letters and Papers of John Stuart Mill
d Henry Solly Collection
Letters of Henry Solly, papers of the *Common Good,* letter from Howell
e Webb Trade Union Collection
Reminiscences of trade union leaders, including Applegarth, Broadhurst, and Shipton
Minute Book of the Conference of Amalgamated Trades, 1867–1871
3 British Museum
a John Bright Papers
b Richard Cobden Papers
c Richard Assheton Cross Papers

  d William Ewart Gladstone Papers
     Letters from Bright, Bruce, Glyn, Howell
 4 Cambridge University Library
   John Malcolm Ludlow Papers
     Letters to Ludlow
     Ms. Autobiography
 5 House of Commons Library
   Notices of Motions (printed)
 6 Imperial College, London
   Thomas Henry Huxley Papers
     Letters from Howell to Huxley
 7 London County Record Office
   Minutes and Papers of the Liberation Society
 8 London Trades Council
   Minutes (Microfilm in possession of Mr Chimen Abramsky)
 9 National Liberal Club
   Minutes of the Election Committee and the General Committee
10 University College, London
   Edward Spencer Beesly Papers

III. *Howell's Published Writings*

 1 Books:
    A Handy Book of the Labour Laws. London, 1876.
    *The Conflicts of Capital and Labour Historically and Economically
       Considered*. London, 1878.
    Trade Unionism New and Old. London, 1891.
    Labour Legislation, Labour Movements, and Labour Leaders.
       London, 1902.
   Edited: *Imperial White Books*. 4 Vols. London, 1886–8. (With
     Herman Cohen), *Trade Union Law and Cases*. London, 1901.
   Contributing Author:
     'Bricklaying', *Report of Artisans Selected by the Society of Arts to
     Visit the Paris Universal Exhibition, 1867*.
     Andrew Reid, ed., *The New Liberal Programme*. London, 1886.
     (with A. J. Mundella), 'Industrial Association, 1833–1887',
        The Reign of Queen Victoria: A Survey of Fifty Years of Progress.
     Thomas Humphrey Ward, ed. 2 vols. London, 1887.
     *Bold Retrenchment; or the Liberal Policy which will save one-half of
        the National Expenditure*. London, 1888.
     'Liberty for Labour', *A Plea for Liberty: An Argument against
        Socialism and Socialistic Legislation*, Thomas MacKay, ed.
        London, 1891.
     Introduction to Lord Brassey, *Work and Wages*. London, 1894.

'Ernest Jones the Chartist' (serialized in the *Newcastle Weekly Chronicle*, January to October 1898).

2 Pamphlets:
> *The London Gas Stokers : A Report by the Committee of their Trial for Conspiracy, of their Defence, and of the Proceedings for their Liberation* (1873)
> *Notes on Books and Reading* (1875)
> *The Labour Laws* (1876)
> *Waste Land and Prison Labour* (1877)
> *Land Tenure Reform* (1879)
> *National Industrial Insurance and Employers' Liability* (1880)
> *Conciliation and Arbitration in Trade Disputes* (1880)

3 Articles (Selected List):
> *Bee-Hive*, 55 articles (1871–8)
> *Contemporary Review*, 6 articles (1876–89)
> *Cooperative Wholesale Society Annual*, 12 articles (1885–1904)
> *Daily Chronicle*, 10 articles (1879)
> *Fortnightly Review*, 2 articles (1887)
> *Fraser's Magazine*, 2 articles (1879)
> *Labour Standard*, 10 articles (1881)
> *New Quarterly Magazine*, 1 article (1878)
> *New Review*, 5 articles (1890–92)
> *Nineteenth Century*, 4 articles (1878–84)
> *North Eastern Leader and Bethnal Green and Hackney News*, 21 articles (1892–4)
> *Reynolds's Newspaper*, 39 articles (1896–1906)
> *Social Notes*, 15 articles (1879–81)

IV. *Newspapers and Periodicals Consulted*

> *Daily News*
> *Manchester Guardian*
> *Reynolds's Newspaper*
> *The Times*
> *Bee-Hive*, 1862–76
> *Bethnal Green News*, 1894–95
> *Buckinghamshire County Chronicle*, 1868, 1874
> *Bucks Advertiser and Aylesbury News*, 1868, 1874
> *Bucks Chronicle and Bucks Gazette*, 1868
> *Bucks Herald*, 1868, 1874
> *Capital and Labour*, 1881–2
> *Common Good*, 1880–1
> *Commonwealth*, 1866–7
> *Eastern Argus and Borough of Hackney Times*, 1885–95

Hackney Standard and Bethnal Green and Shoreditch Chronicle, 1885–95
Industrial Review, Social and Political, 1877–8
Labour Standard, 1881–5
Liberal Home Ruler, 1886–8
Liberal and Radical, 1887–9
The Liberator, 1871–5
Miner and Workman's Advocate, 1865
North Eastern Leader and Bethnal Green and Hackney News, 1892–6
Pioneer, 1883–4
Radical, 1881
Shoreditch Citizen and Hackney and Bethnal Green Advertiser, 1889–90
Stafford Chronicle, 1881
Trade Unionist, 1891–2
Working Man, 1861–2
Workman's Advocate, 1865–6

B. SECONDARY WORKS

1. *Unpublished Material*

Allgood, Henry G. C., 'Stray Leaves from the Past of Our Village: A History of Bethnal Green' [1914], Manuscript in the Bethnal Green Central Library, London.

Bell, Aldon D., 'The Reform League from its Origins to the Reform Act of 1867', D.Phil. Thesis, Oxford University, 1961.

Buchanan, R. A., 'Trade Unions and Public Opinion, 1850–75', Ph.D. Thesis, Cambridge University, 1957

Coltham, Stephen, 'George Potter and the "Bee-Hive" Newspaper', D.Phil. Thesis, Oxford University, 1956.

Crowley, Desmond William, 'The Origins of the Revolt of the British Labour Movement from Liberalism, 1875–1906', Ph.D. Thesis, University of London, 1952.

Harrison, Royden J., 'The Activity and Influence of the English Positivists upon Labour Movements, 1859–1885', D.Phil. Thesis, Oxford University, 1955.

Lamb, William Kaye, 'British Labour and Parliament, 1865–1893', Ph.D. Thesis, University of London, 1933.

McCready, Herbert W., 'Frederic Harrison and the British Working Class Movement, 1860–1875', Ph.D. Thesis, Harvard University, 1952.

Moberg, Donald Read, 'George Odger and the English Working Class Movement, 1860–1877', Ph.D. Thesis, University of London, 1954.

Warner, Arthur Cyrus, 'The Plimsoll Agitation: A Chapter in

Nineteenth Century British Social and Maritime History', Ph.D. Thesis, Harvard University, 1960.

II. *Books and Pamphlets*

Altick, Richard D., *The English Common Reader : A Social History of the Mass Reading Public, 1800–1900*. Chicago, 1963.

Armytage, W. H. G., *A. J. Mundella, 1825–1897 : The Liberal Background to the Labour Movement*. London, 1951.

Ausubel, Herman, *John Bright: Victorian Reformer*. New York, 1966.

Bamford, Samuel, *Bamford's Passages in the Life of a Radical and Early Days*. Henry Dunckley, ed. 2 vols. London, 1893.

Blake, Robert, *Disraeli*. London, 1966.

Bonner, Hypatia Bradlaugh, *Charles Bradlaugh : A Record of His Life and Work*. 3rd ed. 2 vols. London, 1895.

Bowley, Arthur L., *Wages in the United Kingdom in the Nineteenth Century*. Cambridge, 1900.

Briggs, Asa, *Victorian People : A Reassessment of Persons and Themes, 1851–67*. Chicago, 1955.

Briggs, Asa and John Saville, ed., *Essays in Labour History: In Memory of G. D. H. Cole*. London, 1960.

Broadhurst, Henry, *The Story of His Life from a Stonemason's Bench to the Treasury Bench*. London, 1901.

Clegg, H. A., Alan Fox, and A. F. Thompson, *A History of British Trade Unions Since 1889*, Vol. I, 1889–1910. Oxford, 1964.

Cole, G. D. H., *A Short History of the British Working Class Movement, 1789–1927*. London, 1927.

Cole, G. D. H., *British Working Class Politics, 1832–1914*. London, 1941.

Cole, G. D. H., *Chartist Portraits*. 2nd ed. London, 1965.

Cole, G. D. H., *Socialist Thought: The Forerunners, 1789–1850*. London, 1953.

Cole, G. D. H., *Socialist Thought: Marxism and Anarchism, 1850–1890*. London, 1954.

Cole, G. D. H. and A. W. Filson, *British Working Class Movements : Select Documents, 1789–1875*. London, 1951.

Cole, G. D. H. and Raymond Postgate, *The British Common People, 1746–1946*. London, 1961.

Collins, Henry and Chimen Abramsky, *Karl Marx and the British Labour Movement : Years of the First International*. London, 1965.

Cowling, Maurice, *1867 Disraeli, Gladstone and Revolution: The Passing of the Second Reform Bill*. Cambridge, 1967.

Davis, W. J., *The British Trades Union Congress : History and Recollections*. London, 1910.

Documents of the First International : The General Council of the First International, 1864–1870. 3 vols. Moscow, 1963–6.

Dyer, George H., *Benjamin Lucraft : A Biography*. London, 1879.

Elliot, Hugh S. R., ed., *The Letters of John Stuart Mill*. 2 vols. London, 1910.

Ensor, R. C. K., *England, 1870–1914*. Oxford, 1936.

Evans, Howard, *Radical Fights of Forty Years*. London, 1913.

Evans, Howard, *Sir Randal Cremer : His Life and Work*. London, 1909.

Gardiner, A. G., *The Life of Sir William Harcourt*. 2 vols. London, 1923.

Gillespie, Frances Elma, *Labor and Politics in England, 1850–1867*. Durham, N. C., 1927.

Gwyn, William B., *Democracy and the Cost of Politics in Britain*. London, 1962.

Hall, Benjamin T., *Our Fifty Years : The Story of the Working Men's Club and Institute Union*. London, 1912.

Hammond, J. L. and Barbara Hammond, *James Stansfeld : A Victorian Champion of Sex Equality*. London, 1932.

Hanham, H. J., *Elections and Party Management : Politics in the Time of Disraeli and Gladstone*. London, 1959.

Harris, S. Hutchison, *Auberon Herbert : Crusader for Liberty*. London, 1943.

Harrison, Frederic, *Autobiographic Memoirs*. 2 vols. London, 1911.

Harrison, John F. C., *Learning and Living, 1790–1960 : A Study in the History of the English Adult Education Movement*. London, 1961.

Harrison, Royden, *Before the Socialists : Studies in Labour and Politics 1861 to 1881*. London, 1965.

Higenbottam, Samuel, *Our Society's History*. Manchester, 1939.

Hilton, W. S., *Foes to Tyranny : A History of the Amalgamated Union of Building Trade Workers*. London, 1963.

Hobsbawm, Eric J., *Labouring Men : Studies in the History of Labour*. London, 1964.

Hobsbawm, Eric J., *Primitive Rebels : Studies in Archaic Forms of Social Movement in the 19th and 20th Centuries*. 2nd ed. New York, 1963.

Hodder, Edwin, *The Life of Samuel Morley*. 2nd ed. London, 1887.

Hughes, Jonathan R. T., *Fluctuations in Trade, Industry and Finance : A Study of British Economic Development, 1850–1860*. Oxford, 1960.

Humphrey, A. W., *A History of Labour Representation*. London, 1912.

Humphrey, A. W., *Robert Applegarth : Trade Unionist, Educationist, Reformer*. Manchester, 1913,

Hyndman, Henry Mayers, *The Record of an Adventurous Life*. London, 1911.

Inglis, Kenneth S., *Churches and the Working Classes in Victorian England*. London, 1963.

Jefferys, James B., ed., *Labour's Formative Years, 1849–1879*. London, 1948.

Kitson Clark, G. S. R., *The Making of Victorian England*. London, 1962.

Leno, John Bedford, *The Aftermath, with the Autobiography of the Author*. London, 1892.

Lovett, William, *Life and Struggles of William Lovett in His Pursuit of Bread, Knowledge, and Freedom*. 2 vols. London, 1920.

Ludlow, John Malcolm and Lloyd Jones, *Progress of the Working Class, 1832–1867*. London, 1867.

Maccoby, Simon, *English Radicalism, 1853–1886*. London, 1938.

Maccoby, Simon, *English Radicalism, 1886–1914*. London, 1953.

Mack, Edward C. and W. H. G. Armytage, *Thomas Hughes: The Life of the Author of Tom Brown's Schooldays*. London, 1952.

Magnus, Philip, *Gladstone: A Biography*. New York, 1954.

Marx, Karl and Frederick Engels, *On Britain*. Moscow, 1954.

Marx, Karl and Frederick Engels, *Selected Correspondence*. Dona Torr, ed. New York [1942].

Masterman, N. C., *John Malcolm Ludlow: The Builder of Christian Socialism*. Cambridge, 1963.

Masters, David, *The Plimsoll Mark*. London, 1955.

McCabe, Joseph, *Life and Letters of George Jacob Holyoake*. 2 vols. London, 1908.

Mins, L. E., ed., *Founding of the First International (September–November 1864): A Documentary Record*. Moscow, 1935.

Minutes of Evidence of the Royal Commission on Trade Unions. London, 1867.

Monypenny, William Flavelle and George Earle Buckle, *The Life of Benjamin Disraeli, Earl of Beaconsfield*. Rev. ed. 2 vols. New York, 1929.

Morley, John, *The Life of Richard Cobden*. 14th ed. London, 1910.

Morley, John, *The Life of William Ewart Gladstone*. 2nd ed. 3 vols. London, 1912.

Morton, Frederic, *The Rothschilds: A Family Portrait*. New York, 1962.

Mr H. Broadhurst and the Gas Stokers' Fund. Manchester, 1882.

Musson, A. E., *The Congress of 1868: The Origins and Establishment of the Trades Union Congress*. London, 1955.

Owen, David, *English Philanthropy, 1660–1960*. Cambridge, Mass., 1965.

Packe, Michael St John, *The Life of John Stuart Mill*. London, 1954.

Park, Joseph H., *The English Reform Bill of 1867*. New York, 1920.

Pelling, Henry, *A History of British Trade Unionism*. Harmondsworth, 1963.

Pelling, Henry, *America and the British Left: From Bright to Bevan*. New York, 1957.

Pelling, Henry, *Popular Politics and Society in Late Victorian Britain*. London, 1968.

Pelling, Henry, *The Origins of the Labour Party, 1880–1900*. 2nd ed. Oxford, 1965.

Phelps Brown, E. H., *The Growth of British Industrial Relations*. London, 1965.

Postgate, Raymond W., *The Builders' History*. London, 1923.

Rathbone, Eleanor F., *William Rathbone: A Memoir*. London, 1905.

Read, Donald, *Cobden and Bright: A Victorian Political Partnership*. New York, 1968.

Report of the First General Meeting of Members of the National Education League. Birmingham, 1869.

Richards, Cicely, *A History of Trades Councils*. London, 1920.

Roberts, B. C., *The Trades Union Congress, 1868–1921*. London, 1958.

Rutherford, Mark (William Hale White), *The Revolution in Tanner's Lane*. London, 1936.

Saville, John, *Ernest Jones: Chartist*. London, 1952.

Saville, John, ed., *Democracy and the Labour Movement: Essays in Honour of Dona Torr*. London, 1954.

Schoyen, A. R., *The Chartist Challenge: A Portrait of George Julian Harney*. London, 1958.

Shannon, R. T., *Gladstone and the Bulgarian Agitation, 1876*. London, 1963.

Simon, Brian, *Education and the Labour Movement, 1870–1920*. London, 1965.

Smith, B., *The Making of the Second Reform Bill*. Cambridge,. 1966.

Smith, Warren Sylvester, *The London Heretics 1870–1914*. New York, 1968.

Solly, Henry, *These Eighty Years*. 2 vols. London, 1893.

Soutter, Francis William, *Fights for Freedom: The Story of My Life*. London, 1925.

Soutter, Francis William, *Recollections of a Labour Pioneer*. London, 1923.

Tate, George, *The London Trades Council, 1860–1950: A History*. London, 1950.

Taylor, A. J. P., *The Trouble Makers: Dissent over Foreign Policy, 1792–1939*. Bloomington, 1958.

Thompson, Edward P., *The Making of the English Working Class*. New York, 1964.

Thompson, Paul, *Socialists, Liberals and Labour: The Struggle for London, 1885–1914*. London, 1967.

Trevelyan, G. M., *The Life of John Bright*. 2nd ed. London, 1925.

Tsuzuki, Chushichi, *The Life of Eleanor Marx, 1855–1898: A Socialist Tragedy*. Oxford, 1967.

Turner, E. S., *Roads to Ruin: The Shocking History of Social Reform*. Harmondsworth, 1966.

Vincent, John, *The Formation of the Liberal Party, 1857–1868*. London, 1966.

Wallace, Elisabeth, *Goldwin Smith, Victorian Liberal*. Toronto, 1957.

Wearmouth, Robert F., *Methodism and the Struggle of the Working Classes, 1850–1900*. Leicester, 1954.

Wearmouth, Robert F., *Methodism and the Working-Class Movements of England, 1800–1850*. 2nd ed. London, 1947.

Webb, Beatrice, *Our Partnership*. London, 1948.

Webb, Robert K., *The British Working Class Reader, 1790–1848: Literacy and Social Tension*. London, 1955.

Webb, Sidney and Beatrice, *The History of Trade Unionism*. Rev. ed. New York, 1920.

Wilson, Joseph Havelock, *My Stormy Voyage Through Life*. Vol. I, London, 1925.

Young, G. M., *Victorian England: Portrait of an Age*. 2nd ed. London, 1953.

III. *Articles*

Bell, Aldon D., 'Administration and Finance of the Reform League, 1865–67', *International Review of Social History*, X (1965), Part 3, 385–409.

Brand, Carl F., 'Conversion of British Trade Unions to Political Action', *American Historical Review*, XXX, No. 2 (January 1925), 251–70.

Brock, Peter, 'Polish Democrats and English Radicals, 1832–1862', *Journal of Modern History*, XXV, No. 2 (June 1953), 139–56.

Cole, G. D. H., 'Some Notes on British Trade Unionism in the Third Quarter of the Nineteenth Century', *International Review of Social History*, II (1937), 1–22.

Collins, Henry, 'Karl Marx, the International, and the British Trade Union Movement', *Science and Society*, XXVI, No. 4 (1962), 400–21.

Coltham, Stephen, 'George Potter, the Junta, and the *Bee-Hive*', *International Review of Social History*, IX (1964), Part 3 and X (1965), Part 1, 1–85.

Cowling, Maurice, 'Disraeli, Derby and Fusion, October 1865 to July 1866', *The Historical Journal*, VIII, No. 1 (1965), 31–71.

Glicksberg, Charles I., 'Henry Adams Reports on a Trades-Union

Meeting', *New England Quarterly*, XV, No. 4 (December 1942), 724–28.

Harrison, Royden, 'British Labour and the Confederacy', *International Review of Social History*, II (1957), Part 1, 78–105.

Harrison, Royden, 'Practical, Capable Men', *The New Reasoner*, No. 6 (Autumn 1958), 105–19.

Herrick, Francis H., 'The Reform Bill of 1867 and the British Party System', *Pacific Historical Review*, III, No. 2 (June 1934), 216–33.

Himmelfarb, Gertrude, 'The Politics of Democracy: the English Reform Act of 1867', *Journal of British Studies*, VI, No. 1 (November 1966), 97–138.

Leventhal, F. M., 'Notes on Sources: The George Howell Collection', *Bulletin of the Society for the Study of Labour History*, No. 10 (Spring 1965), 38–40.

Marx, Karl, 'A Reply on the First International: Mr George Howell's History of the International Working Men's Association', *Labour Monthly* (September 1954), 417–421.

McCready, H. W., 'British Labour and the Royal Commission on Trade Unions, 1867–69', *University of Toronto Quarterly*, XXIV, No. 4 (July 1955), 390–409.

McCready, II. W., 'British Labour's Lobby, 1867–1875', *Canadian Journal of Economics and Political Science*, XXII, No. 2 (May 1956), 141–60.

Park, Joseph H., 'English Workmen and the American Civil War', *Political Science Quarterly*, XXXIX, No. 3 (September 1924), 432–57.

Saville, John, 'The Background to the Revival of Socialism in England,' *Bulletin of the Society for the Study of Labour History*, No. 11 (Autumn 1965), 13–17.

Smith, F. B., 'Democracy in the Second Reform Debates', *Historical Studies of Australia and New Zealand*, II, No. 43 (October 1964), 306–23.

Tholfsen, Trygve R., 'The Transition to Democracy in Victorian England', *International Review of Social History*, VI (1961), Part 2, 226–48.

Thompson, A. F., 'Gladstone's Whips and the General Election of 1868', *English Historical Review*, LXIII, No. CCXLVII (April 1948), 189–200.

Thompson, Paul, 'Liberals, Radicals and Labour in London, 1880–1900', *Past and Present*, No. 27 (April 1964), 73–101.

Watson, Aaron, 'George Howell', *The Millgate Monthly*, III, No. 2 (August 1908), 665–71.

Wohl, Anthony S., 'The Bitter Cry of Outcast London', *International Review of Social History*, XIII (1968), Part 2, 189–245.

Index